LET THE PEOPLE PICK THE PRESIDENT

LET THE PEOPLE PICK THE PRESIDENT

THE CASE FOR ABOLISHING THE ELECTORAL COLLEGE

JESSE WEGMAN

ST. MARTIN'S PRESS
NEW YORK

First published in the United States by St. Martin's Press, an imprint of St. Martin's Publishing Group

www.stmartins.com

Designed by Meryl Sussman Levavi

Library of Congress Cataloging-in-Publication Data

Names: Wegman, Jesse, author.
Title: Let the people pick the president : the case for
    abolishing the Electoral College / Jesse Wegman.
Identifiers: LCCN 2019043276 | ISBN 9781250221971
    (hardcover) | ISBN 9781250221988 (ebook)
Subjects: LCSH: Presidents—United States—Election. |
    Electoral college—United States. | Voting—United States.
Classification: LCC JK528 .W39 2020 | DDC 324.60973—dc23
LC record available at https://lccn.loc.gov/2019043276

Our books may be purchased in bulk for promotional, educational, or business use. Please contact your local bookseller or the Macmillan Corporate and Premium Sales Department at 1-800-221-7945, extension 5442, or by email at MacmillanSpecialMarkets@macmillan.com.

First Edition: March 2020

10 9 8 7 6 5 4 3 2 1

for my mother

"Democracy is the recurrent suspicion that more than half of the people are right more than half of the time."

—E. B. WHITE

"Democracy is the theory that the common people know what they want, and deserve to get it good and hard."

—H. L. MENCKEN

CONTENTS

A MORE PERFECT UNION

The Last Step Toward American Democracy

At 4:43 a.m. on November 9, 2016, Micheal Baca, a 24-year-old Democratic presidential elector from Colorado, sent an urgent text message to a friend. "I have a plan," Baca wrote.

In retrospect, it was completely insane, but these were insane times.

A few hours earlier, Donald Trump, the Republican nominee for president, had stunned the world by pulling out what may be the most improbable election victory in American history. Trump was losing the popular vote to Hillary Clinton, the Democratic nominee, by more than two million votes, a margin that continued to grow as late returns rolled in. But he'd won where it counted, in the Electoral College. Or he had appeared to.

Baca, a former marine who was earning a living in

Denver that fall as a driver for Uber and Lyft, had no political experience. He knew one thing, though: You might think you're voting for the president when you cast a ballot, but you're not. You're voting for Micheal Baca, or his Republican counterpart. Technically, the presidency wouldn't be decided until the 538 electors voted, as they were scheduled to do on December 19 in state capitals around the country.

The scheme came together quickly in Baca's mind, and he started testing it out. In a text to a fellow Democratic elector in Washington, Bret Chiafalo, he wrote, "We can avoid Trump. But will need 37 Republicans to defect. Call me crazy but this needs to work."

"It's a Hail Mary dude," Chiafalo wrote back. "But it's all we got."

In regular years, the electors' vote is a formality—a ceremonial reaffirmation of the popular vote that most Americans ignore, if they are aware it is happening at all. But in 2016, for the fifth time in the nation's history, the Electoral College and the popular vote didn't match, a phenomenon caused by so-called "winner-take-all" laws. These laws, used in nearly every state, are just what they sound like: they award all of a state's electors to the candidate who earns the most popular votes in the state, no matter how close the margin. The key to Trump's win came in three states—Pennsylvania, Wisconsin, and Michigan—where he beat Clinton by a combined total of just under 78,000 votes out of more than 13 million cast. That's less than the capacity of the University of Michigan's football stadium, but it was enough, barely, to secure all of those states' electors, cross the electoral vote majority threshold of 270, and claim the presidency.

Baca, like millions of other Americans in 2016, including some top Republicans, believed that Trump would be the least qualified president in history. And that wasn't counting the disturbing circumstances surrounding his victory, which included a coordinated cyberattack carried out by the Russian government on Trump's behalf and with his campaign's awareness. As new details of the Russian plot trickled out, Baca became certain that a Trump presidency posed an existential threat to the nation. The vote of the electors was the last thing standing between Trump and the Oval Office, and Baca was determined to keep him from ever getting there.

The good news was that the Constitution's framers had anticipated exactly this scenario. They knew that most people would not be well informed about national candidates and feared they would be easily taken in by a smooth-talking con artist. The Electoral College was the solution. In the *Federalist* no. 68, Alexander Hamilton wrote that the College would ensure that "the office of President will never fall to the lot of any man who is not in an eminent degree endowed with the requisite qualifications."[1] How? By entrusting the choice of the president to a select body of men in each state—men who would "possess the information and discernment requisite to such complicated investigations." These electors, Hamilton assured his readers, would be "most capable of analyzing the qualities adapted to the station, and acting under circumstances favorable to deliberation."

In other words, Hamilton was saying that the electors would think for themselves, reject unqualified candidates however popular they might be, and choose a leader who would govern in the best interests of the nation.

Inspiring words, and in the days after Trump's victory, more than a few shell-shocked liberals latched on to them. Baca and Chiafalo dubbed themselves "Hamilton Electors" and began working to persuade their Republican counterparts not to vote for Donald Trump but instead unite behind a compromise candidate who was actually qualified for the job.

As anti-Trump protestors took to the streets around the country, blocking traffic, chanting "Not my president!" and clashing with police, a quieter protest was developing largely behind closed doors—an unprecedented, loosely coordinated national effort to vindicate the framers' vision, reverse the outcome of the election, and save the republic.

A petition posted on Change.org that called on "Conscientious Electors to protect the Constitution from Donald Trump" by switching their votes from Trump to Clinton drew nearly five million signatures.[2]

Michael Signer, the mayor of Charlottesville, Virginia, at the time, and the author of books about demagogues and James Madison, published an article in *Time* magazine arguing that Republican electors "owe it to all Americans to deliberate on their choice in the manner required by the Constitution"—in short, to "revolt against Trump."[3]

A Harvard law professor named Lawrence Lessig said he had been told of 20 Republican electors, and possibly more, who were considering voting for someone other than Trump, although none ever publicly came forward.[4]

A short video posted to YouTube and viewed more than 1.4 million times featured a solemn parade of TV and movie stars pleading with Republican electors to switch their votes. It opened with Martin Sheen, donning his spectacles and summoning the benevolent didacticism of his alter ego, President Jed Bartlet of *The West Wing*, a liberal's fantasy chief executive who could recite the *Federalist Papers* in his sleep.

"As you know," Sheen said, after quoting Hamilton, "our founding fathers built the Electoral College to safeguard the American people from the dangers of a demagogue."[5]

The rest of the celebrities seemed to be trying to strike a tone somewhere between dire and apocalyptic. "I'm not asking you to vote for Hillary Clinton," several of them repeated. "*Any* eligible person" would do. They assured the electors that "by voting [their] conscience" they would go down in history as brave and heroic patriots. The overall effect sounded like a group of hostages trying to sweet-talk their kidnapper into putting down the gun.

The problem was that the Electoral College has almost never operated as Alexander Hamilton pictured it would. Not since 1792 have electors been independent, deliberative actors who saw their task as picking the fittest person for the job. There isn't even one single body of electors. Instead, each presidential candidate has his or her own "slate" of electors tapped by local party leaders for nothing but their partisan loyalty. Whichever candidate wins a state's popular vote sends all of his or her electors to the state capital, where they cast their ballots for that candidate. And just in case any of them should get a notion to vote for someone else, most states have laws prohibiting them from doing so.

In other words, electors are today, as they have nearly always been, obedient partisan hacks, rubber stamps for their party's candidate. But none of that mattered in the fall of 2016.

| | |

By later November, it seemed as though Democrats had entered a fugue state. Sure, anyone could "like" a video or sign an online petition; but convincing electors—a motley cast of characters made up of former politicians, party insiders, and random activists who happened to know someone powerful—that they suddenly represented the last bulwark of American democracy?[6] It wasn't just a handful of potential mavericks who were needed either. Trump had won states representing 306 electoral votes, which meant that Micheal Baca's Election Night calculation had been right: at least 37 Republican electors would have to agree to switch their vote to someone else to have a chance of stopping Trump.

Even if that happened, it wouldn't guarantee Trump's defeat; it would only deny him a majority of electoral votes and send the election to the House of Representatives, which had not decided a presidential race since 1825. (Trump would likely have won in the House anyway, because the Constitution gives each state a single vote, and a majority of state delegations in 2016 were led by Republicans.)

The Hamilton Electors were undeterred. They knew they would never persuade Republicans to vote for Hillary Clinton, so they suggested John Kasich, the relatively moderate Republican governor of Ohio. Kasich had run for president that year before dropping out in May. If enough Trump electors agreed to switch their vote to him, and they were joined by most or all of Clinton's 232 electors, Trump could be locked out of the presidency. Except for one thing: Kasich himself wasn't on board. "Our country had an election and Donald Trump won," he said.[7]

Hillary Clinton wasn't on board either. Despite her large popular vote lead, her past public statements in favor of a national popular vote, and pleas from some campaign staffers, she was reluctant to sign on to any effort that would make her look like a sore loser.

Michael Signer, the former Charlottesville mayor, told me he couldn't understand Clinton's attitude. "You spent a year saying this guy was an existential threat to the country. This is the exact purpose of the Electoral College. So why don't you go to the mat on it?"[8]

Well, for starters, as the critics of the stop-Trump effort pointed out, everyone knew the rules of the game in advance. All these earnest appeals to electors' consciences may have been sweet music to liberals, but to conservatives they came off as both arrogant and naive, if not treasonous. Democrats were refusing to accept the outcome because they weren't happy with it, something they had warned that Trump would try to do only days earlier.

Then there was the troubling precedent this kind of intervention would set. Imagine a postelection free-for-all every four years in which a few very motivated (and probably very rich) players try to influence the individual electors' votes, while tens of millions of voters watch from the sidelines. Now imagine that it worked, and the presidency was ultimately awarded to someone like, say, John Kasich—a man who was no longer running for the office and who received, nationwide, a smattering of write-in votes on Election Day. It would rightly be seen as a usurpation of the will of the people, whether they had supported Trump or Clinton.

The reviews of the Hamilton Electors were coming in from both left and right, and they were not kind.

"Wildly unrealistic and potentially counterproductive," wrote Ed Kilgore, a longtime liberal political columnist. He called the Hamilton Electors' effort "an impossible plot to overturn an election conducted under long-established if nondemocratic rules."[9]

Meghan McArdle, a libertarian writer, warned that "if you won't accept the results of the elections you lose, then your opponents won't either."[10]

Jonathan Bernstein, a left-leaning political scientist and blogger, wrote, "They should all just stop."[11]

The electors were well aware of the national uproar surrounding them and the job they were about to perform. On December 12, one week before the vote, 10 of them—nine Democrats and one Republican—signed an open letter to the director of national intelligence, James Clapper, requesting a briefing on the status of any investigations into ties between the Trump campaign and the Russian government.[12]

As the days shortened and the odds of success grew longer, the offensive grew more frenzied. There were public entreaties, daily full-page newspaper ads, and passionate op-eds. There were even federal lawsuits challenging state laws forbidding electors to vote for any candidate other than the one they were pledged to.[13] Breaking the law could lead to a fine or even jail time.

Michael Signer described to me the last-minute discussions over how these laws, which were on the books in 29 states but were virtually never invoked, would work in practice. "What would happen that day? You couldn't have a sheriff or someone from the state attorney general's office go and literally force an elector to cast a vote. Would they have substitutes? Could they remove the elector and prevent them from casting their vote?" There were so many unknowns, but the bottom line was clear: "You really would have needed a cohort of rock-ribbed rebels ready to pay a fine or go to jail for a couple of days," Signer said. "And you would've needed 37 of them."[14]

At a press conference three days before the electors convened, President Obama called the Electoral College a "vestige" of the founding era. "There are some structures in our political system as envisioned by the founders that sometimes are going to disadvantage Democrats," he said.[15] And with that, the spell was broken. The president's words, Signer told me, "kind of shut the door on the whole effort."

On December 19, the electors cast their ballots. In Colorado, where Hillary Clinton had won the statewide vote, it was chaos. Micheal Baca crossed out Clinton's name and wrote in John Kasich's, and was immediately disqualified as an elector under state law. When the secretary of state, Wayne Williams, announced that he had in hand eight votes for Hillary Clinton and "one ballot which cannot be received," an angry crowd heckled him and demanded that Baca's vote be counted. Williams said the electors needed to nominate a replacement elector, so they nominated Baca. Williams rejected this. "We need an elector who will cast a vote for the person who received the most votes for president in the state of Colorado," he said. Eventually Baca was replaced by an elector who voted for Clinton.[16]

Nationwide, 10 electors broke their pledges. Three of them, including Micheal Baca, had their votes invalidated by their state. Of the remaining seven, Trump lost two. Hillary Clinton lost five.

Despite the spectacle of the previous six weeks, the Electoral College did exactly what it has done throughout almost all of American history. And why wouldn't it have? The idea that 37 Republican electors would have somehow agreed to switch their votes away from their party's hugely popular nominee—not to mention most or all of Clinton's—had always been preposterous. The only time in history that so many electors had defected at once was in 1872, when 63 of 66 Liberal Republican electors refused to cast their ballot for their party's nominee, Horace Greeley. It was hard to blame them: Greeley had died three weeks after the election.

▌▌▌

The drama of 2016 looks all the more outlandish when you consider that America had endured the same thing less than two decades earlier—and that time it would've taken only three "faithless" electors to change the outcome.

In the weeks leading up to the election of 2000, multiple polls suggested a potential split between the Electoral College and the popular vote: George W. Bush, the Republican nominee, might well win the popular vote but lose the Electoral College to the Democratic nominee, Al Gore.

According to multiple news reports at the time, the possibility was alarming enough to some inside the Bush campaign that there was discussion of a public relations blitz to convince electors to vote for the popular vote winner. It would include newspaper ads, public appeals to local business and community leaders and influential members of the clergy, as well as interviews with radio and TV personalities. The idea, according to an article in the New York *Daily News*, was to capitalize on the anticipated "popular uprising" against the Electoral College's "essential unfairness." The media would help fan the flames, an unnamed Bush aide was quoted as saying, "because the will of the people will have been thwarted."[17]

The Electoral College and the popular vote did indeed split that year, but in the opposite direction—Gore won the popular vote by more than half a million votes, while Bush eked out a victory in the Electoral College.

It was the first time any living American had witnessed the College reject the popular vote winner—the last time was 1888—and it was by a hair: Bush earned 271 electoral votes, only one more than the bare majority he needed. If three Republican electors changed their votes, Bush would have been blocked from the White House. Yet there would be no concerted push to convince electors to "vote their conscience" and save American democracy. Democrats' fury over the split vote was diverted and diluted by the month-long drama over the recount in the absurdly close Florida race, which ended up being decided by the Supreme Court—by a 5–4 vote—in favor of Bush.

A week later, the historian Arthur Schlesinger Jr. wrote in the *Washington Post* that the split election "puts the republic in an intolerable predicament. It is intolerable because it is undemocratic. And it is intolerable because it imposes a fatal burden on the minority president."[18]

Across the country, Americans retreated to their political tribes. A newspaper account from Tallahassee, Florida, in the eye of the storm, described how locals used to have civil, leisurely chats with one another, but no longer. "You can feel the tension," a business owner said. "Now the chats have changed into partisan verbal brawls and then into stony silences."[19]

In Washington, members of the Congressional Black Caucus boycotted the counting of the electoral votes. John Lewis, a Georgia representative, stayed home on Inauguration Day because, the *Washington Post* reported, "he doesn't believe Bush is the true elected president."[20]

In the end, only one elector broke her pledge—Barbara Lett-Simmons, a Democrat from Washington, D.C., who withheld her vote from Gore in protest of the District's lack of representation in Congress.

Nine months later, terrorists attacked the World Trade Center and the Pentagon, killing thousands and quickly overshadowing any lingering bitterness over the election.

The debate over the Electoral College didn't disappear entirely. Many Americans, who had never before considered how the College operated, were shocked that Bush's 537-vote victory in the Florida popular vote had given him all 25 of the state's electors, while Gore got none. Over the following year, legislatures in nearly two dozen states debated switching their method of allocating presidential electors to a system that awarded electors instead by congressional district.[21] None ended up making the change.

In the eyes of many Democrats, Bush remained an illegitimate president throughout his first term, but as the wars in Iraq and Afghanistan moved to the center of the nation's consciousness, the Electoral College drifted out of it.

2016 was a different story. For one thing, Hillary Clinton's popular vote margin was more than five times as large as Gore's had been, giving Donald Trump the distinction of losing by more popular votes than any winning president in history.

There was the polarization of the American electorate, which had been increasing for decades, turning every issue into a scorched-earth battle between liberals and conservatives, who saw each other not as fellow Americans to negotiate with but as enemies to be vanquished.

And there was Trump himself—this proudly crude, race-baiting, retrograde reality TV star whose candidacy had enthralled, enraged, and divided Americans like none before. The fact that the nation had now endured not just another popular vote loser entering the White House but this *particular* loser triggered a fresh, intense debate over the legitimacy of our entire electoral system.

On January 21, 2017, the day after Trump was inaugurated, Americans turned out in cities and towns across the country to march in opposition to the new administration. Final estimates put the total number of marchers at between three and five million.[22] It was the largest one-day protest in American history. It also served as a visual representation of the magnitude of Hillary Clinton's popular vote margin, as though the marchers were saying, "You want to know what three million votes look like? This is what they look like."

Even President-elect Trump agreed a popular vote would be better. In an interview on *60 Minutes* five days after Election Day, Trump said, "I would rather see it, where you went with simple votes. You know, you get 100 million votes, and somebody else gets 90 million votes, and you win."[23] (Two days later he tweeted, "The Electoral College is actually genius in that it brings all states, including the smaller ones, into play."[24])

Meanwhile, the Electoral College stayed in the news,

buoyed by a popular-vote movement that hadn't existed in 2000, and had been building momentum over the previous decade. "The Electoral College is an abomination," read a characteristic headline in the *Washington Post*, "and Democrats should keep talking about it."[25]

The College was "a pro-slavery tool," said one constitutional historian, and it "lurks in our political backyard, like some horrible monster waiting to spring on us and undermine the very notion of democratic government in the world's oldest constitutional democracy."[26]

Conservatives raced to the College's defense, arguing that it was a key element of the framers' brilliant design, and that any effort to change or abolish it is "an attack against our republican form of government."[27]

"Without the Electoral College," went one common refrain, "the presidential election would be dominated by California, Texas, New York and Florida, while states like Wyoming, Vermont, Alaska and Delaware would vanish from the political landscape."[28]

Choosing the president by national popular vote would "make America more like the Third World,"[29] and could even spell "the end of our constitutional system as we have known it since 1787."[30]

III

For all its intensity, the fight over the Electoral College reflects an even deeper national divide between two competing narratives about American history and how popular participation in a self-governing republic was meant to work.

The conservative narrative says, in brief, that the founding fathers got it mostly right. They didn't trust unfettered democracy, and believed it was necessary to channel and constrain the people's voice in order to prevent a tyrannical majority from trampling the rights of minorities. Some of these constraints were good, like a two-tiered system of government with checks on majorities and filters of the popular will. Others were not good, like the denial of voting rights to nearly everyone but white male property owners. Many of these restrictions have been lifted, and while most modern conservatives agree with those changes, they were nearly all controversial at the time that they were made. Since the tendency of these reforms has been to remove checks against direct popular rule, any new reforms, like abolishing the Electoral College, are best approached with caution and skepticism.

The liberal narrative, on the other hand, emphasizes the egalitarian ideal at the heart of the Declaration of Independence. We are all created equal, and we should govern ourselves that way. Yet for most of our history, those were just words on parchment—the founders erected barriers to democracy not because of legitimate constitutional principles but because of immoral prejudices. When those barriers have been eliminated, as has happened in various spurts of moral progress throughout our history, it is cause for celebration. Democratic legitimacy depends, at its core, on all votes being treated the same. The real story of America, according to this narrative, has been the hard-won progress of democratization—bringing our practices into line with our founding principles.

The second narrative, by and large, has won out. With some important exceptions, the arc of American history has bent in one direction: toward more inclusivity, more equality, more participation—in short, toward democracy. It didn't have to happen that way, but it has. And if we want to know where we're headed, it's important to remember how we got here.

The arc toward greater democracy was underway even as the Constitution was being ratified. At the time, only adult white men, usually those who owned property, were eligible to vote—no women, no enslaved blacks, no Native Americans, and in many states, no poorer white men. But states soon began eliminating property qualifications for voting and holding office, expanding the meaning of "the people." Into the early nineteenth century, these restrictions continued to fall, and they were virtually gone by the presidency of Andrew Jackson, who ran on a platform of universal suffrage—universal for white men, anyway.

During the same period, states began to include regular citizens more directly in picking the president. In 1800, a majority of state legislatures chose their state's electors themselves, with no input at all from the voters.[31] But as some states started to adopt direct voting for electors, it became politically impossible for the others not to follow suit. By 1832, all states but one, South Carolina, had adopted a popular vote for their presidential electors.

Of course, the vast majority of the population still could not vote. That began to change after the Civil War, with the passage of the Thirteenth, Fourteenth, and Fifteenth Amendments, which freed the slaves, made them citizens, and guaranteed their right to vote. The Reconstruction Amendments are referred to as the "Second Founding" because, in rejecting the framers' three-fifths compromise and its entrenchment of slavery, they represented as much of a revolution as the Declaration of Independence and the Constitution themselves.

Black people were now free citizens, equal to whites in theory but not in practice. With the collapse of Reconstruction and the rise of Jim Crow, southern blacks were made electorally invisible, whether through restrictive voting practices like poll taxes and literacy tests or by campaigns of terrorism and state-sanctioned murder. It took another century before the guarantees of these amendments would be enforced in a meaningful way.

And yet with almost every new amendment, the Constitution was evolving from a charter of exclusion to one of inclusion. More of the American people were getting a more direct say in the functioning of their government. The arc was continuing to bend.

The Seventeenth Amendment, ratified in 1913, gave the people the right to vote directly for their U.S. senators, rather than leaving the job to state lawmakers, as the founders had designed it. In 1920, the Nineteenth Amendment gave women the right to vote, doubling the number of eligible voters, at least in theory. The Twenty-Third, Twenty-Fourth, and Twenty-Sixth Amendments, ratified between 1961 and 1971, gave the residents of Washington, D.C., a say in choosing the president, barred racist poll taxes, and lowered the voting age from 21 to 18.

And in a series of cases in the early 1960s, the Supreme Court established the principle of one person, one vote, transforming representative democracy in America by forcing states to redraw their legislative districts, which had long been massively skewed in favor of sparsely populated (and overwhelmingly white) rural areas. "Legislators represent people, not trees or acres," the Court wrote.[32] The rule applied only to legislative elections, but the Court's language was unmistakable in its sweep. "The conception of political equality from the Declaration of Independence, to Lincoln's Gettysburg Address, to the Fifteenth, Seventeenth, and Nineteenth Amendments can mean only one thing: one person, one vote."[33]

Today, with the important exception of some people with criminal records, every American 18 and older is automatically eligible to vote. In 200 years, we went from a country in which less than one-fifth of adults were allowed to vote to one in which virtually every adult citizen has that right.

It's an astonishing story of democratic transformation. The founders, rightly or wrongly, believed the constraints they imposed on public participation in our government were wise, or at least inevitable. Today, we can point to the founders' own words to say, with confidence, that they are neither.

Maybe this is the real American exceptionalism: our nation was conceived out of the audacious, world-changing idea of universal human equality. And though it was born in a snarl of prejudice, mistrust, and exclusion, it harbored in its DNA the code to express more faithfully the true meaning of its founding principles. Over multiple generations, and thanks to the tireless work and bloody sacrifices of millions of Americans—some powerful but most just regular people who wanted to be treated the same as everyone else—that code has been unlocked, and those principles, slowly but surely, have found expression.

This evolution has brought us to a point at which all Americans now carry around the basic expectations of people living in any modern democracy: we are political equals, and our elections are decided by majority rule. We are quicker to notice the antidemocratic nature of institutions like the Senate, which was not meant to represent the people in the first place, but which has only grown more skewed as Americans cluster more tightly in a handful of states. And we are quicker to denounce partisan gerrymandering, an age-old practice in which lawmakers draw warped district maps to entrench themselves and their party in power, no matter what voters want.

In both of these cases, there's not much we can do. The Senate, which is effectively unamendable by the Constitution's own terms, is here to stay. So are partisan gerrymanders, which have become more distorted than ever with the help of modern technology, but which the Supreme Court has refused to block.

Then there's the Electoral College. It too violates the core democratic principles of political equality and majority rule. We may all be eligible to vote for president now, yet all of our votes do not count the same, and the candidate who gets the most votes can lose.

That brings us to the central point of this book: if the arc of American history bends toward more equality, more participation, and more democracy, then the national popular vote is the last major point on that arc. The Electoral College is the final obstacle remaining from the imperfections and built-in inequalities of the nation's founding. And, unlike the

Senate and partisan gerrymandering, we can do something about it.

III

But what, exactly, can we do?

People have been trying to answer that question for more than two centuries. Since the first proposed amendment to the Electoral College was introduced in Congress in 1797, there have been more than 700 attempts to reform or abolish it—more by far than for any other provision of the Constitution. Only one has succeeded: the Twelfth Amendment, which was ratified in 1804 to fix a technical flaw in the College's design but left it otherwise intact.

In the late 1960s, an amendment abolishing the College and replacing it with a national popular vote passed the House of Representatives and came extraordinarily close in the Senate, but was blocked by a filibuster. At the time, 80 percent of the American public supported switching to the popular vote, as did President Richard Nixon and other top Republicans and Democrats.

To some, this litany of failure speaks for itself. "I think it is a waste of time to talk about changing the Electoral College," former president Jimmy Carter said in 2000. Carter had supported a national popular vote in the 1960s and 1970s. "I would predict that 200 years from now, we will still have the Electoral College."[34]

Was President Carter right? Is it simply our fate as Americans to remain trapped by the historical quirks of a Constitution that is too easy to revere and too hard to change?

Especially after the failed effort in the 1960s, when

American politics was far less polarized than today, and there was no simple partisan divide over the issue, it's clear that a constitutional amendment is not in the cards. But there may be another way.

It's called the National Popular Vote Interstate Compact—an agreement among states to award all of their electors to the winner of the national popular vote, rather than the winner of their statewide vote. The compact will take effect when it is joined by states representing a majority of electoral votes, 270, thus guaranteeing that the candidate who wins the most votes in the country becomes president.

The ingenuity of the compact is that it doesn't touch the Constitution. Its target is the statewide winner-take-all rule. Currently in use by 48 states (Maine and Nebraska are the exceptions), this rule is what makes presidents out of popular vote losers. It incentivizes presidential campaigns to ignore more than 100 million American voters living in noncompetitive states, turning what should be a national electoral contest into a series of bitter, hyperlocal brawls. It focuses nearly all campaign spending and policy proposals on a few battleground states, where even a small shift in voting can lead to an electoral jackpot for one side or the other.

That familiar red and blue map we all obsess over every four years? It's nothing but a visual representation of state winner-take-all rules, with each state stamped Democratic or Republican, as though that is its "true" identity, regardless of how many voters from the other party cast a ballot there.

This is bad for democracy, and it should concern all Americans, no matter where they live or which political party they support. In contrast, when candidates know that all votes are equal, and they need a majority of them to win, they are forced to seek the support of all Americans and craft policies that appeal to as many as possible.

The popular vote compact was launched in 2006 and got its first member state, Maryland, the following year. As of October 2019, 15 states and the District of Columbia, together representing 196 electoral votes, had joined—74 more and the compact takes effect. So far, only Democratic-majority states have joined the compact, and while the 2016 election dealt a significant setback to efforts to enlist Republican-led states, lawmakers of both parties around the country continue to support it, and Republican-led chambers have passed it in four states.

Critics of the compact effort call it an "end run" around the Constitution. It's true that the Constitution's framers never mentioned something like a popular vote compact. They also never mentioned the winner-take-all rule, but that didn't stop the majority of states from rapidly adopting it to benefit themselves. That's the whole point of the compact: the framers gave states near-total control over how to allocate their electors.

The fact that the compact is an agreement among states also means that, unlike a constitutional amendment, which is effectively permanent, member states may back out if they later decide they don't want to be a part of it.

Opponents of the popular vote argue that no matter how you might achieve it, it's not the way our country is built. As the popular saying goes, we're a republic, not a democracy. The Electoral College is one of the core republican elements of the framers' constitutional design—like the Senate and the

Supreme Court—which are there precisely to prevent majorities from running rampant. In other words, majority rule is not our only organizing principle, and perhaps not even our most important.

There are two problems with this argument. The minor one is on the surface, and involves terminology. The United States is both a republic and a representative democracy. The two terms describe the same thing: a government in which the people hold the ultimate power but elect representatives to make laws, policies, and other decisions on their behalf. The founders used the term "republic" to distinguish what they were building from a monarchy. For them, "democracy" generally referred to the direct variety, as in Ancient Athens or the New England town meeting, where the people literally make the laws themselves. But American politics at the national level has never been and will never be a direct democracy. So any distinction between the terms today is meaningless. As one political columnist put it, "To say that the U.S. is a republic, not a democracy, is like claiming to eat beef and pork but not cows and pigs."[35]

The bigger problem with the saying is the implication that lies beneath it. By insisting that we are not a democracy, it seems to be making the case that we should be guided only by the "republican" features of our government, such as checks and balances, and not by the "democratic" ones, such as political equality and majority rule. And yet the founders themselves wouldn't agree with this. It's true that they were concerned about too much public participation in government, but they also understood majority rule to be the essence of republican government. And when they adopted the

Electoral College, they did so not for fear of the people—whom, after all, they trusted to vote directly for the House of Representatives—but for a mix of reasons specific to the historical moment they lived in. These included the limitations of travel and communications, the fight for power between larger and smaller states, and the battle between the North and the South over the institution of slavery and its impact on representation.

These are just some of the misunderstandings, and in some cases outright myths, that have propped up the Electoral College for decades. Others include the idea that the Constitution was an artful design created by a room full of geniuses; that the College forces candidates to campaign and win support in all areas of the country; that abolishing the College would benefit large states over small ones and cities over rural areas; that minor tweaks to the College would be better than outright abolition; and that a popular vote would be nothing but a free pass to the White House for Democrats.

In the coming chapters I dispel these myths, and in the process arm you with facts to cite and stories to tell the next time you find yourself in a debate over how we pick the president, whatever your politics, and wherever you live. This is a debate that we, the people, have been having for more than two centuries. It's time to finish it.

∎∎∎

I realize I'm writing this book at a dicey moment. Even just a few years ago it would have been an academic exercise, but today, after the popular vote loser has won the presidency in two of the past five elections, it is an issue of immediate concern to millions of Americans. Anyone weighing in on either side will be accused of being partisan.

So it wouldn't surprise me if you're thinking, Of course this guy wants to abolish the Electoral College. He's on the *New York Times* editorial board—a card-carrying member of the elite liberal media. He spends his days floating inside the dark-blue bubble of a coastal metropolis, fantasizing about a progressive takeover of America. Next he'll want to take away all our guns and force everyone to get gay married.

I will admit it's predictable for someone like me to write a book like this. I've been eligible to vote in seven presidential elections, and in two of them—nearly one-third!—the candidate I supported won more votes and still lost the presidency. I'd be lying if I said these experiences didn't whet my appetite for electoral reform.

At the same time, my politics are progressive, not nihilistic. I'm not a burn-it-all-down type. I value traditions and established institutions—when they work for people. I went to law school to study the Constitution, and I recognize that it is a brilliant, transformative document. Still, I cherish it not because of what it was 230 years ago but because of who it has allowed us to become.

That's why what galled me most in 2000 and 2016 were the violations of two fundamental democratic principles. One is political equality—meaning every vote counts the same. The other is majority rule, meaning the person who gets the most votes wins. I can accept losing under a system like that. I might not be thrilled with the outcome, but I would regard it as fair. That's the key point: whether our side wins or loses, we must see the outcome to be fair. And outcomes are seen as fair when the process that led to them is seen as just. If it isn't, the entire system loses legitimacy, and then we're in for real trouble.

All of this started to come together in my mind the day I first saw the purple blob.

It was a few months before Election Day 2004, and I was aimlessly surfing the Web when I came across a series of political maps of the United States that I'd never seen before. They were on the personal website of a physicist from the University of Michigan named Mark Newman, who had, as many scientists do these days, a side interest in electoral systems.[36]

The first map was the one we all know: the standard binary representation of the country under the statewide winner-take-all rule. Frankly, it looked pretty bad for liberals: America was awash in red, with only a few spotty patches of blue on the coasts and in the upper Midwest.

In the next map, Newman kept the colors intact but adjusted the size and shape of the states to reflect their population rather than their geographical size. The states were now squishy, unrecognizable inkblots, and yet the country as a whole was starting to look more like it does in reality— roughly equally divided between red and blue.

Newman then showed the same two maps again—one based on geography and one on population—using voting results from each county rather than from entire states. Now, instead of large red and blue blocks, there were dozens of blue spots of different sizes scattered against a red backdrop.

The most revealing map Newman saved for last. He took the population-based map, but rather than coloring states red or blue according to the winner-take-all rule, he substituted county-level voting results, and he used shades of purple to represent each party's relative margin of victory. The result was astonishing—there were still some clearly blue spots representing cities, and there was still an unmistakable red lattice across the middle of the country. But the overwhelming impression was of purple everywhere.

My first reaction was to smile. Look at all those people! Disagreeing deeply about politics but living right next to each other. It reflected the political diversity of the country I lived in.

I know I'm not the only one who feels this way. Long before anyone could create complex maps and post them online, Americans understood the basic unfairness of a winner-take-all Electoral College.

If we really thought the Electoral College was the best way to choose a president, we wouldn't have tried to reform or abolish it more than 700 times. We wouldn't have expressed a consistent and overwhelming support for the popular vote, as has been the case since polling on the question began in the 1940s. Democrats wouldn't have fought to convince electors to choose the popular vote winner in 2016, and Republicans wouldn't have planned to do the same in 2000.

And Donald Trump wouldn't have tweeted, as he did on Election Night 2012, when for a moment it looked like his candidate, Mitt Romney, might win the popular vote but lose the presidency, "The electoral college is a disaster for a democracy."[37] (He followed that one up with another tweet that he later deleted: "More votes equals a loss . . . revolution!")[38]

It's simple: Americans from the founding fathers onward have always considered majority rule to be the lodestar of our political system. That's the way we run every election in the country—except the most important one of all.

So why has the College survived? More than anything else, because one party or the other, and sometimes both, believes it gives them a systematic advantage. As the political scientist James MacGregor Burns said in 1963, "The Electoral College is not just a technical electoral procedure. It is steeped in politics—it affects the balance of parties, the power of interest groups, the strength of ideologies, the fates of politicians. Hence it cannot be considered apart from the political context in which it operates. It is part of the whole solar system of our Government, and any effort to change it will disturb the whole system."[39]

While this is clearly true, it's also true that the country cannot tolerate the College's effects under the winner-take-all rule much longer. Pundits tend to dismiss the elections of 2000 and 2016 as anomalies, but what's remarkable is not that a split between the Electoral College and the popular vote has happened twice in the past two decades, it's that it hasn't happened far more often. In sixteen other elections, a shift of 75,000 votes or fewer in key states—just slightly less than Trump's total victory margin in Pennsylvania, Michigan, and Wisconsin—would have made the popular vote loser president. Six times, a shift of fewer than 10,000 votes would have done the trick.

The odds of a split are only going up as the country grows more polarized and razor-thin vote margins become the norm. Two recent studies have found that, in an election decided by a popular-vote margin of 2 percent or less (roughly 2.6 million votes), there is a one-in-three chance that the Electoral College will be won by the popular-vote loser.[40]

At the same time, we are witnessing a sea change among the newest generation of voters—the millions of teenagers now entering the American electorate, all of them born long after the Constitution was amended to guarantee their right to vote at age 18. They believe in the legitimacy of the democratic process. Think of the students from Marjory Stoneman Douglas High School in Parkland, Florida, who transformed the unfathomable trauma they endured into a national movement for political change. They're invested in the idea of active democratic citizenship, and they want their peers to be too. How will those students feel when they realize that their vote for president doesn't matter, simply because they happen to have moved to California, or Texas, or South Carolina, or New York—or any other noncompetitive state?

Thus it's no surprise that in 2020, for the first time in American history, the future of the Electoral College is a live issue in the presidential race. Nearly a dozen of the original Democratic candidates called for abolishing it and replacing it with a national popular vote. President Trump himself has agreed, at least in theory. "I would rather have a popular election," he said as late as 2018. "To me, it's much easier to win the popular vote."

As this book went to press, there were all kinds of conflicting data about what might happen in the 2020 election. On one hand, polls showed President Trump either leading or locked in a tight race with top Democratic candidates in the battleground states he needs to win, giving him a plausible path to another Electoral College victory, even if he loses the popular vote by more than he did in 2016.[41] On the other hand, he remains deeply unpopular nationally. A Fox News national poll found the president running well behind all top Democrats, and also found that Democratic voters are more motivated to vote in 2020 than Republicans.[42]

All of this could change in the coming months. A war or a spike in the economy could improve Trump's chances; a depression or a natural disaster could hurt them. And we haven't even gotten to impeachment. But whatever happens, one thing is certain: the Electoral College under the winner-take-all rule will force the candidates to ignore the vast majority of Americans. The Democrats will game out which voters to focus on to repair the mistakes they made in 2016, while Trump will try to shore up his base in the states that delivered him victory before.

It is, as Donald Trump would say, a disaster for a democracy.

III

For the people behind the 2016 attempt to resurrect the framers' Electoral College in the hope of stopping a Trump presidency, the searing experience of those six weeks in November and December drove home the depth of the dysfunction in America's presidential election system.

"When you lift the hood and look at what the Electoral College actually is, there's no way it can serve its function," Mike Signer, the former Charlottesville mayor, told me. "There's not even a unitary 'it.' There are 50 different groups under 50 different state laws with hundreds of different people selected by these congressional districts. So there wasn't a way to treat it as one thing that could do something different."[43]

Micheal Baca, the Colorado elector who ultimately cast his electoral ballot for John Kasich, was rewarded for that act of conscience with a string of death threats and an eight-month investigation by the state attorney general's office. By breaking the state law that bound him to vote for Clinton, Baca had committed felony perjury, a crime punishable by up to nine years in prison. In the end, no charges were filed.

"I do feel like I opened up a Pandora's Box," Baca told me. He understood people's anger toward him. "Doing what I did, I feel that if it wasn't me, I would feel uneasy. I'm not someone with the requisite knowledge to make choices of this magnitude for other people."

What concerned Baca even more than the anger was the ignorance. Now and then one of his Uber customers would recognize him from television, he said, and yet still "most didn't know what the Electoral College was. They were amazed that we don't elect the president by popular vote."

Nearly three years after his electoral ballot was invalidated, a federal appeals court decided that Baca had been right all along. In late August 2019, the United States Court of Appeals for the Tenth Circuit, based in Denver, ruled that the state of Colorado had violated Baca's constitutional rights when it removed him as an elector for refusing to vote for Hillary Clinton.[44]

News headlines made the ruling sound calamitous: "Appeals Court Opens the Door to Electoral College Chaos"; "A Court Ruling Just Changed How We Pick Our President"; and so on. On television and radio, across Facebook and Twitter, pundits and regular citizens were aghast at the idea that some random elector could defy the will of the people on a whim.[45]

That's an understandable reaction. In practice, however, the ruling is unlikely to change much. Even when there is no threat of prosecution, as is the case in roughly two dozen states without elector-binding laws, electors virtually never break their faith, and for a simple reason: they don't want to.

Remember, there isn't one single, neutral set of electors in each state, patiently awaiting instructions from the voters. Rather, months or more before Election Day, each candidate has assembled his or her own slate of electors, chosen precisely because they commit to support that candidate. Micheal Baca's case is the exception that proves the rule. He began his campaign to get electors to vote for John Kasich not because he suddenly decided Kasich would make a better president than Hillary Clinton. He did it as a last-ditch effort to stop Trump from entering the White House, knowing that he could never convince a majority of Republican electors to choose Clinton. When that campaign failed, he cast a protest vote for Kasich.

As this book went to press, the Supreme Court was weighing whether to take up the faithless-elector question and issue a ruling in time for the 2020 election.

III

More than half a century ago, when America was last embroiled in a deep debate about the full scope of its democracy, the Supreme Court wrote, "The weight of a citizen's vote cannot be made to depend on where he lives." And yet under the winner-take-all Electoral College today, it does. In 2000, 537 votes in Florida weighed more than 537,000 votes in the rest of the country. In 2016, fewer than 78,000 votes in three states in the upper Midwest counted for more than three million votes nationwide.

Wouldn't it be thrilling to go to the polls on Election Day knowing that your vote will count just as much as everyone else's, no matter where you live? Isn't it exciting to think about candidates competing everywhere for votes, and parties calibrating their platforms to appeal to all Americans, rather than to the interests of a few targeted constituencies in a few battleground states? In reality, the United States is one big battleground, and the people who want to lead it should have to treat it like one.

This isn't to diminish the importance of states in our federal system. To the contrary, that system recognizes that every American enjoys a kind of dual citizenship. You are a citizen of the United States and you are, in a sense, a citizen of your state. When you vote for your governor, or your local and state lawmakers, or your senators and members of Congress, you are voting as a citizen of your state. When you vote for the president—the only person whose job it is to represent all Americans equally—you should be voting as a citizen of the United States.

Everyone knows the famous opening words of the Constitution's preamble—"We the People of the United States . . ." What most people don't know is that those words weren't in the first draft. In its original form, the preamble read, "We the People of New-Hampshire, Massachusetts, Rhode-Island . . ." and so on. That's how it stood until the closing days of the convention, when Gouverneur Morris, a Pennsylvania delegate, changed the words to the ones we know today. The point was to emphasize what, above all, the framers were creating: one nation, indivisible.

In that spirit, I hope you approach this book not as a liberal or a conservative, not as a Republican or a Democrat, not as a Texan or a Californian or a Kansan or a New Yorker, but as an American.

1

DID THE FOUNDERS FEAR DEMOCRACY?

The Radical Democratic Vision of James Wilson

On Monday morning, October 4, 1779, a crowd of almost 200 radical revolutionaries gathered at Paddy Byrne's Tavern, on Tenth Street in Philadelphia, to drink and plot an attack.[1]

They had good reason to be upset. Just three years earlier and a few blocks to the south, America's founding fathers had signed the Declaration of Independence and launched a new nation. Now, in the middle of a brutal and bloody war with Britain to secure that independence, the city's economy was in bad shape. Merchants were gouging their struggling customers on essential goods like flour, tea, sugar, and wood— "getting rich by sucking the blood of this county," as the leader of a local militia said.[2] The militia had spent months petitioning the Pennsylvania state government to set price controls, but the appeals went nowhere. It was time for direct action.

By midafternoon, the tavern crowd was drunk on liquor and rage. Armed with bayonets and muskets, they set out in search of the higher-profile members of the merchant class—to rid the city of what the militia called "un-American elements."[3] They marched down Arch Street, turned south, and stopped in front of a solid, two-story brick house at the corner of Third and Walnut Streets—the home of James Wilson and his wife, Rachel, who was then eight months pregnant with the couple's fourth child.

Everyone in Philadelphia knew James Wilson, and most had strong opinions about him. Only 37 years old, he was already one of the most politically and financially prominent figures in the country.

Wilson had come far from his origins in every sense: he was an immigrant, having sailed over from Scotland when he was 23, poor and jobless, yet full of ambition and classical learning.

Soon after settling in Pennsylvania, Wilson apprenticed in the law before opening his own practice. By 1779 he had been elected to the Continental Congress, signed the Declaration of Independence, served as a brigadier general in the state militia, and become one of the country's most successful lawyers and authoritative legal scholars. He was also a fixture in Philadelphia's business community, among whom he was most at ease. He made a lot of money and he lived like it.

Wilson's taste for the high life made him an easy target of the radical revolutionaries, who saw him as a typical conservative aristocrat who cared little for the concerns of regular people. But their suspicions of his motives and loyalties had been floating around for years, driven by his tendency to take political positions that were easily misinterpreted or misunderstood.

For example, in 1776, as a Pennsylvania delegate to the Second Continental Congress, he forced a short delay in the vote on the Declaration of Independence. He did so in order to secure the authorization of the Pennsylvania Assembly. But the delay infuriated the most radical revolutionaries, and he was suspected of harboring a secret allegiance to Great Britain. That wasn't remotely true. He was as strongly in favor of independence as any founder, and had published one of the most influential pamphlets challenging the British Parliament's legal authority over the colonies.

After independence, Wilson infuriated the revolutionaries yet again when he opposed Pennsylvania's democratic new constitution. That constitution was the world's most radical at the time. It had one popularly elected house of the legislature, with no executive, and nearly universal suffrage among white men. But Wilson thought it failed to establish a sufficient separation of powers—a nuance lost on his opponents, who voted him out of Congress in 1777.

The last straw came in 1778, when he provided legal representation to a group of Quakers and Tory sympathizers charged with treason, and managed to get most of them acquitted. He considered this doing his job as a lawyer. The radicals saw it differently. There was a war on, and he was suspected of aiding the enemy.

When Wilson got word of what was developing in the streets on that Monday morning in October, he gathered a few dozen of his merchant friends and barricaded them inside his house. As the mob approached, one of Wilson's crew, Captain Campbell, leaned out a second-floor window and called for the militia to disperse. He was shot and killed, and the fighting began. The radicals shouted "Get Wilson!" as they stormed the front door and fired a cannon. Wilson's friends returned fire from inside.

The siege ended only when Joseph Reed, the president of Pennsylvania's supreme executive council—essentially, the state's governor—rode in with city troops and dispersed the angry crowd. In all, six or seven people were dead and nineteen wounded. Wilson escaped the city in the middle of the night, hiding out for weeks before he could return safely.

The Fort Wilson Riot, as the battle soon became known, traumatized the city, particularly the members of the upper class who understood they were its targets. "Our streets for the first time were stained with fraternal blood," wrote Benjamin Rush, a friend of Wilson's who was also a prominent Philadelphia doctor and signer of the Declaration.[4]

Henry Laurens, a former president of the Continental Congress, wrote, "We are at this moment on a precipice, and what I have long dreaded and often intimated to my friends, seems to be breaking forth—a convulsion among the people."[5]

Laurens was right: the politics of the revolutionary period could be convulsive, combustible, and frequently violent. It reached a climax in the fall of 1786 and into 1787, when hundreds of indebted farmers in western Massachusetts began a series of anti-tax protests at local debtors' courts that ultimately led to an armed uprising against a federal armory. Quelling the attack, known as Shays' Rebellion, was a job for the federal government, but under America's first constitution, known as the Articles of Confederation, that government was so underfunded as to be useless. The state militia stepped in and shut down the rebellion, with a hand from a private militia. It was a stark and terrifying reminder for many of the founding fathers, who were preoccupied with the idea that the very people for whom they were designing a government might smother it in the cradle, and there would be nothing they could do.

III

The ever-present threat of political violence—and a federal government unequipped to respond to it—was one of two inescapable realities confronting the 55 men who gathered in the assembly room of the Pennsylvania State House in the hot summer of 1787 to hammer out the details of a new national charter. The other was the physical circumstances of the country and its residents.[6]

Late eighteenth century America was almost entirely rural: 97 percent of the population lived on farms and plantations or in small villages and towns. Only five cities had more than 10,000 residents. Philadelphia, the second largest, had 28,000. There was, of course, no electricity or indoor plumbing.

Few people had much in the way of formal education. Newspapers were beginning to spread, but they were mostly devoted to classified ads and local news.

Traveling beyond one's immediate region was daunting at best. Even by stagecoach, the jetliner of its day, getting from New York to Boston could take almost a week in bad weather. Under those circumstances, most Americans stayed close to home.

And, perhaps most important, the vast majority of them were not allowed to vote.

Only a decade earlier, America had declared independence based on the radical premise of human equality. But in practice, if you were anything other than a well-off white man, it was still just a premise—some nice-sounding words scratched on a piece of parchment. When it came to the right to vote, and thus to have a political voice in society, there was no equality at all. Not for the indigenous peoples of the continent, or for the close to 700,000 people of African descent held in bondage, or for white men who weren't fortunate enough to own property, or for white women who made up roughly half of the three million white people in the country at the time.

To comprehend the magnitude of these numbers, think of them in modern terms. At late eighteenth-century rates, modern America would hold about 58 million slaves. Add to that about 120 million white adult women and several tens of millions more lower-income white men. Now imagine that none of these people can cast a ballot.

The electorate in 1787 was, in short, minuscule. It consisted almost entirely of wealthy, well-educated, landowning white men—men like the delegates to the constitutional convention, more than one-third of whom owned slaves themselves.

These were the facts on the ground—some out of the framers' control, some they had helped to create—that would shape every part of the debates over the Constitution. America would survive as a self-governing nation, they believed, only by keeping the government at some distance from the public. Democratic rule was inherently unstable in their eyes because they considered most people to be poorly informed. A functioning republic required leadership by wise, learned men who could make decisions in the best interests of the entire country.

Uprisings like Shays' Rebellion only drove the point home: angry men, left to their own devices and discontents, could cause a whole lot of trouble. The problem was that state lawmakers weren't much better. Drawn increasingly from the ranks of the common people, they were passing economic policies that were too friendly to debtors and too hostile to wealthier creditors, men of the framers' class.[7]

The framers were no fans of monarchy, of course, nor were they interested in a pure aristocracy—but by the mid-1780s it was clear to them that simple democracy wasn't the answer. It was, in the words of Benjamin Rush, "the devil's own government."

This sentiment was expressed by many at the Philadelphia convention. "The evils we experience flow from the excess of democracy," said Elbridge Gerry, a Massachusetts delegate who was still shaken by what he'd seen play out in his home state. He called regular people "the dupes of pretended patriots."[8]

Some delegates were against popular elections even in the lower house of Congress—what we now call the House of Representatives, or "the People's House." "The people immediately should have as little to do as may be about the Government," said Roger Sherman of Connecticut. "They want information and are constantly liable to be misled."[9]

The framers knew they were smarter and more discerning

than the average man, and they designed a new system based on those presumptions. The final product was built for the people, legitimized by their approval, and at the same time kept at a remove from them. In the words of the historian Gordon Wood, it was an "aristocratic document designed to curb the democratic excesses of the revolution."[10]

In many ways, that system has been a remarkable success. It gave us a written Constitution, ratified by the people themselves, that establishes a national government and yet exists above it, protecting the rule of law from would-be tyrants (or so we have hoped). It gave us a system of separated powers designed to check and balance each other, ensuring that no one branch of government can ride roughshod over the others. It gave us a judiciary with the power to enforce individual rights against the government and, eventually, to strike down those laws that conflict with the Constitution.

But this vision of America wasn't the only one in the Pennsylvania State House that summer. There was another vision—of a far more democratic nation, in which the people themselves voted directly for all their representatives, including the president—and it was promoted by James Wilson. Far more than any other framer, Wilson, who had nearly been killed by the people just eight years before, made the insistent and passionate case for giving as much power as possible to the people themselves.

III

The odds are decent that you hadn't heard of James Wilson until now. Most Americans haven't, which is curious, because he was one of the main architects of our national charter, along with James Madison, the founder who is generally credited as the "father of the Constitution."

Why doesn't Wilson get any credit? It has nothing to do with his role at the convention but with what happened in the years afterward, when he was brought down by crippling debt he incurred through his longtime addiction to land speculation. He died a wretched, solitary death in a small cabin in the woods of North Carolina in 1798. The nation he had been central in helping to build was barely a decade old.

Wilson's pitiable end is the reason for his near total erasure from our national narrative. That's both a disservice to him and a tragedy for us, because when it comes to the evolution of American democracy, no one foresaw where we would be today more accurately than he did. He saw a country that was democratic, extensive, inclusive, and egalitarian to a degree almost no one else in Philadelphia dared imagine. In the words of a political scientist writing in 1897, Wilson was "filled with the democracy of the next century."[11] If we are going to take the last step in our slow evolution toward a truly representative democracy and let the people pick the president, it's first necessary to resurrect him.

Before I began researching and writing this book, I knew essentially nothing about James Wilson. As I learned more about him, about his radical political philosophy and his attempts to win over the other founding fathers to it, I was struck by how modern he sounded.

Wilson believed that the right to vote should be "extended as far as considerations of safety and order will possibly admit,"[12] and he opposed all property qualifications for voting and for holding elected office. He fought for more lenient residency requirements for immigrants who, like him, wanted to serve in government. He demanded that the Constitution be approved by the people themselves, in ratifying conventions, rather than by state legislatures.

He argued for a national legislature that would represent the people according to their numbers, and that would be elected by them, not by the states. And more than any other framer, Wilson insisted that the president should be chosen directly by the people.

But what explains his undying commitment to these ideals? Why would a man who faced down a bloodthirsty mob intent on killing him have any faith in the wisdom of the people, let alone a desire to give them more political power? That was my question, and I found part of the answer in where he came from.

Wilson, like Alexander Hamilton, was a poor immigrant whose boat landed on the shore's edge of the American Revolution. He was born into a religious farming family in the lowlands of Scotland in 1742 and had two early influences that would forever animate his thinking—and guide much of the shape of the Constitution.

The first was religious: Wilson was raised in the Presbyterian Church, where power flows up to the church elders from the congregants, who choose their pastor and ruling leaders themselves. This is a far less hierarchical structure than the Church of England, a towering layer cake of increasing power with bishops, archbishops, and a monarch at the top.

Wilson's second major influence was educational. By the age of 15, he was studying on a scholarship at the University of St. Andrews, getting a solid classical education in Latin, Greek, moral and political philosophy, and theology. It was the peak of the Scottish Enlightenment—a period of rapid intellectual development and innovative thinking about politics and human nature that would exert a profound influence on the American founders.

Scotland in the late eighteenth century was a far more democratic society than England, and the top thinkers of the era, including David Hume, Francis Hutcheson, and Adam Smith, were consumed with questions about the nature of human progress, the design of national governments and economies, and the rights of human beings. Hutcheson wrote that people had the right to rule themselves and, if necessary, declare their independence from faraway countries. He was thinking of Scotland's own relationship to England, but as far as James Madison and Alexander Hamilton were concerned, Hutcheson was preaching the gospel. Of course, these men were only schooled in Scottish thought; Wilson was literally raised in it.

Wilson's Scottish education, his Presbyterian upbringing, his exposure to the relatively democratic societies of Scotland and, later, of the Pennsylvania frontier, seem to have instilled in him the root of what would become his political philosophy: a deep faith in the wisdom, dignity, and equality of regular people.

Wilson carried these beliefs with him when he crossed the ocean from Scotland to New York in 1765. He arrived in the middle of protests over the Stamp Act, a law that had just been passed by the British parliament imposing a direct tax on paper documents in the colonies—everything from newspapers and pamphlets to wills and playing cards—to pay for British troops stationed there. For the colonists, who were unrepresented in parliament, "No taxation without representation" became the rallying cry, and they physically attacked British officials who tried to collect the tax. The stage for revolution was set, and Wilson would soon be standing in the middle of it.[13]

In 1768, when Wilson was just 26, he wrote a lengthy essay arguing that the British parliament didn't just lack the authority to pass the Stamp Act—it had no legislative authority at all over the colonies.[14] The essay wasn't published until 1774, when it became an instant hit, providing a clear and powerful legal basis for American independence and transforming Wilson into a leading revolutionary thinker.

It also caught the eye of a 31-year-old lawyer from Virginia named Thomas Jefferson, who copied parts of the essay into his *Commonplace Book*. One passage in particular stuck with him:

> All men are, by nature, equal and free: no one has a right to any authority over another without his consent: all lawful government is founded on the consent of those who are subject to it: such consent was given with a view to ensure and to increase the happiness of the governed . . .[15]

Jefferson was almost certainly channeling Wilson's words as he drafted the most famous lines of the Declaration of Independence a couple of years later:

> We hold these truths to be self-evident, that all men are created equal, that they are endowed by their Creator with certain unalienable rights, that among

these are Life, Liberty, and the pursuit of Happiness. That to secure these rights, Governments are instituted among Men, deriving their just powers from the consent of the governed . . .'[16]

On August 2, 1776, a month after the Declaration was first unveiled, Wilson stood beside Jefferson and several dozen other men in the Pennsylvania State House and signed his name to the document that he had partly inspired.

Over the next decade, Wilson's legal practice grew rapidly, as did his reputation and wealth. He indulged in one of his favorite hobbies, speculation, buying up massive tracts of land, much of it in the new western territories.

He served as a representative in the Continental Congress but grew frustrated at its inability to get anything done. And he participated in the earliest debates over the nation's first constitution, known as the Articles of Confederation, which were drafted with the primary purpose of protecting the power and independence of the states.

It was during these debates that Wilson began to develop his case for equal representation of people and to express his bafflement at his colleagues' intense attachment to their states. "It has been said that Congress is a representative of states, not of individuals," Wilson said. "It is strange that annexing the name of 'State' to ten thousand men, should give them an equal right with forty thousand. This must be the effect of magic, not reason."[17]

Of course, Wilson's home state of Pennsylvania was the most populous in the country at the time, which made it easier to argue in favor of representation based on population.

But his opposition to state equality had more to do with his ingrained political philosophy and his background as an immigrant, born an ocean away and holding no allegiance to any state or region. Wilson's address may have been in Pennsylvania, but he considered himself, above all, an American.[18]

III

This was the fully developed philosophy Wilson brought with him to the Pennsylvania State House in late May of 1787. The essential idea was known as "popular sovereignty"—that is, the people themselves are the ultimate source of all political power and authority in society. Any government of those people is legitimate only to the extent that they have consented to its rule.

"If we are to establish a national government, that government ought to flow from the people at large," he said. The reason, he explained, was that "no government could long subsist without the confidence of the people."[19]

Throughout the summer, Wilson hammered away at this idea in his distinctive Scottish brogue. According to James Madison's notes, Wilson spoke 168 times, more than any other delegate but one. A "fiery energy went into his declamations," said Benjamin Rush, a friend and fellow signer of the Declaration. "Though his voice was not melodious, it was powerful, and his blue eyes gleamed through heavy spectacles rimmed in metal."[20] Years later, Rush would write of Wilson, "His mind, while he spoke, was one blaze of light."[21]

As he had during the debates on the Articles of Confederation, Wilson reserved his greatest disdain for the claim that individual states should retain significant power under the new system. "The general government is not an assemblage of states, but of individuals, for certain political purposes," Wilson said on June 25 during one of many battles over the shape of the national legislature. To him, it was obvious that population should be the measure of representation. After all, he said, the legislature was the voice of the people, and "the individuals, therefore, not the states, ought to be represented in it."[22]

When delegates from New Jersey demanded that every state have an equal vote in at least one house of Congress, Wilson shot back in anger. "Shall New Jersey have the same right or influence in the councils of the nation with Pennsylvania? I say no. It is unjust—I never will confederate on this plan," he said. "If no state will part with any of its sovereignty, it is in vain to talk of a national government."[23]

This approach didn't endear Wilson to his colleagues, who might have been forgiven for wanting to keep the powers they had enjoyed under the Articles of Confederation. And why was he being so dismissive of the states? It was the states, after all, that had declared independence from Britain. It was the states that had sent their sons to fight the redcoats. John Dickinson, a delegate from Delaware and a skeptic of centralized national power, compared the federal system to "the solar system, in which the states were the planets." Wilson, he said, wanted to "extinguish these planets."[24]

As Wilson saw it, if America was going to work as a true republic, then living, breathing humans had to count more than artificial political lines. "All men, wherever placed, have equal rights and are equally entitled to confidence," he said on July 13—the day the Continental Congress passed a law establishing a government in the Northwest Territory and creating a way for new states carved out of that territory to be admitted to the union.[25]

What if those new states ended up containing most of the population? Not a problem, Wilson said. "The majority of people, wherever found, ought in all questions to govern the minority." Otherwise, America would just be repeating Britain's mistakes. "The fatal maxims espoused by her were that the colonies were growing too fast, and that their growth must be stinted in time," Wilson reminded the other delegates. "What were the consequences? First, enmity on our part, then actual separation."[26]

In practice, Wilson's principles had their limits. He was one of the convention's strongest voices against slavery, and yet, like other antislavery delegates, he kept a slave himself—a man named Thomas Purcell, who was his domestic servant for 26 years until Wilson freed him in 1794, possibly at the urging of his second wife, Hannah, a Quaker.[27]

Then there was the three-fifths clause, which allowed states to count each of their slaves as three-fifths of a free white person for purposes of representation in Congress. The number came from a similar deal made under the Articles of Confederation regarding the calculation of states' wealth for tax purposes.[28] The delegate who proposed it was James Wilson. At first he saw it simply as a way to secure the slave states' approval of the Constitution. But it ran against his egalitarian values, and eventually he backed away, challenging his colleagues to justify such unequal treatment. "Are they admitted as citizens?" he asked of the slaves. "Then why are they not admitted on an equality with white citizens? Are they admitted as property? Then why is not other property admitted into the computation?"[29]

Wilson nevertheless accepted the "difficulties" presented by the three-fifths ratio because, he said, of "the necessity of compromise."[30]

By the end, the Constitution was covered in Wilson's fingerprints—literally. With his remarkably tidy handwriting, Wilson was selected to be the scribe who wrote the first drafts of the charter.

In some ways, his vision for a more democratic America prevailed. After days of debate, a majority of the delegates agreed to adopt popular elections for the House of Representatives, which was expected to be the most powerful branch. The framers also agreed to present the Constitution for ratification directly to the people—who would assemble in state conventions—rather than to state legislatures.

But in other ways, the final product fell far short of his ideals. There would be a Senate with equal votes for all states, which he considered an abomination. And there would be no popularly elected president.

No matter his losses, Wilson was committed to the nationalist cause, and he knew the Constitution was the best and only hope for its survival. He remained a loyal soldier, returning to the Pennsylvania State House in October, only weeks after the convention adjourned, to address a large crowd gathered in the front yard. In a long and passionate speech almost eight years to the day after the attack on his house, Wilson defended the new charter, answering the critics' main objections one by one.

In the final words of his speech, Wilson acknowledged

his doubts, but he also seemed to be looking beyond his own life and toward the nation's future. "I am not a blind admirer of this plan of government, and that there are some parts of it which, if my wish had prevailed, would certainly have been altered," he said. And yet, "if there are errors, it should be remembered that the seeds of reformation are sown in the work itself."[31]

I I I

For a time after the convention, Wilson's political stature continued to rise. He was appointed by George Washington to be an associate justice on the first Supreme Court—although he had hoped desperately for the job of chief justice. In 1790 he began an influential series of lectures on the foundations and philosophy of American law at the College of Philadelphia. He never finished delivering them.

Behind the scenes, Wilson's life was falling apart. His compulsive land speculation had driven him to buy up more than four million acres, an area larger than the size of Connecticut. It had also driven him deep into debt. By the 1790s much of his wealth was locked in massive land deals secured with loans from friends and colleagues. When the economy turned in 1796, Wilson's creditors came calling. In August 1797 he was jailed briefly in New Jersey for unpaid debts, the first and only sitting Supreme Court justice to be incarcerated.

When the Supreme Court's new term began that fall, Wilson's seat sat empty. He had skipped town—this time, he was running not from a violent mob but from his creditors. He made his way to eastern North Carolina, where he hid in a small cabin in the woods near the home of James Iredell, his fellow justice and friend. It didn't work. One of his debts—of $197,000, or nearly $4 million in today's dollars—was to Pierce Butler, a fellow convention delegate from South Carolina. Butler tracked Wilson down and got him thrown in jail again. Wilson emerged from his second stint behind bars a broken man. He was still a sitting Supreme Court justice, but he was disgraced, penniless, and very sick. On August 21, 1798, Wilson died of malarial fever in Edenton, North Carolina. He was buried there, in a small plantation cemetery. More than a century passed before his body was exhumed, given a statesman's funeral, and reinterred in the churchyard at Christ Church in Philadelphia.[32]

Even if the man was largely forgotten, his ideas have remained alive, echoing in every step we take toward a more expansive and inclusive democracy. He would never get to see it himself, but James Wilson understood where America's founding principles inevitably pointed. They were right there, in the words of the Declaration of Independence that he had inspired. Long ignored in practice, those words were embedded in our national DNA, and with each new generation a little more of their full meaning has emerged into view.

Consider all the ways in which Wilson's vision has been vindicated: in the expansion of the franchise to include black former slaves, all women, and virtually all adults over 18; in the elimination of property qualifications for voting and holding office; in the right of the people to elect their senators directly; in the Supreme Court's adoption of the principle of one person, one vote. In all these ways and more, America has slowly come into line with what Wilson envisioned in 1787.

On the matter of a national popular vote for president,

however, he was so far ahead of his time that we still haven't caught up.

III

Wilson's premature death also deprived him of the chance to witness the personal evolution of some of the framers he had worked alongside in Philadelphia. As the United States entered the nineteenth century, several of them became more receptive to ideas of political equality and majority rule than they had been at the time of the founding. They came to see these features as not only compatible with republican government but essential to it.

James Madison's transformation began early. In the *Federalist Papers*, published in the months after the convention ended, Madison famously warned of the dangers of "factions"—his term for political parties, which he believed looked out for themselves at the expense of the public interest and were thus destructive to republican government.

Just a few years later, he recanted. In a series of newspaper essays, Madison explained that he had been wrong. Parties are not just "unavoidable" in any political society but could be useful to a functioning democracy—so long as there is "political equality among all." He also argued in favor of laws that, "without violating the rights of property, reduce extreme wealth towards a state of mediocrity, and raise extreme indigence toward a state of comfort." "If this is not the language of reason," Madison wrote, "it is that of republicanism."[33]

Madison's overriding goal at the convention was to filter the voice of the people and prevent what he saw as the dangers of too much democracy. But he had the good fortune to live nearly 50 years after the summer of 1787, longer than any other founder, and in that time he was able to see his political theories play out in practice—an experience that changed his mind on several key issues, including the right to vote. In 1821, as he prepared his notes from the convention for general publication, he felt it necessary to add a footnote. The views he expressed in Philadelphia, he wrote, "do not convey" his "more full and matured view of the subject. The right of suffrage is a fundamental article in republican constitutions."[34]

In 1833, three years before his death, Madison wrote that "the will of the majority" is "the vital principle of republican government."[35]

And then there is Thomas Jefferson, who missed the convention itself while serving as ambassador to France. Jefferson's views on democracy were deeply influenced by his firsthand experience of the French Revolution, which he initially saw as a benign reflection of the American one. "The nation has been awaked by our revolution, they feel their strength, they are enlightened, their lights are spreading, and they will not retrograde," he wrote to George Washington in 1788.[36] Jefferson's sympathies with the French radicals persisted even after the revolution descended into executions and massacres. This put him at odds with Federalists like John Adams, who saw France's bloodshed as evidence of what could happen if democracy were left unchecked. "Men could never be governed but by *force*," Adams said in 1793, after learning of the latest violence in France, according to Jefferson's notes. "Neither virtue, prudence, wisdom nor any thing else sufficed to restrain their passions."[37]

Jefferson eventually came to see the horrors of the French

Revolution for what they were, but he never let go of his belief in the people's will. In an 1816 letter to his friend Samuel Kercheval, Jefferson, by then an ex-president, recalled the immense pressures of the revolutionary period and recounted how they warped his and the other founders' thinking. This led them to make many mistakes, he said, as did their overall "inexperience of self-government."[38]

"In truth, the abuses of monarchy had so much filled all the space of political contemplation, that we imagined everything republican which was not monarchy," Jefferson wrote to Kercheval. "We had not yet penetrated to the mother principle, that 'governments are republican only in proportion as they embody the will of their people, and execute it.'"

Jefferson then proposed seven amendments to the Constitution, which he believed would "secure self-government by the republicanism of our constitution, as well as by the spirit of the people." "I am not among those who fear the people," Jefferson wrote, using words that, as in the Declaration, seemed to carry more than a hint of James Wilson's vision.

Jefferson's first proposed amendment would guarantee "general suffrage"—that is, broad access to voting. His second would require "equal representation in the legislature," the current lack of which he referred to as "republican heresy." Both proposals would have brought a smile to James Wilson's face. As would have Jefferson's third: "An executive chosen by the people."

2

THE FRAUGHT ORIGINS OF THE ELECTORAL COLLEGE

A Last-Minute "Frankenstein Compromise"

James Wilson was one of the Constitution's most tireless and aggressive advocates. Throughout the fall of 1787, he gave speech after speech highlighting its strengths and methodically rebutting its critics.

When it came to the Electoral College, however, Wilson was less than enthusiastic.

On December 11, several weeks into Pennsylvania's ratification debate, he said in a speech, "The Convention, sir, were perplexed with no part of this plan so much as with the mode of choosing the President of the United States."[1]

"Perplexed" was putting it mildly. From the start of the constitutional convention until the very end, four months later, the delegates battled continuously over the issue of presidential selection. They debated it on 21 different days, considered a wide range of proposals, and held 30 separate votes—more than for any other single topic in the Constitution. Every time the matter arose, it triggered long, exasperating, and often circular arguments. Should Congress choose the president? No, that would make the president dependent on another branch of government. Maybe it was better left to the state legislatures, or to their governors? No, they'll just play favorites. Why not let the people themselves vote directly? Too risky and impractical. Around and around it went.

The final product—a system of specially appointed, state-based electors that we today call the Electoral College—was a complicated, halfhearted arrangement cobbled together in the convention's final days by a few exhausted delegates in a side room of the Pennsylvania State House. It ran to 346 words over two paragraphs, the longest, most convoluted clause in the whole charter.

In a letter to a friend years later, James Madison recalled the last scrambled hours of the debate. "As the final arrangement of it took place in the latter stage of the session," he wrote, "it was not exempt from a degree of the hurrying influence produced by fatigue and impatience in all such bodies."[2]

Any informed debate about how and why we have an Electoral College must begin with these often forgotten circumstances of its birth. It was not, as many of us learned in school, a brilliant part of the framers' plan. It did not reflect any coherent political theory but flowed instead from deals the delegates had made in response to the specific conflicts they faced at a particular moment in history. It was settled on only after every other method failed to win enough support. It was, in the words of one constitutional scholar, a "Frankenstein compromise," adopted mainly so the delegates could finish their work and go home. And all of them knew that no matter what method they finally agreed to, George Washington was virtually certain to be the nation's first president.[3]

The convention of 1787 was actually the second stab at crafting an American constitution. The first, the Articles of Confederation, had been in effect for just six years, and everyone agreed that the system was not working.

The Articles had been drafted at the same time as the Declaration of Independence, in the middle of the war, and they were concerned far more with protecting the sovereignty of individual states than with establishing a strong or even functional national government. The states were entering into "a firm league of friendship with each other," the Articles said, language that sounded like a treaty among independent nations. That's effectively how the Articles operated: 9 of the 13 original states had to agree in order to pass any law, and all 13 had to agree to pass an amendment. There was a Congress, but it had almost no power to perform even the most basic tasks, like running an army, making international treaties, or levying taxes to pay war-related debts.

It was a recipe for failure. If America was going to endure, the system needed to be fixed.

But how? There were two camps. The Federalists—Washington, Madison, Wilson, Hamilton, and the other names most Americans know today—argued that the most urgent task was to build a strong, well-funded, and supreme national government. "I came here as a representative of America," Pennsylvania's Gouverneur Morris, one of the most committed nationalists, said. Morris "wished gentlemen to extend their views beyond the present moment of time; beyond the narrow limits of place from which they derive their political origin," and not simply "to truck and bargain for our particular States."[4]

The Anti-Federalists, as they came to be known, were a more varied group. They were more or less content with the existing system because they shared a general suspicion of centralized power, which they believed would lead inevitably to corruption and tyranny. Their main concern was protecting individual liberties and preventing faraway governments from meddling in local affairs. They were enraged at the nationalists, "those furious zealots who are for cramming it down the throats of the people," as one Anti-Federalist wrote of the new Constitution in a Boston newspaper. "I had rather be a free citizen of the small republic of Massachusetts, than an oppressed subject of the great American empire."[5]

It soon became clear that the Federalists had the winning argument. The Articles couldn't just be tweaked; America needed an entirely new constitution and a national government that was supreme over the states.

Beginning in late May, 55 delegates gathered each morning in the assembly room of the Pennsylvania State House on Chestnut Street. First, they laid down ground rules: no absences without permission, and a vow of total secrecy until the job was finished. Armed guards stood watch outside, and the State House's windows were sealed shut in case anyone tried to listen in.

Next, they ticked off the central problems with the Articles of Confederation. In addition to a weak central government, there was no judiciary to resolve disputes between the states. And there was no president.

This last point was especially sensitive. In 1787, the fear of executive power was very real. America had just fought a war to win independence from King George III, a despotic, unelected monarch who ruled at his whim from across the ocean. No one was eager to replace him with a homegrown tyrant. Even though most states had governors, they were generally weaker than the legislature.

Still, America as a whole was not functioning without a national executive. The question was what that executive would look like, what powers it would hold, and how it would be chosen.

On these counts, the delegates had no clear model to work from. But they did have George Washington, the revered war general, sitting right there in front of them. At the urging of his friends who knew he would bring a special gravitas to the proceedings, Washington had reluctantly agreed to preside over the convention. He barely spoke a word over the course of that summer, but he had a profound effect on the delegates' debates over the nature of the executive simply by being in the room.

▮▮▮

It was June 1, a Friday morning one week into the convention, when the delegates took up the proposal to establish a "national executive"—part of a broader plan James Madison had sketched out for a national government. James Wilson stood and called for this national executive, the president, to be a single person.

According to contemporaneous notes kept by Madison, who had appointed himself the convention's unofficial stenographer, Wilson's call was followed by "a considerable pause."

What was going through the delegates' minds in those awkward, silent moments? Having a single person act as president is obvious to us today, but it wasn't to the delegates. Some, surely picturing King George, were wary of placing so much power in one person. They wanted the job spread among multiple people, an executive panel. Others felt uncomfortable debating the issue in front of General Washington.

At the same time they couldn't simply ignore Wilson, a tall, intense presence with glasses always perched at the tip of his nose. By 1787 Wilson was the most respected legal scholar in the country, and one of just six delegates at the convention to have signed the Declaration of Independence. He wasn't an eloquent speaker, but he was brilliant, insistent, and forceful, and as educated in politics and philosophy as any delegate besides Madison.

The convention's chairman broke the silence and tried to put Wilson's proposal to a vote. Benjamin Franklin told him to wait. At 81, Franklin was a national icon and the only delegate whose star power rivaled Washington's. The nature of the executive, Franklin said, was "a point of great importance," and he wanted to hear what the other delegates thought before any votes were taken. Whatever the reasons for their silence, the men knew they had to respond.

Several spoke up in opposition. Edmund Randolph, a delegate from Virginia, warned that a single chief executive would be the "fetus of monarchy" and that Americans had "no motive to be governed by the British government as our prototype."[6]

It was a provocative challenge, and Wilson could have backed down right then. He didn't. To the contrary, he replied, a single president "would be the best safeguard against tyranny." Not only would that person be easier to control and hold accountable, he argued, but—and this next part "he was almost unwilling to declare" out of a fear that it would seem impossible to achieve—that person, the president, should be chosen directly by the people.[7]

Popular election was the most appropriate way for a self-governing society to choose its leaders, Wilson said—not just in the executive branch but in the legislative branch too. It would make all parts of the government "as independent as possible of each other, as well as of the states."[8] Massachusetts and New York chose their governors by direct vote, he pointed out, and they were operating just fine.

No one came to Wilson's side that day, and the convention put off any decisions on the matter until later. Much later, as it turned out.

The delegates who met in Philadelphia in 1787 were as distinguished, educated, and experienced a group of men as could be found anywhere in the country at the time. Many had fought in the revolution. They were well versed in political theory, moral philosophy, and world history going back to the ancient Greeks and Romans. And yet when it came to deciding the best way to elect a leader of their new nation, they were stumped.

III

The framers had good reasons to struggle so much over the question of how to choose a president. The issue didn't just trigger the concerns at the heart of the fight for America's independence; it was also tangled up in the two central clashes of the convention, both of which involved representation in Congress.

These two clashes provoked the most acrimonious battles of the summer, and more than once they threatened to topple the entire convention. There were charges of extortion and threats of treason. Gouverneur Morris, the Pennsylvania delegate and a fierce Federalist, later said that until these disputes were resolved, "the fate of America was suspended by a hair."[9]

And while the delegates couldn't know it at the time, the

resolution of the debates over Congress would seal the fate of the popular vote for president.

One debate was between the larger and the smaller states. The nationalists—men like Madison, Wilson, and Morris—who tended to come from more populous states, insisted that population be the measure of representation; states with more people, they felt, should get more representatives. It was simple and fair. The delegates from the smaller states, meanwhile, were just as insistent that states be equally represented, regardless of their population.

The debate got ugly. In a private conversation with Madison, Delaware's John Dickinson warned, "You see the consequences of pushing things too far." The small states, he said, "would sooner submit to a foreign power than submit to be deprived of an equality of suffrage in both branches of the legislature, and thereby be thrown under the domination of the large states."[10]

Dickinson's fellow Delawarean Gunning Bedford made the point out loud. "The large states dare not dissolve the confederation," he said on the convention floor. "If they do the small ones will find some foreign ally of more honor and good faith who will take them by the hand and do them justice."[11]

This type of talk infuriated the nationalists. "State attachments and state importance have been the bane of this country," Gouverneur Morris said. "We cannot annihilate the states, but we may perhaps take out the teeth of the serpents."[12]

Morris charged the small states with having "extorted from the large ones an equality of votes" in the drafting of the Articles of Confederation. "Standing now on that ground, they demand under the new system greater rights as men, than their fellow citizens of the large states."[13]

Alexander Hamilton was on the same page. "As States are a collection of individual men, which ought we to respect most, the rights of the people composing them, or of the artificial beings resulting from the composition," he asked on June 29. "Nothing could be more preposterous or absurd than to sacrifice the former to the latter. It has been said that if the smaller States renounce their equality, they renounce at the same time their liberty. The truth is it is a contest for power, not for liberty."[14]

These criticisms were being made at a time when the biggest state, Virginia, was only 13 times as big as the smallest, Delaware. (The ratio was six to one if you counted only eligible voters.) Today, the largest state has 70 times the population of the smallest.

However valid the complaints, the extortion worked. The nationalists knew they were over a barrel. On July 16, the delegates agreed to the so-called Great Compromise, which established the Congress largely as we know it. The upper house—the Senate—would be composed of equally weighted states, with senators chosen by their state's legislatures. The lower house—the House of Representatives—would be elected by the people and apportioned by population.

Gouverneur Morris never managed to extract the teeth of the serpents, but he did get his way in one respect—by extracting the serpents themselves from the Constitution's preamble. The first draft read, "We the People of New-Hampshire, Massachusetts, Rhode-Island and Providence Plantations, Connecticut, New-York, New-Jersey, Pennsylvania, Delaware, Maryland, Virginia, North-Carolina, South-Carolina, and Georgia, do ordain, declare and establish the following constitution for the government of ourselves and our posterity." When Morris got a spot on the committee tasked with hammering out the Constitution's final wording, he made a key edit: "We the People of the United States, in order to form a more perfect union . . ." It may have seemed like a consolation prize at the time, but measured by the lasting echo of those words over the centuries, Morris had struck one of his most influential blows in favor of the union.

III

The battle over the Senate was vicious enough, but as James Madison saw early on, the most significant divide at the convention was not between the large and the small states. It was between the slaveholding and non-slaveholding states. "The great danger to our general government is the great southern and northern interests of the continent, being opposed to each other," Madison said on June 29.[15] "Look to the votes in congress, and most of them stand divided by the geography of the country, not according to the size of the States."

By 1787, those divisions were only growing. States like Pennsylvania and New York were slowly emancipating their own slaves, and others, like Vermont and New Hampshire, had virtually none. Meanwhile, slavery was the economic engine of the South, which held about 90 percent of the country's almost 700,000 slaves. The southern delegates were perfectly aware of the dislike many northerners had for their "peculiar institution," and they were adamant that it not be taken from them.

The main fight at the convention was over how to count slaves for purposes of congressional representation. The southern delegates wanted to count them the same as free citizens, thus giving their states more representatives in the

House. The northern delegates didn't want the slaves to count for anything.

The day after his first remark on the subject, Madison was more blunt. "The States were divided into different interests not by their difference of size, but by other circumstances; the most material of which resulted partly from climate, but principally from the effects of their having or not having slaves. These two causes concurred in forming the great division of interests in the United States. It did not lie between the large & small states: It lay between the Northern and Southern."[16]

In case anyone missed it, he repeated himself on July 14: "The institution of slavery and its consequences formed the line of discrimination."[17]

The day before that comment, the delegates had agreed to the other major compromise of the convention: an agreement to count each slave as 60 percent of a free white person for purposes of both taxation and representation in Congress. We call it the Three-Fifths Compromise, but "compromise" isn't quite the term. The South got an enormous boost in political power and gave up essentially nothing in return.[18]

As one delegate to the South Carolina ratifying convention would later say, the three-fifths clause was "an immense concession in our favor."[19]

I I I

Once the debates over Congress had been resolved, however unsatisfactorily to the nationalists, the convention was able to return at last to the question of the presidency.

Wilson's original call for a popular vote on June 1 had gone nowhere. But he hadn't forgotten about it, and by the middle of July he had some powerful friends in tow. His nationalist comrades, James Madison and Gouverneur Morris, were still smarting from their recent defeats, and they soon came to agree with the logic of a national popular vote.

The president "ought to be elected by the people at large," Morris said on July 17. They will "never fail to prefer some man of distinguished character," of "continental reputation." If the legislature were to make the choice, on the other hand, "it will be the work of intrigue, of cabal, and of faction."[20]

Charles Cotesworth Pinckney, of South Carolina, was confused. Hadn't this proposal been rejected the first time around? Anyway, he said, the choice was best left to Congress. If it were given to the people, they "will be led by a few active and designing men." Then he added, "The most populous states by combining in favor of the same individual will be able to carry their points."[21]

Pinckney's first point wasn't about voters' intellectual capacity—after all, the delegates were happy to allow direct election of the House of Representatives, which they considered the most important branch. Rather it was a matter of practicality: How much information could regular citizens be expected to know about national candidates?

It was a reasonable concern, and one shared by many other delegates. In late eighteenth-century America, education was limited, transportation was slow, and mass communication was almost unheard of. Under these conditions, it was difficult for most people to get any reliable information about candidates beyond their local districts, and the framers feared that they would be inclined to vote for a charlatan, a smooth talker who was unfit to hold such a powerful job.

Pinckney's second point was more curious. Why would he

be so concerned about an advantage for the "populous" states? After all, South Carolina, his state, had about 250,000 residents at the time of the convention, enough to be considered "populous." But Pinckney wasn't referring to a state's total population; he was referring to its voting population. And 100,000 of South Carolina's residents were in chains.[22]

Hugh Williamson, a North Carolina delegate, made the point more directly. "The people will be sure to vote for some man in their own state, and the largest state will be sure to succeed," he said. "This will not be Virginia, however. Her slaves will have no suffrage."[23]

Morris called for a vote on the popular election of the president, which lost, nine to one, with only Pennsylvania voting in favor.

Two days later, Morris tried again. The president "should be the guardian of the people, even of the lower classes, against legislative tyranny," he said. And "if he is to be the guardian of the people, let him be appointed by the people."[24] This won over a few more delegates, and Wilson said he was pleased to see his idea gaining ground.

Then Madison chimed in. A direct popular vote for president "was in his opinion the fittest in itself," and would be as likely as any method to produce an executive of "distinguished character."[25] This was a coup for Wilson. Madison was by all accounts the most important delegate at the convention. He had also been consistently wary of placing too much power directly in the people's hands, preferring instead what he called "successive filtrations" of the popular will.[26] This was his first public comment on the popular vote.

Madison wasn't finished. There was "one difficulty however of a serious nature" regarding a popular vote. He picked up the point Hugh Williamson had made a couple days earlier and carried it to its logical conclusion. "The right of suffrage was much more diffusive in the Northern than the Southern States," Madison said, "and the latter could have no influence in the election on the score of the Negroes. The substitution of electors obviated this difficulty and seemed on the whole to be liable to fewest objections."[27]

In other words, Madison was saying, the method of choosing the president, like the design of Congress, would need to accommodate the demands of slaveholders. However the president would be picked, it would not be by the people.

But what was this about the substitution of "electors"? It was an idea that had originally been pitched by James Wilson, of all people—back on June 2, one day after he had proposed a direct popular election of the president. How he came up with the scheme is not clear,[28] but what is clear is that he considered it a second-best option, a way to give the people some voice in the process while also ensuring that Congress wouldn't make the choice.[29]

Wilson's proposal—a system of electors chosen by eligible voters only—was voted down easily in June. Now the idea was back, this time with a way to include the slave population, which likely made it more appealing to the southern delegates.

On July 25, Madison spoke again in favor of a popular vote. As he saw it, there were two concerns. The first was the plight of the small states, which he acknowledged would lose out because voters tended to get behind their home-state candidates. The second was "the disproportion of qualified voters in the Northern and Southern states, and the disadvantages which this mode would throw on the latter."

This would not be a problem, he said, because the South's

population would grow more quickly than the North's. Either way, he said, "local considerations must give way to the general interest," and as a slave-owning southerner himself, "he was willing to make the sacrifice."[30]

It was typical Madison—trying to please everyone. It was also in vain. The fight over how to choose the president would continue for more than a month, but the mid-July compromises were critical to its final shape. The small states and slave states had just won a disproportionate share of power in Congress, and they weren't about to leave their prize on the doorstep of the executive branch.

George Mason, a Virginia delegate and a slaveholder himself, put it simply during one of the final debates over representation in Congress: "From the nature of man we may be sure, that those who have power in their hands will not give it up while they can retain it. On the contrary we know they will always when they can rather increase it."[31]

▮▮▮

As July turned into August, the delegates were no closer to figuring out how to pick a president. At the same time, the nationalists were still stewing at their losses on both of the major compromises over Congress. Gouverneur Morris raged against slavery, calling it a "nefarious institution" and "the curse of heaven in the states where it prevailed."[32]

Weeks after the Three-Fifths Compromise had been agreed to, Morris was still trying to undo it. "Upon what principle is it that the slaves shall be computed in the representation?" he asked, echoing Wilson's remarks of several weeks earlier. "Are they men? Then make them Citizens and let them vote. Are they property? Why then is no other property included? The houses in this city are worth more than all the wretched slaves which cover the rice swamps of South Carolina."[33]

Morris said he "would sooner submit himself to a tax for paying for all the negroes in the United States, than saddle posterity with such a Constitution."[34] It was righteous talk, but it was just talk. Morris wanted a union as much as any nationalist, and he wasn't going to walk away from the last real chance to achieve it. Posterity would be saddled with such a Constitution, and he would sign it.

Meanwhile the newly emboldened slavers were defending their "nefarious institution" as both natural and indispensable.

"If slavery be wrong," South Carolina's Charles Cotesworth Pinckney said, "it is justified by the example of all the world." From Ancient Greece and Rome to modern France, England, Holland, and more, he said, "in all ages, one half of mankind have been slaves."[35] As a matter of history, Pinckney was right. What he neglected to mention was that none of those other societies had premised their right to self-government on the principle of human equality. Within a few decades, Pinckney's state would join 10 others in seceding from the union over this issue, plunging the United States into a brutal civil war that left more than 600,000 dead.

For now, Pinckney could comfortably stifle that point. And just to be clear about who had the leverage, he followed up with a familiar threat. "An attempt to take away the right as proposed will produce serious objections to the Constitution which he wished to see adopted"—specifically, that the free citizens of the South would refuse to ratify it. "South

Carolina and Georgia cannot do without slaves," he said.[36] Unlike Morris, he was prepared to back it up.

By late August, the delegates were exhausted and anxious to be done. Some had abandoned the convention over disagreements with the process or the document. A successful convention was still not a sure thing.

On August 31, a committee of 11 delegates, one from each state, convened to try to resolve the last outstanding issues, which included the method of selecting the president. Led by David Brearley of New Jersey, it was known as the Committee on Unfinished Parts.

Four days later, the committee presented its resolution to the full convention: the president would be a single person, would serve a term of four years, and would be eligible for reelection.

On the most difficult point—the manner of election— the resolution called for it to be done not by Congress or state legislatures or the people directly but by specially appointed electors in every state. These would be "the most enlightened and respectable citizens," in the later words of Alexander Hamilton, and would "possess the information and discernment" necessary for such a solemn task.

Each state would get as many electors as it had senators and members of Congress combined—so Massachusetts, which had two senators and eight representatives in the first Congress, started out with 10 electors.

Every four years, the electors would gather in their respective state capitals on a given day and cast their ballots for president. Each elector would vote for two candidates, at least one of whom had to live in a different state from the elector. The candidate with the most votes would become president. The runner-up would become vice president. If no candidate won a majority of electors' votes, the Senate would choose the president from among the top five vote-getters.

The framers did not call their invention the Electoral College. That name came into use many years later, and is somewhat misleading, since the design of the system—with electors gathering fleetingly in state capitals to do a single job—is hardly "collegiate."

In the last hours of the convention, the plan seemed like it would be acceptable enough to pass, with one important change: deadlocked elections would get decided not by the Senate but by the House. This change was made at the urging of James Wilson, who was still trying to keep the election as close as possible to the people. To appease the smaller states, it was agreed that in the event of an election decided by the House, each state delegation would get a single vote.

The final product was clunky, it was complicated, it was nonintuitive—and it was enough to get the votes. On September 6, the convention voted to approve the committee's proposal. Every state but Delaware voted yes.

Once again, the slave states and the small states got an electoral boost. The slave states got an electoral-vote bonus equaling 60 percent of their slaves, which could also serve as an incentive to enslave even more people, since more slaves meant more electors.

The small states got to repurpose the two extra votes for their senators in the vote for president. More important, they got the backup plan, which would throw contested elections to the House, where the small states would now be on equal footing with the large states. Some framers imagined that this wouldn't be a backup plan at all in practice. They thought the House would end up deciding virtually every election, because it would be hard for any one candidate to win a majority of electors. In that scenario, the larger states would benefit in the first round, because they had more electors, while the smaller states would get the advantage in the second round, where they had an equal vote in choosing among the top electoral vote finishers.

How much did the institution of slavery determine the way we choose our president? Even today, leading scholars of the founding era disagree with one another—and sometimes with themselves—on this question. In a *New York Times* op-ed in April 2019, Sean Wilentz, a history professor at Princeton, wrote that he had been mistaken to claim in a recent book that slavery was the key to the College's adoption.[37] "I've decided I was wrong," Wilentz wrote, arguing that the benefit the College gave slave states through the three-fifths clause was incidental. Two days later, Akhil Reed Amar, a constitutional law professor at Yale Law School, wrote his own *Times* op-ed arguing the other side. Given the various democratic features of the Constitution, like the popularly elected House of Representatives and the absence of federal property qualifications for voting and holding office, why not elect the president by popular vote? Because, Amar wrote, "Direct election would have been a dealbreaker for the South."[38]

What no one disputes is that the Constitution's framers gave speeches connecting slavery to the Electoral College, that the College gave extra electoral votes to the slave states, and that this inequity persisted throughout the years leading up to the Civil War.

But even apart from slavery, another question remains.

If the Electoral College was so hastily conceived and confusingly designed, why did Madison, Wilson, Morris, and the other nationalists agree to it? It wasn't because they thought it was the best way to pick a president. It was because they needed to finish writing the Constitution.[39]

|||

Less than two weeks after the method of electing the president was finalized, the convention voted to adopt the Constitution. Then came the real challenge: convincing the states to buy in. In late September the delegates returned to their home states and shifted gears from statesmen to salesmen.

Federalists like Madison, Wilson, Morris, and Hamilton promoted the Constitution as the best way to organize and run a diverse and rapidly expanding country. The Anti-Federalists challenged almost every part of the new charter, particularly its lack of a bill of rights, which they insisted was needed to protect the people against a newly empowered national government.

Both sides appealed to the power of the people—an easier lift for the Federalists when the subject was, say, the House of Representatives. Making a populist case for the Electoral College was harder.

At Virginia's ratifying convention, James Madison sold it as a pragmatic compromise. He would have preferred a popular vote for president, he said, but that was "impractical" given "the extent and population of the states."[40]

He also emphasized the provision that would send a deadlocked election to the House. "The lesser states, and some larger ones, will be pleased by that mode," he said. Without it, "the interest of the small states might be neglected or sacrificed."

Alexander Hamilton, writing in the *Federalist Papers,* praised the Electoral College as "almost the only part of the system, of any consequence, which has escaped without severe censure, or which has received the slightest mark of approbation from its opponents."[41]

For anyone who had been present and awake in the State House that summer, this was an amusing way to describe it.

Hamilton's argument was that, by giving the final choice of president to a temporary body assembled in each state for that purpose alone, the College would prevent "cabal, intrigue, and corruption," which he called the "most deadly adversaries of republican government." Moreover, it was a "moral certainty" that the system would prevent the election of "any man who is not in an eminent degree endowed with the requisite qualifications."

"Talents for low intrigue, and the little arts of popularity, may alone suffice to elevate a man to the first honors in a single State," Hamilton wrote, "but it will require other talents, and a different kind of merit, to establish him in the esteem and confidence of the whole Union."

James Wilson led the charge at Pennsylvania's ratifying convention, although when it came to the method of choosing the president, he was careful with his words. It "is not objected to," he said, and "therefore I shall say little on that point." During the convention itself, he had spoken with more candor: "This subject has greatly divided the House, and will also divide people out of doors. It is in truth the most difficult of all on which we have had to decide."[42]

But now, as a salesman, he defended electors, who would bring the vote "as nearly home to the people as is practicable" while making corruption unlikely and offering "little time or opportunity for tumult or intrigue."[43] Of his valiant push for a direct popular vote, Wilson added, perhaps with a wink, "other embarrassments presented themselves."[44]

The Anti-Federalists weren't buying any of it. George Mason, the Virginian delegate who had refused at the last minute to sign the Constitution, called the Electoral College a "deception" that deluded the people into thinking they were choosing the president themselves. In one Anti-Federalist newspaper, a writer identified as "A Columbian Patriot" claimed that the president would be elected by "an aristocratic junto" that could combine easily across state lines and install "the most convenient instrument for despotic sway."[45]

The slave states, meanwhile, were largely satisfied with the final document, and for good reason: it protected their most valuable property. At South Carolina's ratifying convention, Charles Cotesworth Pinckney said of the Constitution as a whole, "Considering all circumstances, we have made the best terms for the security of this species of property it was in our power to make. We would have made better if we could; but on the whole, I do not think them bad."[46]

In the end, any reservations about the Electoral College were overtaken by the larger fight over a bill of rights. James Madison argued strongly against the need for one. In his mind, the Constitution already protected citizens' rights, and any attempt to write out a list of specific rights would have the opposite effect, by making it easier for the government to claim that if a right wasn't on the list, it didn't exist. This argument didn't sway the Anti-Federalists, who remained wary of a central government with the executive power vested in a single person. They insisted on a bill of rights as the price of ratification.

Madison eventually agreed. He would draft a bill of rights—including the freedom of speech and religion, the right to a speedy trial and due process of law, and the right not to be subjected to cruel and unusual punishments. But because the Constitution had already been signed in Philadelphia, these rights would have to take the form of amendments. As he developed those amendments, the ratification process continued quickly. On June 21, 1788, New Hampshire became the ninth state to ratify the Constitution, officially establishing the charter as the foundation of the new American government. That December, the first presidential election got underway. In February 1789, the 69 electors cast their two votes each. As expected, all of them used one vote to pick George Washington. No popular vote was officially tallied, but it is estimated that roughly 43,000 men around the country, or less than 2 percent of the total population, cast ballots.

3

DID THE ELECTORAL COLLEGE EVER REALLY WORK?

Not Like the Framers Expected It To

When the framers of the Constitution dreamed of their ideal presidential elector, surely they pictured someone like Samuel Miles.

Miles was 56 years old when he was nominated for the job in 1796. By then he had served as an officer in the Revolutionary War, an appeals court judge, a trustee of the University of Pennsylvania, and the mayor of Philadelphia, one of the nation's largest cities. He was an upstanding, well-regarded citizen with deep knowledge of both local and national politics, so it was no surprise that Pennsylvania's voters chose him, along with 14 other men, to help select the next president.

The race that year was between John Adams, the sitting vice president, and Thomas Jefferson, the former secretary of state. When the time came to cast his ballot, Miles did what he believed the framers had intended him to do—consider the choices before him and pick the candidate who, in his judgment, would govern in the best interests of the country.

For Miles, that meant voting for Jefferson over Adams. It was a close call. He thought highly of both men and assumed either would make a competent executive. But he was tired of living through constant armed conflict, and with the United States appearing to be on the eve of war with France, Miles believed Jefferson, who had previously served as the ambassador to France, would be more likely than Adams to steer the two countries to a peaceful outcome.

"I had not fully made up my mind," Miles wrote some years later, but "I thought it my duty to vote for the man that appeared to me most useful for the public good, without any regard to party views."[1]

Miles was right: that was how many of the framers intended the Electoral College to work. And it was how the College had in fact worked in each of the first two elections, in 1789 and 1792, when the electors unanimously chose George Washington, the revered war general.

The problem for Miles—and for the framers—was that it was no longer working this way. Washington was so broadly popular in part because he had deliberately kept his distance from partisan politics out of a belief that the young nation needed leaders who would unite a diverse and growing population. But by 1796 there were two established national political parties: the Federalists, who believed in a strong central government and supported John Adams, and the Democratic-Republicans, which

Jefferson had recently founded with his fellow Virginian James Madison to oppose the Federalists' national ambitions and preserve state power.

Faced with two incompatible platforms, electors could no longer justify playing the role of neutral arbiter; they had to take sides. Samuel Miles was a Federalist, and the Federalists who voted for him expected him to toe the party line. In their eyes, his high-minded rationale for bucking them and choosing Jefferson was beside the point. He had betrayed the party at a moment when the stakes could not have been higher. Adams ended up winning a bare majority of electors, 71 to Jefferson's 68. If just two other electors had followed Miles's path, Jefferson would have won.

Federalists were furious. One wrote to his local newspaper, "What, do I choose Samuel Miles to determine for me whether John Adams or Thomas Jefferson shall be president? No! I choose him to act, not to think."[2]

No one today would blink at that statement; for us, the Electoral College has never operated any other way. It's not hard to imagine a similar letter to the editor being written by, say, a Democratic voter in 2000 if an elector pledged to Al Gore had instead chosen to vote for George W. Bush, who won by a margin nearly as narrow as Adams's.[3] But in the closing days of the eighteenth century, it was a new sentiment.

And it shows that within less than a decade of the Constitution's ratification, the framers' main public rationale for the Electoral College—that it would act as a body of learned men who would deliberate and choose the fittest man for the job—was dead in the water.

I I I

The beginning of the end of the framers' Electoral College came on September 19, 1796, only a few weeks before Miles and his fellow electors cast their ballots. On that Monday, the *American Daily Advertiser* published a 6,000-word open letter to the American people from George Washington, who was nearing the end of his second term and had decided he would not run again.

Washington was the most respected and beloved American of his day, and he was as committed to the primacy of the new union as any founder. In his letter, now commonly known as his Farewell Address, he exhorted his fellow countrymen to think of themselves, above all, as Americans—and not as residents of any particular state or region.

"Citizens, by birth or choice, of a common country, that country has a right to concentrate your affections," Washington wrote. "The name of American, which belongs to you in your national capacity, must always exalt the just pride of patriotism more than any appellation derived from local discriminations."[4]

This ideal was fully in keeping with Washington's nationalist, nonpartisan mission, but even before he stepped down, that mission was increasingly coming under assault. The country's politics were fracturing and reshaping themselves in ways that neither he nor the other framers had anticipated. As a result, the election of 1796 would not only be the first without George Washington on the ballot but also the first to feature candidates from two opposing parties.

This new world of partisan politics had two immediate

consequences for presidential elections. First, candidates started to run on tickets, joining with a vice presidential candidate from their own party and of their own choice, in the expectation that electors would cast their two votes for the team. In 1796 Adams ran with Thomas Pinckney of South Carolina, while Jefferson chose New York senator Aaron Burr.

Second, the electors began to run on party lines. Samuel Miles had run as a Federalist, but he didn't believe that prevented him from honoring the framers' intent. He was swimming against the tide.

Over the last two centuries fewer than 170 electors have dared to follow Miles's lead and cast their ballots for someone other than their party's preferred candidate. Never have any of these so-called faithless electors come close to influencing the outcome of an election, and yet the mere threat of partisan disobedience has led more than two dozen states to pass laws binding their electors—and punishing them with fines or other sanctions if they break ranks.

The framers assumed that electors would generally choose the most qualified candidates, which is why they saw no risk in giving the presidency to the electoral vote winner and the vice presidency to the runner-up. It made sense to install the two best men at the head of government. The moment opposing parties entered the picture, however, that logic fell apart. When Jefferson placed second in the 1796 electoral vote count, sneaking ahead of Adams's fellow Federalist Thomas Pinckney, it triggered the first unintended consequence of the Electoral College: a president and vice president with fundamentally different views of governance.

In a sense, 1796 was America's first modern presidential

election—a showcase of fierce partisan combat that did not at all resemble the framers' original vision for the presidency. It also revealed the fallacy of the claim that states would align themselves with one another according to population size, which small-state delegates had asserted repeatedly at the constitutional convention. In reality, the voting breakdown in 1796 had nothing to do with state size. Instead, as Madison had pointed out years earlier, the real dividing line was between the North and the South, and their opposing views on the institution of slavery. Adams—one of just two presidents in the nation's first half century who did not own slaves (the other was his son, John Quincy Adams)—swept the northern states, with the exception of Pennsylvania; Jefferson, a Virginia slaveholder, took almost all of the South. This result held even though both candidates chose a running mate from the other region in the hope of generating wider appeal.

And yet the electoral complications that first presented themselves in 1796 were minor compared to what would happen four years later. The 1800 election featured a rematch between Adams and Jefferson, which created enough tension on its own. Then a quirk of the Electoral College got in the way, setting off a wave of political chaos that nearly toppled the young nation and required a constitutional amendment to repair. The drama was all the more agonizing because it was entirely predictable. Indeed, Alexander Hamilton himself had foreseen it.

III

In public at least, Alexander Hamilton was one of the Electoral College's biggest cheerleaders.

In *Federalist* no. 68, which Hamilton published in early 1788 during the ratification debates over the Constitution, he wrote, "if the manner of it be not perfect, it is at least excellent."

For more than 200 years, defenders of the Electoral College have pointed to Hamilton's words as direct evidence of the founders' faith in the wisdom of their convoluted mechanism for electing the president. But the *Federalist Papers*, which Hamilton churned out with his fellow Federalists James Madison and John Jay in the months after the Philadelphia convention, were essentially one extended advertisement selling the Constitution to skeptical New Yorkers. And Hamilton, like any good salesman, knew how to talk up the benefits of his product. Behind the scenes, though, he was panicking.

In a private letter to James Wilson on January 25, 1789, before the electors had met to cast their ballots in the first election, Hamilton raised the alarm. Writing with "a degree of anxiety about a matter of primary importance to the new government," he pointed out a major flaw in the College.[5]

"Everybody is aware of that defect in the constitution which renders it possible that the man intended for Vice President may in fact turn up President," he wrote. How could that happen? The Constitution gave each elector two votes but no way to indicate which vote was for which office. The general expectation—and Hamilton's strong desire—was that George Washington would win the most votes. John Adams would most likely come in second, with the remainder of the votes divided among the other candidates, one of whom, New York governor George Clinton, was an Anti-Federalist.

But even though Washington was very popular, there had never been a nationwide election for president before, and it didn't take a mathematician to figure out that the new system could easily be gamed. As Hamilton wrote, "unanimity in Adams as vice president and a few votes insidiously withheld from Washington might substitute the former to the latter."

He didn't consider this to be a hypothetical. The opponents of the Constitution were still angry at their failure to defeat it, and Hamilton expected them to do whatever they could—"machinations of anti-Federal malignity," as he put it—to undermine its success.

"What in this situation is wise?" Hamilton asked Wilson. Luckily, he had a solution: "I conclude it would be prudent to throw away a few votes, say 7 or 8" in Adams-friendly states like Connecticut and New Jersey—enough to ensure that Adams remained in second place but not so many that he fell into third, possibly elevating to the vice presidency a candidate who would be hostile to the nationalists' project.

The irony was thick: Hamilton had marketed the Electoral College as the best way to prevent "cabal, intrigue and corruption," and yet here he was, not even a year later, trying to use the College to create a cabal.

No matter: in the end, all 69 electors cast one of their votes for Washington, making him the first president. Adams finished second with 34.

When Washington stood for reelection in 1792, he was again chosen by every elector, and concerns about flaws in the Electoral College quieted down. But Hamilton had been right: the defect was in plain sight. In the wake of the 1796 election, which resulted in a president and vice president from opposing parties, it became clear that the problem was worse than he had thought.

❙❙❙

On January 6, 1797, only weeks after the 1796 election had ended, the first amendment to the Electoral College was proposed in Congress. Its sponsor, a South Carolina representative named William L. Smith, advocated changing the Constitution to let electors designate separately their picks for president and vice president.[6] In this way, political opponents like Adams and Jefferson wouldn't be forced to govern together, and "great inconveniences" would be avoided. Smith's resolution failed.

Three years later, the "great inconveniences" became a reality. In the 1800 race, President Adams ran for reelection, this time with Charles Pinckney, Thomas's brother; Jefferson ran again with Aaron Burr. This time Jefferson prevailed, 73 electoral votes to Adams's 65. But that wasn't the problematic result. Partly in reaction to the behavior of Samuel Miles in 1796, the Democratic-Republican electors were uniformly faithful to the party, each one casting one vote for Jefferson and one for Burr. That left the two men with 73 electoral votes each. Alexander Hamilton's nightmare had come true—and it hadn't even required any intentional partisan mischief.

Under the Constitution's rules, the House of Representatives would now break the tie, with each state getting a single vote—a major advantage for the small states, which would find themselves on equal footing with states many times their size. Each state's vote would go to whichever candidate was preferred by a majority of the state's delegation; if a delegation split evenly, it lost its vote. To become president, a candidate had to win an absolute majority of states.

Jefferson was the Democratic-Republicans' unequivocal choice for president, so the process should have been quick. But the ambitious Burr, aware of how close to power he suddenly was, refused to stand aside in the face of intense pressure from party leaders.

On Wednesday, February 11, 1801, in the middle of a snowstorm, the House took its first vote for president. With 16 states participating, nine were needed to win the presidency. The tally was eight states for Jefferson and six for Burr. Two states, Vermont and Maryland, split their votes and had to cast blank ballots. Jefferson was one state short of victory.

Six more ballots were taken, all with the same result. One Maryland lawmaker, Joseph Hopper Nicholson, was so ill he was carted into the chamber on a bed to cast his vote. Massachusetts's Harrison Gray Otis observed the scene and said that although he wouldn't risk his life for any president, he had "no objection to staying [t]here all night" since he was in good health.[7]

The voting continued for the next several days as members of Congress huddled behind closed doors to haggle over votes. The Federalists despised Jefferson, and the state delegations that they controlled voted for Burr in order to keep Jefferson out of the White House. The Democratic-Republicans, meanwhile, stayed faithful to their man.

The unfairness of the system was obvious: Delaware, then the smallest state in the union, had one representative in the House, a Federalist named James A. Bayard; Virginia, the largest, had 19 representatives. And yet when it came time to cast their ballots, Bayard's vote, which went for Burr in the first rounds, was equal to that of Virginia's entire delegation, which went overwhelmingly for Jefferson.

Over the course of a week, the delegations cast 36 separate ballots. In each of the first 35, the outcome was identical: Jefferson eight, Burr six, two abstentions. Inauguration Day was March 4, less than a month off, and representatives were beginning to fear they would never reach a conclusion, even as they dug their heels deeper with each successive ballot. "No man's reputation would be safe, should he now change," Connecticut senator Uriah Tracy said.[8]

It might have gone on like that forever, but Alexander Hamilton—who by now could have had a side business in gaming the Electoral College—was feverishly working the levers, trying to convince Federalists to vote for Jefferson over Burr. Hamilton and Jefferson disagreed intensely, but Hamilton still had respect for him as a statesman, which he did not have for the opportunistic Burr.

On February 17, Hamilton's ploy finally worked: on the thirty-sixth ballot, no Federalist cast a vote for Jefferson, but Delaware's Bayard abstained from voting, which took Delaware out of Burr's column. Federalists in Maryland and Vermont who had supported Burr also sat out, breaking the ties in those states, pushing them to Jefferson and giving him the presidency.

In theory, this was how many of the framers of the Constitution had expected most presidential elections to be decided. The debacle of the 1800–1801 election showed that, in practice, it was a disaster.

The public was starting to catch on. One letter to the editor of the *Philadelphia Aurora*, the most influential Republican newspaper in the country, called the framers' design a "puerile and circuitous mode" meant to avoid "some imaginary evils." The writer urged an amendment "that the presidential election be held on the same day throughout the union, and the choice be made *immediately by the people, without the intervention of electors.*"[9]

The system was clearly broken in more ways than one, but as far as Jefferson and his fellow Republicans were concerned, the most pressing item on the agenda was to prevent a repeat of the 1800 election. While they had pulled that one out of a hat, they had seen the chaos it triggered and weren't eager to leave their fate to future House delegations. They also knew that the Federalists, while electorally weak, could still scuttle Jefferson's reelection by strategic electoral voting—that is, if enough Federalist electors threw their votes to Jefferson's running mate, they would vault that person over Jefferson and into the White House.

In December 1803, Republicans in Congress passed the Twelfth Amendment, which required electors to cast separate ballots for president and vice president. It both fixed the design flaw in the Electoral College and effectively ensured Jefferson's reelection in the process. The states ratified the amendment barely in time for the 1804 election. Jefferson, running this time with a more reliable number-two in George Clinton, won handily.

But the Twelfth Amendment did more than fix a quirk of the original Electoral College. By dramatically reducing the likelihood that an election would be thrown into the House of Representatives, it took away the one meaningful advantage the framers had given to the smaller states.

By accommodating the new reality of organized parties and joint tickets, it ensured that the presidency would become a national political office, appealing to, and being supported by, national coalitions.

And by tweaking the College's design while refusing to address the pro-slavery distortions of the three-fifths rule—which gave more than a dozen extra electoral votes to the southern states because of their slaves, and which was responsible for Jefferson's victory in 1800—the Twelfth Amendment helped entrench slavery in America for another 60 years.[10]

III

More than 200 years after its ratification, the Twelfth Amendment remains the only successful constitutional reform of the Electoral College, out of more than 700 efforts to alter or abolish it. But it wasn't the only way the College was transformed in the nation's early years. These transformations, which were as consequential as anything that could be done by a constitutional amendment, can be summed up in two questions: Who picks electors? And how are those electors allocated?

These two matters are central to the way the Electoral College operates, and both are left entirely to the states to decide. The Constitution sets the number of electors each state gets—one for each representative and senator—but beyond that, it's a state-run operation.

From the moment national political parties entered the

scene, the states took advantage of their control over these features of the College, constantly revising their rules to give an edge to one party or the other. Combined with the transformations wrought by the Twelfth Amendment, the states' decisions created the Electoral College we use today—one that is far different from what the founders thought they were designing.

First, who picks? State lawmakers may keep the power for themselves—in which case voters have no role at all in electing the president—or they can let their citizens vote.

In the first election, in 1789, six states chose their electors either with no input from eligible citizens or, in the case of two (Massachusetts and New Hampshire), with an indirect role for them. Four states—Delaware, Maryland, Pennsylvania, and Virginia—let their eligible citizens (that is, white men, usually with property) choose the electors directly.

Of the remaining three states at the time, two—Rhode Island and North Carolina—had not yet ratified the Constitution. New York had, but it cast no electoral votes because lawmakers there were still debating how to appoint their two senators, and they had agreed that whatever system they chose would apply equally to their electors. Since they had no system in place for choosing senators, they couldn't choose electors.

Over the next several decades, states experimented freely, sometimes changing methods depending on who was in power at the time or on what they believed was in their political best interests. Massachusetts has changed its method of allocating electors 11 times.

By 1800, a majority of state legislatures still appointed

their electors themselves. But as more states began switching to popular election, it became harder for the holdouts to deny their own voters a say in the presidential race.

By 1824, all but six states let their voters choose the electors directly. For reasons we will get to in a moment, the election that year provided the last big push in favor of popular voting for electors. By 1828 only two states resisted, and by 1832 there was only one—South Carolina, which refused to let its voters cast a presidential ballot until 1860.

The last time a state denied its people the ability to vote for presidential electors was in 1876, when Colorado, which had been admitted to the union earlier that year, had the legislature appoint its three electors. As it turned out, those three votes would be crucial to the outcome of the election.

The switch to popular voting for electors was an important step toward democracy because it gave the people—or the eligible voters of the time, at least—a more direct role in choosing their leader. At the same time, it made it hard to argue that the Electoral College was an essential element of the nation's federal system.

When state legislatures chose the electors themselves, they could claim that their decision represented their state's political sovereignty—similar to the way they once chose senators, a power that was at the heart of the original federal scheme.

That logic collapses as soon as you move to a popular vote. Average citizens don't cast their presidential ballots (or even their Senate ballots) based on what state they live in; they vote based on their party preference. Democrats in 2016 voted for Hillary Clinton whether they lived in California,

Nebraska, or Maine. Republicans in Florida picked Donald Trump not because they lived in Florida but because they wanted him to be the president.

III

Just as important as *who* gets to choose a state's electors is *how* those electors are allocated. At the founding, states used one of two basic approaches to allocation. Under the district system, a state tallied the popular vote in its congressional districts and awarded one elector to whichever candidate won each district. In the "general ticket" system, what we call winner-take-all today, the candidate who got the most votes in a state got all of that state's electors, no matter the margin of victory.

Of the two methods, the district system more accurately reflects a state's political makeup: no state gives 100 percent of its popular vote to one candidate. But in a world with clearly defined national political parties, district-based allocation is almost guaranteed to hurt a state's preferred candidate. Thomas Jefferson found this out the hard way in 1796 when he lost a handful of electors in states like North Carolina, Pennsylvania, and his home state of Virginia, where he had won a majority of the popular vote, because those states used the district system to allocate their electors. In each state there were enough Federalist districts to give Adams the extra electors he needed to squeeze out a majority and win the presidency.

Jefferson didn't like winner-take-all on principle—in the states that used it, "the minority is entirely unrepresented," he wrote to James Monroe, Virginia's governor, in January 1800. Still, he saw what had happened in 1796, and he wasn't about to let it happen again. In his letter to Monroe, he added that "all agree that an election by districts would be best, if it could be general; but while 10 states choose either by their legislatures or by a general ticket, it is folly and worse than folly for the other 6 not to do it."[11]

Virginia lawmakers got the memo. They passed a law switching the state from the district system to winner-take-all—just in time for the 1800 election. That year, Virginia was one of only two states, along with Rhode Island, to use the winner-take-all rule. By 1832 every state but one used it—South Carolina, again, was the lone holdout.

But Jefferson wasn't the only founder discomfited by winner-take-all, which offended basic notions of republican government. In a letter to a friend, James Madison wrote that he would support a constitutional amendment banning the practice and requiring states to allocate their electors under the district system, which he said "was mostly, if not exclusively in view when the Constitution was framed and adopted."[12]

The main problem with winner-take-all, Madison explained, was what Jefferson had identified: it created a race to the bottom. As one state after the next adopted the method, it became "the only expedient for baffling the policy of the particular States which had set the example." The result was that the states became "a string of beads." If the district system were required, Madison hoped, it would "break the force of those geographical and other noxious parties."

But there was a deeper unfairness to winner-take-all— its effect on individual voters. This effect was best described by Thomas Hart Benton, a Missouri senator from 1821 to 1851. "To lose their votes is the fate of all minorities; and it is their duty to submit," Benton said in 1824. "But this is not a case of votes lost, but of votes taken away, added to those of the majority, and given to a person to whom the minority is opposed."[13]

Winner-take-all rules harmed the country by "segregating the states, drawing them up against one another, like hostile ships in battle," Benton said. "This alienates the states from each other, and fills them with hostile feelings, and the president elected must become the president of the states which choose him, and look with coldness and resentment upon those which oppose him."

In the first decades of the nineteenth century, Congress considered multiple amendments that would prohibit the use of winner-take-all and require states to use the district system. Three passed the Senate, but none made it through the House of Representatives.

During an 1816 debate over one of the amendments, Abner Lacock, a Pennsylvania senator, suggested abolishing the College outright and replacing it with the national popular vote—the first time this idea was introduced in Congress. Lacock could "see no reason why these agents"—the electors—"should be employed between the people and their votes."[14] Governors are chosen by popular vote, he pointed out, and it works perfectly well in that context. He rejected the idea that direct election "would produce popular fermentation"—or civic unrest, which he considered to be a figment of lawmakers' imaginations. "The people at home will remain unmoved, and on the day of election will, at their respective polls, soberly and dispassionately decide the question." Lacock won a few supporters, but in the end his motion was voted down.

Over the years, a few states have returned to the district system. Michigan did so briefly in 1892, when Democrats took control of the state legislature and realized they could pick off a few electors in a Republican-dominated state. This change led to a lawsuit that went all the way to the Supreme Court. The opinion in that case, *McPherson v. Blacker*, still stands today for the proposition that "the appointment and mode of appointment of electors belong exclusively to the states."[15]

Today, two states use the district system. Maine adopted it in the wake of the tumultuous 1968 election, a three-way race that raised serious questions about the fairness of the winner-take-all system. In 1992 Nebraska followed suit, hoping to make its electors more competitive and thus turning the traditionally Republican-dominated state into more of a "player" in presidential elections. It didn't work. After the 2000 race, one state official said, "We didn't get a presidential candidate this year or a vice presidential candidate. We didn't even get the presidential candidates' wives. We got the vice president's wife."[16]

Aside from these exceptions, every state since 1880 has appointed its electors by popular vote using the winner-take-all rule. Periodically, lawmakers in the minority party of a state have tried to replace winner-take-all with the district system—Republicans in California attempted it in 2007, as did Republicans in New York in 2011. Those efforts have failed for a simple reason: no state wants to unilaterally disarm by giving up its influence on behalf of the majority-party candidate. As Thomas Jefferson realized more than 200 years ago, you'd be crazy to do it.

■ ■ ■

The framers' unhappiness with winner-take-all, which never came up during the convention, was understandable. But the parts of the College that the framers had explicitly agreed to weren't looking very good, either.

Madison particularly regretted signing on to the provision sending deadlocked elections to the House of Representatives, with its one-vote-per-state rule—a ghost of the Articles of Confederation, under which all states had equal power. He referred to this as an "evil" and said it was "so great a departure from the republican principle of numerical equality" that it needed to be eliminated from the Constitution.[17] Knowing this would infuriate the smaller states, Madison suggested an amendment with something for everyone. Get rid of winner-take-all, which gave the larger states an advantage, and get rid of the House-decided election, which benefited the smaller states. The idea never went anywhere.

Thomas Jefferson shared Madison's aversion to letting presidential elections be decided by the House. Even though he had been the beneficiary of one, he had seen up close the chaos it produced and had no desire to see it happen again. In 1823 Jefferson wrote that the one-vote-per-state provision was "the most dangerous blot in our Constitution, and one which some unlucky chance will someday hit."[18] Barely a year later, it did.

The election of 1824 was the first to have a meaningful count of the national popular vote, because it was the first time a majority of eligible citizens could vote directly for presidential electors. About 360,000 voters turned out to cast a ballot that year, and they had a clear favorite: Andrew Jackson, a decorated army general from Tennessee, won about 150,000 votes, or a little more than 41 percent of the electorate. That put him well ahead of his nearest rival, John Quincy Adams, the secretary of state and son of the second president, who pulled in about 31 percent. Behind them were William Harris Crawford, the treasury secretary; and Henry Clay, the Speaker of the House. All four were Democratic-Republicans, since the Federalist Party had disintegrated in the early 1820s.

In addition to his popular-vote lead, Jackson held a comfortable lead in the Electoral College, with 99 electoral votes to Adams's 84. But the four-man race divided the electors widely enough to deprive any one candidate of the necessary majority. Under the provisions of the Twelfth Amendment, the House would choose among the top three finishers—Jackson, Adams, and Crawford. Clay, who finished fourth, was disqualified.

Unlike the first time this happened, in 1800, the balloting didn't drag on for days, but the final outcome was nearly as controversial. Adams won a majority of state votes on the first ballot, and he became the nation's sixth president. Jackson, despite being a clear favorite in the popular vote and the Electoral College, went home empty-handed. And, as in 1800, there were questions about why lawmakers had voted as they did—especially after Clay, who detested Jackson and played a central role in corralling enough votes for Adams to win, wound up getting named Adams's secretary of state. Whether or not it was the product of a backroom deal, it certainly smelled like one. Jackson was livid, and his supporters called it a "corrupt bargain."

Over the next four years, Jackson plotted his revenge, riding the first great wave of democratization in America—the trend among the states to eliminate property requirements for voting and holding office. This was a natural fit for Jackson, who saw his loss in 1824 as an unjust usurpation of the people's democratic will.

It sounded a little like what James Wilson would have argued, although it's worth noting that Wilson would have been the first to be kicked out the door by Jackson. If the founders were concerned primarily with toppling the monarchy, Jackson was out to topple the aristocracy the founders represented. He built a movement around veneration of the common man and vilification of entrenched elites and their grip on money and power.

In 1828 Jackson easily won a rematch with Adams, taking the popular vote by 56 percent to 44 percent and the Electoral College by 178 to 83.

He cared far more about the former statistic than the latter—so much so that in his first message to Congress, in December 1829, Jackson called for replacing the College with a national popular vote. "To the people belongs the right of electing their chief magistrate," he said. Engaging in a little historical revisionism, he added, "It was never designed that their choice should in any case be defeated either by the intervention of the electoral colleges or by" the House of Representatives. "The first principle of our system," Jackson said, is "that the majority is to govern—it must be very certain that a President elected by a minority can not enjoy the confidence necessary to the successful discharge of his duties."[19]

Once he was settled in office, Jackson made "universal suffrage" a centerpiece of his platform—although "universal" still meant only adult white men. Jackson, a slaveholder himself, had no interest in emancipation, let alone racial equality. To him, the growing antislavery movement was little more than a distraction. (Even his appeal for a direct popular vote recognized that the three-fifths clause would still somehow have to be honored.[20])

Still, the Jacksonian era fundamentally changed the way Americans think and talk about the presidency. Under his tenure it became a truly national office, the only one that represented the people—however narrowly defined that term remained—as a whole. It also became a more expansive one, as Jackson wielded the powers of the presidency more aggressively than his predecessors.

Speaking of John Quincy Adams, he returned to government after his 1828 defeat, winning election to Congress from Massachusetts and serving nine terms, but he never stopped thinking about the odd circumstances that had propelled him to the White House. In his diary entry for April 28, 1841, he made note of a letter he had recently received suggesting yet another amendment to the Electoral College. He wrote, "This election of a chief magistrate for the whole Union will never be settled to the satisfaction of the people."[21]

4

THE SECOND FOUNDING

Black People and Women Get the Vote

On the afternoon of February 25, 1870, Hiram Rhodes Revels, a newly elected Republican senator from Mississippi, sat in the Capitol building in Washington, D.C., waiting to take the oath of office.

"There was not an inch of standing or sitting room in the galleries, so densely were they packed," the *New York Times* reported in its dispatch from that day.[1]

Swearing-in ceremonies for senators are not usually standing-room-only affairs. But this was different: Revels was black. Once admitted, he would be the first black member of Congress in the nation's history. "When the Vice-President uttered the words, 'The Senator elect will now advance and take the oath,' a pin might have been heard drop," the *Times* reported.

Almost immediately, George Vickers, a Democratic senator from Maryland, rose to challenge Revels's eligibility to serve. The Constitution requires each senator to have been an American citizen for at least nine years, he pointed out. But the Supreme Court had said in *Dred Scott v. Sandford* that black people could never be American citizens, and the Fourteenth Amendment, which effectively overturned that decision, had been ratified only two years earlier. Revels's supporters argued that he had been born to free black parents in North Carolina and had held lifelong citizenship until *Dred Scott* wrongly rescinded it.

Southern Democrats like Vickers were still seething at the prospect of blacks having any role at all in American public life, let alone an equal one, and they weren't about to let technicalities get in the way. But in the wake of the Civil War, antislavery Republicans dominated Congress. Senator Vickers's challenge was rejected, and Revels was sworn in. As the *Times* described it, "Mr. Revels showed no embarrassment whatever, and his demeanor was as dignified as could be expected under the circumstances. The abuse which had been poured upon him and on his race during the last two days might well have shaken the nerves of any one."

Revels's election, and the transformation in black political participation it represented, was so meaningful not only because of the horrors of slavery but because of how much that institution had warped political power in the national government in favor of the South—both in Congress and in the choosing of the president.

The distorting mechanism in both cases was the same: the Constitution's three-fifths clause. Under the clause, slaves were counted as three-fifths of a free white person for the purposes of representation. This gave the slaveholding states more representatives in Congress than they would have had if they were only counting their eligible voting population. And it gave them more influence in picking the president, because a state got as many presidential electors as it had representatives and senators in Congress. In 1790, for example, Virginia and Pennsylvania had nearly the same number of free white men, but thanks to its almost 300,000 slaves, Virginia had six more House seats—and thus six more presidential electors.[2]

Over time, this disproportionate weight was given a name: the Slave Power. And the slaveholding states' bonus votes in the Electoral College were often referred to metaphorically as their "Negro electors." It wasn't a small bonus, either. In the first half of the nineteenth century, the slave population in several southern states approached 50 percent of the total population.

The Slave Power made itself felt almost immediately, in the third presidential election, in 1800, which ended up sending Thomas Jefferson to the White House. That election is remembered today for its chaotic resolution in the House of Representatives, but Jefferson was only able to push it that far in the first place because of the extra, slave-based electoral votes he received from the southern states. Jefferson, who was the favorite throughout the slaveholding states, beat John Adams, the sitting president, by eight electoral votes, 73–65—but an estimated 12 to 14 of Jefferson's haul were "Negro electors."[3]

The role of the Slave Power in Jefferson's victory in 1800 was accepted wisdom at the time. In early 1801, the Boston newspaper *Mercury and New-England Palladium* wrote that Jefferson had made his "ride into the TEMPLE OF LIBERTY, on the shoulders of slaves."[4]

The *Gazette of the United States*, in Philadelphia, was even harsher. "There are above 500,000 negro slaves in the United States, who have not more voice in the Election of

President and Vice-President . . . than 500,000 New-England horses, hogs, and oxen. Yet," the *Gazette* wrote, "their masters for them choose 15 Electors!"[5]

John Quincy Adams, the son of John Adams and the sixth president, later wrote, "The election of Mr. Jefferson to the presidency was, upon sectional feelings, the triumph of the South over the North—of the slave representation over the purely free."[6]

Southern whites certainly weren't trying to downplay the extra power they got for treating other human beings as property. On the contrary, they were proud of it. During a Senate debate in 1816 over whether to adopt a popular vote for president, Virginia senator James Barbour lashed out against what he said would be a "destruction of the balance of power" in the nation. "It has pleased God to give the Southern country a population anomalous, having the double character of person and property," he said. "Other states had none such."[7]

By 1820, the southern states had 18 more representatives in Congress than they would have had without counting their slaves.[8] The slave population kept growing, and thanks to the three-fifths clause, it didn't just mean more free labor, but increasing political power, because more slaves equaled more representatives.

Overall, the number of slaves in the southern states sextupled in the half century after the Constitution's ratification.[9] The effects of this growth could be felt everywhere. Up through 1850, the slaveholding states enjoyed an average of one-third more seats in Congress than they would have if free citizens only were counted. For most of the country's first four decades, the Speaker of the House was a slaveholder, as were 18 of the first

31 Supreme Court justices, including a majority of those who issued the Court's opinion in *Dred Scott,* which helped trigger the Civil War and is remembered today as the most morally abhorrent decision in the Court's history.[10]

The Slave Power also played a decisive role in the adoption or defeat of major federal legislation, and in the shape of the country itself—driving slavery-friendly outcomes in, among other things, the admission of Missouri as a slave state in 1820; Andrew Jackson's Indian Removal Act of 1830; the House "gag rule" of 1840, which protected slavery in the District of Columbia; the defeat of the Wilmot Proviso in 1847, which would have banned slavery in the formerly Mexican territories; and the Kansas-Nebraska Act of 1854, which permitted slavery in new territories where it had been previously prohibited, helping set the stage for the Civil War.[11]

And, of course, the Slave Power showed up in the Electoral College. It wasn't just Thomas Jefferson who benefited. For the first 36 years of the United States' existence, the South's "population anomalous" helped ensure that every president but one—John Adams—was a Virginia slaveholder. It took the election of Abraham Lincoln in 1860 for the country to be forced at last to reckon with its original sin. Lincoln won despite not receiving a single vote in the southern states, which kept him off their ballots. In the six months following his election, eleven southern states seceded, claiming they had the constitutional right to do so. Lincoln disagreed, and shortly after his inauguration, in April 1861, the Civil War began.

With the North's victory in the war and Lincoln's Emancipation Proclamation, roughly four million enslaved people were guaranteed their freedom. By the end of the decade,

the nation had ratified three new amendments—known together as the Reconstruction Amendments. The Thirteenth
Amendment banned the practice of slavery; the Fourteenth
Amendment made the newly freed slaves citizens and eliminated the three-fifths clause; and the Fifteenth Amendment
guaranteed the former slaves' right to vote.

Together these amendments were as revolutionary as the
Declaration of Independence and the Constitution themselves, because they were the first attempt from within American government to live up to the nation's founding ideals.
And they represented the greatest expansion of democracy
in the country's history.

⦚⦚⦚

Since the three-fifths clause was at the root of the pre–Civil
War distortion in American politics and government, you
might think that when the clause was removed from the
Constitution, the distortion disappeared. After all, almost
four million black people were now full legal members of
society—five-fifths of a person—and their votes (or those of
the adult males, anyway) would count just as much as those
of their white neighbors.

But after the Civil War, the discrepancies only got worse.
The reason is that while the Constitution had changed, white
supremacy had not. One of the great ironies of American
history is that the end of slavery actually made the white
power structures in the former slave states stronger.

How did that happen? By numbers alone, black Americans should have come to dominate southern politics. Blacks
represented a majority of the population in post–Civil War
Louisiana, Mississippi, and South Carolina, and 40 percent

or more in Alabama, Florida, Georgia, and Virginia. Within a few years after the end of the war, and particularly after the passage of the Fifteenth Amendment, black enfranchisement and political participation skyrocketed. Across the South, blacks were voting at remarkably high rates, winning hundreds of state legislative seats and dozens of seats in Congress. Mississippi alone had two black U.S. senators, including Hiram Rhodes Revels, and a black lieutenant governor.

In theory, at least, the Union's victory in the Civil War had reaffirmed the supremacy of the national government over the states. But of course the states of the former Confederacy had not come back willingly. They rejoined the union at gunpoint, and only after being forced to ratify the Fourteenth Amendment and rewrite their state constitutions to ensure equal rights for newly freed blacks. Even then, it took the constant presence of federal troops, who fanned out across the South, to fight off attempts by the newly formed Ku Klux Klan and other white supremacists to intimidate, terrorize, or murder black citizens who dared try to cast a ballot.

The drafters of the Reconstruction Amendments had anticipated this sort of resistance and had devised a simple and elegant solution: Section 2 of the Fourteenth Amendment, which lays out the consequences for any state that denies any of its adult male citizens the right to vote or abridges that right in any way. Those states, the amendment says, will see their representation in Congress "reduced in the proportion which the number of such male citizens shall bear to the whole number of male citizens twenty-one years of age in such State."[12]

This was the official eradication of the three-fifths clause: if you prevent eligible voters from voting, you don't get to count them toward your representation in Congress. The punishment was straightforward and sensible. That, at any rate, was the hope. As of 2020, Section 2 of the Fourteenth Amendment has never been enforced.

III

The failure to hold southern states politically accountable for disenfranchising their black citizens came to a head in the election of 1876—the most chaotic and disputed election in American history, and the second time the Electoral College awarded the presidency to the popular-vote loser.

For four months after Election Day, the candidates battled over who was the rightful winner, nearly triggering a constitutional crisis in the process.

In the end, Rutherford B. Hayes, the Republican nominee, won by a single electoral vote, even though his Democratic opponent, the New York governor Samuel Tilden, won a majority of the nationwide popular vote, 51 percent to Hayes's 48 percent. As in 1824, the last time this had happened, the final outcome was widely viewed as the product of a "corrupt bargain." But this time the beneficiary wasn't just Hayes, it was the entire South, which leveraged the tortured negotiations over the election's resolution to kill off Reconstruction for good.

By the early 1870s, with the Fifteenth Amendment and federal troops at their backs, southern blacks weren't just voting in record numbers; they were voting overwhelmingly for the Republican Party, which had formed shortly before the Civil War in opposition to slavery.

This represented an existential threat to southern Democrats, because newly freed and enfranchised blacks now represented an electoral majority in many southern states. As one former Confederate general said in a speech shortly before the election, "South Carolina is a white man's state, and in spite of nigger majorities the Democrats are going to rule it."[13]

Words like that were mild compared to the spasms of violence carried out by whites against blacks trying to exercise their right to vote. In one of the most brutal incidents, on Easter Sunday, 1873, armed white supremacists in Colfax, Louisiana, slaughtered as many as 150 freedmen, following a dispute over the state's gubernatorial election. Up to a third of those murdered had already surrendered.[14]

It was in this tense political moment that more than eight million Americans streamed to the polls in November 1876, representing nearly 82 percent of all eligible voters— the highest-percentage election turnout in American history. In the days after the election, it was clear that Tilden had won the popular vote, and he appeared to have won more than enough electoral votes, leading several newspapers to crown him the winner.

In fact the battle had just begun. Tilden had secured 184 electoral votes, one short of a majority. Hayes was well behind, with 165 votes. But in three southern states— South Carolina, Louisiana, and Florida—the electoral vote was in dispute. Democrats had won the popular vote in all three states, but Republicans charged they had done so only through voter intimidation and ballot fraud.

This was standard operating procedure in the waning days of Reconstruction. White Democrats intent on regaining control of state governments did whatever they could to control and suppress black voters. When asked how they would manage to secure a win for Tilden in a state like South Carolina, which at the time had a sizable majority of Republican voters, the former Confederate general quoted above referred to what he called the "shot-gun policy": "That policy is to plainly tell the negroes that the Whites are again in command of the state. We Democrats do not want their votes, but they will vote against us at their peril. We must warn the leaders that 'the tall poppies will fall first.'" The general added, "We must be prepared to shoot rather than be prevented from redeeming the State from Radical rule."[15]

In addition to outright violence and intimidation, white voters stuffed ballot boxes with fake ballots for Tilden and other Democrats. A black representative from North Carolina later recalled one election in the small town of Halifax, where "the registered Republican vote was 345, and the total registered vote of the township was 539, but when the count was announced it stood 990 Democrats to 41 Republicans, or 492 more Democratic votes counted than were registered votes in the township."[16]

In response to this type of blatant fraud, Republican-led canvassing boards got creative in their vote counting, tossing out hundreds of Democratic ballots on minor technicalities, such as a finding that election inspectors had left ballot boxes unattended during a dinner break.[17]

Together, South Carolina, Louisiana, and Florida represented 19 electoral votes. An unrelated dispute in Oregon over the eligibility of one of that state's electors meant that in all there were 20 electoral votes up for grabs. Tilden and the Democrats needed only one more vote to prevail. If Hayes was going to win, he needed all twenty.

The problem was that the Constitution set out no method for resolving disputed vote counts. To make matters more complicated, Congress was divided, with Democrats holding the House and Republicans in control of the Senate. For months, the parties fought over who would count the votes and how. By January 1877, with no end in sight, Congress created a 15-member commission to resolve the election. The commission consisted of 10 senators and representatives, evenly divided between Republicans and Democrats, and five Supreme Court justices. Two of the justices had been appointed by Republican presidents and two by Democrats; together, those four would agree on a fifth.

They chose Justice David Davis, a political independent who seemed to represent the best chance for something resembling a fair outcome. But Davis would never serve on the commission. In late January, Democratic lawmakers in Davis's home state of Illinois chose him to fill a recent vacancy in the Senate. The idea was to secure Davis's support for Tilden, but the plan backfired when Davis immediately resigned his seat on the Court to take the job as senator. In his place, the justices chose their colleague Joseph Bradley, another Republican.

With Bradley as the deciding vote and only days until inauguration, the commission heard arguments from both sides, then voted 8–7 on strict party lines to give all 20 of the contested electoral votes to Hayes.

Enraged Democrats tried to delay the final electoral vote tally, in the hope of stalemating the election and forcing it into the House, where Democrats held the advantage and could anoint Tilden the winner. One representative held up an envelope that he claimed contained a certified slate of electors from Vermont, which had already submitted its electoral votes to the Senate. When Thomas Ferry, the Republican senator from Michigan who was presiding over the counting of the electoral votes, refused to accept the second slate, Democrats erupted. One "shrieked wildly, threw his arms about, and for a time refused to come to order." In a House session the following day, one Democratic representative climbed across four desks to impress his views on the Speaker, while others grabbed for their guns, and the Speaker had to call in the sergeant-at-arms.[18]

At last, a Louisiana Democrat named William Levy announced that he and other Democrats had met with Hayes, and had gotten assurances that "in the event of his elevation to the Presidency he will be guided by a policy of conciliation toward the Southern States, that he will not use the Federal authority or the Army to force upon those State governments not of their choice."[19]

With that, the conflict ended. Democrats stood down, and the final electoral vote tally was taken: 185 for Hayes, 184 for Tilden. It was the closest Electoral College finish in history. The commission finished its work on March 2, two days before inauguration day.

But the Democrats weren't finished. On March 3, the House passed a resolution declaring that Tilden was in fact the "duly elected President." It was legally meaningless, but it gave them a last chance to express their outrage.

Democratic voters around the country were no less furious. Decrying the ballot-counting shenanigans, they called Hayes "His Fraudulency" and "Rutherfraud B. Hayes." But especially in the South, Democrats came to understand the significance of the concessions they had won in exchange for backing down: the removal of the last remaining federal troops from South Carolina and Louisiana signaled the official end of Reconstruction, allowed for the almost immediate reassertion of white political dominance throughout the South, and introduced the Jim Crow era, which would effectively disenfranchise millions of black citizens for the next 80 years.

It remains one of the most shameful episodes in American history: at the moment when newly freed black citizens depended on the federal government to protect them, they were abandoned by it.

In many ways, the story of the election of 1876 reflects the broader pattern of America's halting progress toward democracy. The lurches in the direction of greater equality and inclusion are always impeded by the more regressive tendencies—generally in the form of pushback from those grasping to hold onto their own disproportionate power.

But there was another factor that influenced the outcome of the 1876 race, separate from the disputed electors. It happened on August 1, the day Colorado was formally admitted to the union—just three months before the presidential election.

Colorado, like a number of other states, owed its admission primarily to partisan politics. As Democrats forced their way back to power in the South, Republicans began seeking out new places to develop their political power in order to offset those losses. The new, sparsely populated western states offered the best opportunity. In 1870, the territory of Colorado had fewer than 40,000 residents, many of them engaged in the silver mining industry.[20] That number was growing fast, but it was barely enough to qualify as a state at all. Before Democrats in Congress realized what was happening, Republicans had gotten themselves a Republican-led legislature in Colorado and, just as important, three brand-new electoral votes. As soon as the Colorado legislature convened, it decided it didn't have time to organize a popular vote. When the election came, the legislature awarded its three electors to Hayes, and he needed every one. It was the last time in American history that a state's electors were not chosen by popular vote.[21]

III

The next three presidential elections after 1876 were all marked by intense political polarization, very high turnout, exceedingly close popular-vote margins, and constant charges of fraud.

In 1880, James Garfield, the Republican nominee, won the popular vote by fewer than 10,000 out of more than nine million ballots cast, or about one-tenth of 1 percent. (Federal government records put the final margin at under 2,000 votes; the discrepancy is due to the fact that states did not officially certify their popular-vote totals.)[22]

Garfield's margin in the Electoral College was much more comfortable, in part because he won the key state of New York by about 20,000 votes. Democrats claimed that the same number of votes had been cast illegally, many by voters whom Republicans had allegedly smuggled into the state from Vermont, Massachusetts, Pennsylvania, and even Canada.[23] There was an unverified claim that 5,000 Democratic ballots had ended up in the Hudson River.

In 1884, the national popular vote margin was again less than 1 percent. This time the Democrat, Grover Cleveland, prevailed. But it took two weeks for the result to be finalized, because Cleveland's margin of victory in New York, once again the tipping-point state, was just 1,047 votes out of more than 1.1 million cast.

And then in 1888, for the second time in 12 years, the

Electoral College overrode the results of the popular vote. Once again, party support was closely aligned with geography: Grover Cleveland, the sitting president, swept the South, while his Republican opponent, Benjamin Harrison, took almost every state in the North and West, with the exception of New Jersey and Connecticut.

The decisive factor that year would be the winner-take-all rule. Cleveland won the popular vote by a little more than 100,000 votes, or roughly 1 percent of the total, but he came up just short in his home state of New York, which was the nation's largest swing state (as it often was into the middle of the twentieth century). Out of more than 1.3 million votes cast in New York, Harrison won by just over 14,000—enough to walk off with all 36 of the state's electoral votes, and the White House.

Allegations of fraud again poured in from both sides: Democrats said Republicans had bought as many as 40,000 votes in New York. According to one Republican, Harrison would never know "how close a number of men were compelled to approach the gates of the penitentiary to make him President."[24] But none of the charges were verified, and Cleveland let the results stand without challenge. Four years later he ran again, and won.

███

Meanwhile, the southern states, newly freed from the constraints of Reconstruction, continued their mad dash backward in time. They called it the Redemption—and it was swift and brutal. If they couldn't enslave black people, at least they could erase them from political life. Around the turn of the century, the former Confederate states held new constitutional conventions in which they dumped the post-war charters they had been forced to adopt, and replaced them with new ones designed specifically to disenfranchise their black citizens. They did it through poll taxes, literacy tests, and other measures that targeted blacks' poverty and lack of education. White politicians were not shy about what they were doing. "Let us tell the truth if it bursts the bottom of the Universe," the president of the Mississippi convention announced. "We came here to exclude the Negro."[25] This was exactly what Section Two of the Fourteenth Amendment was designed to block—if anyone had ever bothered to enforce it.

Along with the adoption of explicitly racist state constitutions and Jim Crow laws came a coordinated campaign of state-sponsored intimidation, terror, and murder by the Ku Klux Klan and other groups, acting with the assent, and often the cooperation, of state and local authorities. The goal was to re-establish white supremacy—and it worked. By the 1940s, the entire South was a one-party region. Registration among voting-age black citizens hovered around 3 percent, at best. Those blacks who managed to vote were effectively silenced by state winner-take-all rules. In the 11 presidential elections held between 1908 and 1948, 44 percent of all minority votes in the country were not represented by a single electoral vote.[26] According to one calculation, at the turn of the twentieth century the southern states got an Electoral College bump of 7 percent over what they should have had if the Fourteenth Amendment had been enforced.[27]

This erasing of black voters' voices in the South continued in the wake of the Civil Rights Act of 1964, when white southerners began to abandon the Democratic Party. Black southerners turned away from Republicans and toward the

Democrats—but thanks to state winner-take-all rules, they still had essentially no political representation. In the 1968 election, nearly 600,000 black voters in the South picked the Democratic nominee, Hubert Humphrey—but in the Electoral College, all of those votes were converted into votes for the Alabama governor and segregationist George Wallace. In the words of a 1979 Senate report, "it was as if they had never voted."[28]

But the South's regression in the late nineteenth and early twentieth centuries was only one side of the coin. During the same period, between about 1890 and 1920, the country saw widespread social, economic, and political reforms, many in response to the gross inequalities of the Gilded Age. In what became known as the Progressive Era, Congress passed child labor and food safety laws; restraints on business monopolies, political corruption, and entrenched party machines; as well as expansions of civil rights and women's rights.

This democratic evolution changed how Americans thought about their role in politics and in electing their leader, which in turn forced the Constitution to become more democratic, shedding more of its early barriers to inclusivity and participation.

Many of these changes started at the local or state level but eventually came to be absorbed into the Constitution itself. The two most significant were reflected in the Seventeenth and Nineteenth Amendments, which were adopted within a decade of each other, and together represented the biggest expansion of American democracy since Reconstruction.

In 1913, the states ratified the Seventeenth Amendment, giving the American people the right to vote directly for their United States senators. It was an astonishing repudiation of the framers' original bicameral design of the legislature, which had established the Senate as an anti-democratic counterweight to the House of Representatives. House members were elected directly to two-year terms, and were allocated according to population, making them more responsive to the people's demands, but also to their whims. In contrast, the Senate was insulated from the people. Senators were chosen by state legislators, not voters, and they served six-year terms, encouraging them to be more focused on states' interests. The framers' intent was to elevate a more distinguished group of men who could then serve as a check against an overbearing federal government.

In other words, a popularly elected Senate would have been a contradiction in terms to most of the delegates at the Philadelphia convention—with the exception of James Wilson, who argued consistently for the direct election of senators, just as he did for the presidency.

Wilson lost both arguments. But by the mid-1800s, Americans were becoming increasingly aware of the opportunities for corruption built into the system. State lawmakers, many of whom were not themselves paragons of civic virtue, were cutting sweetheart deals to get their preferred candidates into the Senate. Sometimes they couldn't agree on a pick, leaving seats open for months or even years.

In the final decades of the century, states had begun involving their citizens more directly in the choice of senators. Some states held direct primaries. In Oregon, citizens voted in a nonbinding election for senator, and then candidates for the state legislature were required to agree to abide by the results of that election. This was mostly an acknowledgment of reality. As the federal government grew in size and power, the makeup of the Senate grew more important. Voters were already weighing how their vote for state lawmakers would influence the choice of their senators; Oregon's nonbinding election just let them be explicit about it.

When Oregon switched to direct vote for its senators in 1908, more than half the states allowed some degree of public involvement in Senate elections. Whatever the framers had intended the Senate to be more than a century earlier, the public had moved on. Within five years, the practice was written into the Constitution, and America took yet another step toward democracy and away from the nation the framers had designed.

▌▌▌

The Progressive Era would deliver one other major democratic advance: the enfranchisement of women.

The Declaration of Independence, for all its prescient brilliance, suffered from a central logical flaw (even beyond its tolerance of slavery): How could a statement of universal equality be limited to just half the population?

In 1848, at a chapel in Seneca Falls, New York, the women's suffrage movement held a convention at which it introduced the "Declaration of Sentiments," a tweak of the original that read, "We hold these truths to be self-evident, that all men and women are created equal . . ."

While the Civil War delayed the movement, the Reconstruction Amendments gave it new focus. The suffragists Elizabeth Cady Stanton, Susan B. Anthony, and Lucretia Mott pushed to include women in the Fourteenth and Fifteenth Amendments, but failed. Section 2 of the Fourteenth Amendment is restricted to "adult male citizens"—the only provision of the Constitution that explicitly discriminates on the basis of sex, although as we saw above, that particular provision never helped the men it was intended to help. Regardless, the tension between blacks and women as both fought for voting rights would never go away.

Through the 1870s the suffragists pushed on, arguing in the courts that the language of the Fourteenth and Fifteenth Amendments implicitly included women, but the Supreme Court rejected that claim. An amendment giving women the right to vote was proposed in Congress in 1878, but failed.

The suffrage movement realized that if it were going to make any progress, it would need to focus its attention on the states. In 1869, the territory of Wyoming gave the vote to all women 21 and older, then maintained that right when it became a state in 1890. Into the twentieth century, more than a dozen states, most in the west, followed suit.

As the United States entered World War I and women became more deeply involved in the war effort, it became impossible to justify denying them the vote as a constitutional matter. In 1918, the push for an amendment got the backing of President Woodrow Wilson. It passed Congress in June 1919, and the states quickly began to ratify it. The primary opposition to women's suffrage was the same as it was for black suffrage: southern white Democrats, most of whose states would refuse to ratify the Nineteenth Amendment until the 1950s. Mississippi held out until 1984.

But if southern whites were still terrorizing black men into silence, they couldn't stem the tide of the women's vote. On August 18, 1920, Tennessee became the thirty-sixth state to ratify the Nineteenth Amendment, which was certified eight days later. For the first time in U.S. history, and more than 130 years after the Constitution's framers had set the course of a new nation, virtually all adult citizens in the country were eligible to vote. Twenty-six million women were suddenly enfranchised under the Constitution, and eight million voted in that fall's presidential election.

It was a remarkable transformation for a country that had allowed, at its birth, only a fraction of the population to vote. And yet 130 years is a long time to deliver on a nation's founding premise. One reason it took so long can be found in the design of the Electoral College itself. Because each state gets its prescribed number of electors based on total population, not on how many of its residents cast a ballot, there is no incentive to expand the electorate. Why bother letting more people vote when it doesn't give your state any additional influence? Imagine how much sooner America might have confronted slavery, or the disenfranchisement of women— half of the entire population!—under a popular vote system in which every vote counted.

Speaking of disenfranchisement, the Nineteenth Amendment did essentially nothing for millions of black women throughout the South who remained, like their male counterparts, locked out of political participation by poll taxes, literacy tests, and violent intimidation by white supremacists. For these women, who had now been twice left behind, it would take what amounted to a second Reconstruction—the adoption of the Civil Rights and Voting Rights Acts of the 1960s—for them to be included in American democracy.

And none of the amendments passed between the Civil

War and the Progressive Era did anything for Native Americans. The federal government had granted them citizenship in 1924, but individual states continued to deny them the vote until the 1960s.

III

At the same moment that the Nineteenth Amendment was finding its way into the Constitution and bringing the nation closer to its founding principles, a new crack was opening, revealing the next great chasm separating Americans from true representative democracy: for the first time, the 1920 decennial census showed more Americans living in urban areas than in rural ones.

This fact—a massive shift in where people lived—would be the basis for the next great battle in the American struggle for more democracy and fairer representation, a struggle that would play out over the next 50 years. The fight wasn't just about numbers, but color. Cities were growing in both size and diversity, as those in the North, particularly, absorbed increasing numbers of black refugees escaping the Jim Crow South, as well as waves of immigrants from eastern and southern Europe.

During this same period, the country's total population was also exploding. The 1920 census counted 14 million more people living in the United States than 10 years earlier. Nearly all that increase was in the cities, which grew by 19 million people; rural areas actually lost 5 million.

Rural lawmakers, who had long dominated American politics, fought back against this threat to their grip on power in two ways. At the state level, they refused to redraw legislative district lines to more accurately reflect where people lived.

And in Congress, they froze the size of the House of Representatives itself, in the hope of locking in their numerical advantage in Washington as it slipped away everywhere else.

Before 1920, Congress had virtually always expanded the House to keep up with the growing population. In 1911, that meant increasing the House to 435 members. In 1921, it would have led to the addition of nearly 50 more seats, primarily in the cities. But rural lawmakers blocked the decennial reapportionment of the House of Representatives that year. Today, with a national population more than three times as big as it was in 1920, the House remains stuck, effectively, in 1911. If it had continued to expand as it had for more than a century before, it would now consist of more than 1,500 members.

In 1928, Emanuel Celler, a representative from New York, observed how the power struggle between urban and rural America infected every part of the House's deliberations. The "thread of controversy," he said, "runs through immigration, prohibition, income tax, tariff. It is the city versus the country. The issue grows more and more menacing."[29]

Celler was right. The urban-rural clash would continue to intensify into the middle of the twentieth century. It reached its climax in the early 1960s, when in a string of decisions the Supreme Court established the fundamental democratic principle of one person, one vote. The firestorm set off by these decisions transformed representative democracy in America, and in the end nearly toppled the Electoral College itself.

5

ONE PERSON, ONE VOTE

Four Words That Nearly Brought Down
the Electoral College

A few minutes after 1:00 p.m. on September 29, 1970, an unseasonably cool Tuesday in the nation's capital, the last serious attempt to abolish the Electoral College from the Constitution died on the floor of the U.S. Senate.

Just one year earlier, a national popular vote for president looked like it was on the brink of becoming a reality. Roughly 80 percent of Americans supported it, as did President Richard Nixon, top Democrats and Republicans, and interest groups across the political spectrum, from the AFL-CIO to the Chamber of Commerce. Even the loudest critics of electoral reform had come to accept that it was inevitable—calling it "a bad idea whose time has come."

In September 1969, the House of Representatives held its first meaningful floor debate on the Electoral College in 150 years, then voted overwhelmingly in favor of passing an amendment to abolish it. Surveys suggested support among a majority of lawmakers in at least 30 states, and possibly as many as 40, which would have been more than enough to ratify it.

The last remaining hurdle was the Senate. If two-thirds of the senators joined the majority of their House colleagues and voted yes, the amendment would go to the states.

The popular vote advocates, led by Birch Bayh, a Democratic senator from Indiana, tried again and again through late 1969 and into 1970 to bring the bill to a vote in the Senate; again and again they were thwarted. The opposition was led by a bloc of southern senators who used every trick in the book, including the filibuster, to delay and distract until the momentum behind the effort was snuffed out.

The vote on September 29 was a procedural one—the second attempt in as many weeks to end the southerners' filibuster. If it failed, the amendment was dead.

An editorial in that morning's *New York Times* was dire. The Electoral College is "archaic, undemocratic, complex, ambiguous and dangerous," the editors wrote. Leaving it in place "threatens electoral chaos."[1]

Even under the best circumstances, amending the Constitution is a monumental task. Every piece has to fall into place at the right moment, or the entire project can stall and crash. A vote against ending the filibuster was, as the *Times* editorial warned, "a vote against any reform of the Presidential electoral system within the foreseeable future."

But if Bayh could get the bill over this hump, anything was possible. While many senators refused as a matter of principle to vote to break a filibuster, several told Bayh's staff that they supported the amendment and would vote yes if it made it to the floor.[2]

Bayh needed 58 votes to end the filibuster. He got 53—five votes short. Since that day, no effort to abolish the Electoral College has come anywhere near as close.

The story of how America almost adopted a national popular vote for president in 1969 and 1970 is largely forgotten today. But it illustrates how naturally it seemed to flow out of the waves of democratic transformation in that period—from the Supreme Court's one person, one vote rulings, to the Civil Rights and Voting Rights Acts, to the constitutional amendments prohibiting poll taxes, giving electoral votes to Washington, D.C., and lowering the voting age from 21 to 18—the last of which Bayh also sponsored.

The effort's ultimate collapse shows how the same forces that have always preserved the Electoral College succeeded in blocking Birch Bayh too.

▌▌▌

Birch Bayh entered the Senate in early 1963 as a mainstream Democrat—progressive, but not too progressive. He was 34, affably handsome, with a head of thick, dark hair and sharp blue eyes. Back home in Indiana, where he was the youngest-ever Speaker of the state House of Representatives, he had earned a reputation as a genial, no-nonsense farm boy who got along with everyone. The radical reform of the American presidency was not on his agenda.

But three unrelated events, one in each branch of the federal government, would soon combine to turn Bayh into the leader of a national movement to abolish the Electoral College. First, he would end up getting the most important job in the Senate for someone inclined to amend the Constitution. Second, the Surpeme Court would establish the one person, one vote principle, transforming how Americans thought about representative government. Third, the 1968 presidential election, which nearly ended up getting thrown into the House of Representatives, would show millions of Americans just how dangerous and unpredictable our presidential election system was.

Bayh couldn't have anticipated any of this as he settled into his first term in Washington. Then, in August 1963, Estes Kefauver, the veteran Tennessee senator, died suddenly. Kefauver left behind, among many other assignments, the chairmanship of the constitutional amendments subcommittee of the Senate Judiciary Committee. Running this subcommittee was, at least in theory, a big job—drafting amendments to the Constitution and introducing them into Congress. In practice it was a sleepy affair, and the subcommittee had done little of note since the days of Prohibition.

The subcommittee was in the process of being disbanded by James Eastland, the Mississippi Democrat who led the Judiciary Committee, when Bayh, looking for an assignment that would help him build his influence in the Senate, approached him and asked to run it. When Eastland balked, Bayh offered to pay for the subcommittee out of his own office account. Eastland changed his mind, kept the subcommittee alive, and gave Bayh the job.

Bayh was officially named chair on September 30. The former law student in him thought it would be an interesting experience, but he didn't expect much excitement. "It was a graveyard," Bayh recalled in 2010. "How often do you amend the Constitution, for heaven's sakes?"[3] (For the record: 27

times, the first 10 of which, known collectively as the Bill of Rights, were adopted almost before the original Constitution's ink was dry. Since then, we've ratified a new amendment on average once every 13 years.)

Fifty-three days later, President John F. Kennedy was assassinated in Dallas. And like that, a graveyard job was about to become one of the most important in the country.

Bayh was faced with a suddenly urgent issue: what to do if a president becomes incapacitated while in office. Previous presidents had informal arrangements in place to deal with such a scenario, but the Constitution itself provided no next steps. It said only that if a president can't serve, the vice president takes over, and any further details can be hammered out by Congress.

The nation was still absorbing the shock of Kennedy's death when Bayh got to work. On December 12, he introduced a resolution to amend the Constitution by adding clear rules for presidential and vice presidential succession in cases of emergency.

Under Bayh's guidance, the bill passed both houses of Congress and went out to the states for ratification. The Twenty-Fifth Amendment went into effect in February 1967, a little more than three years after Bayh first introduced it. It was a remarkable accomplishment for a junior senator who, in the words of a 1970 *New York Times* profile, "had flunked his bar exam the first time and had practiced law only a couple of months before coming to Washington."

Bayh's success on the Twenty-Fifth Amendment transformed him into a respected lawmaker whose opinions mattered, particularly when it came to the Constitution.

It wasn't long before he'd get his second shot. Even before Bayh took his seat in Congress, the Supreme Court had begun deciding a string of cases on political representation that would transform American democracy, and in the process inadvertently raise serious questions about the supposed wisdom of the Electoral College.

III

"One person, one vote"—four words that sound like common sense today. But when the Supreme Court first put them to paper, on March 18, 1963, in a decision on an election law case out of Georgia, they triggered a political earthquake.

In a series of rulings over the next two years, the Court's expansion of this principle forced lawmakers across the country to redraw legislative district lines, redistributing political power to reflect where people actually lived. It thrust the nation into what two political scientists called "the greatest peace-time change in representation in the history of the United States, perhaps in the history of democracy."[4] And while it wasn't obvious at first, those four words would change forever the way we talk about electing our president.

Why were these rulings necessary in the first place? By the early 1960s the nation was at the tail end of a massive population shift in which millions of Americans, many of them black, migrated from farms and rural areas to rapidly growing cities. But this shift was not being reflected in Congress or state governments, because the people who decided where the district lines were drawn—most often rural lawmakers—refused to cede their power by redrawing the districts. The result was entrenched minority rule: small numbers of rural voters had the same representation as much larger numbers of urban voters, and often more.

The problem—known as malapportionment—had existed since at least 1920, the first year that the U.S. census found more Americans living in urban areas than rural ones. By the middle of the century, the power imbalance had grown far worse. In Vermont, a town of 38 residents got one state representative; so did the state's capital, Burlington, which held 33,000 people. The same was true in California, where six million people living in Los Angeles County had the same number of state senators (one) as a little more than 14,000 people living in three of the least populated counties in the state.[5]

But malapportionment was especially bad in the South, where white rural lawmakers held a death grip on political power that grew only tighter as their numbers shrank.

This was a classic breakdown of the political process. In a liberal democracy like the United States, citizens are expected to express their preferences at the ballot box and to change the system if they don't like it. What are they supposed to do if the system itself is rigged to prevent them from expressing those preferences?

The effects of malapportionment were felt in all areas of public life. City residents, who were disproportionately racial or ethnic minorities, saw popular policy priorities lose again and again—from expanding workers' rights to reducing overcrowded schools, from adding more housing to improving urban roadways. In 1956, when the rural-dominated Virginia legislature opted to close public schools rather than integrate them, the 21 lawmakers voting for closure represented fewer people than the 17 voting for integration.[6]

And yet despite repeated legal challenges to these discrepancies, the Supreme Court's answer had consistently been, "Tough luck." The justices saw full well what was going on, but they considered legislative boundary drawing to be a natural part of politics—what Justice Felix Frankfurter had called the "political thicket"—over which they had no authority.[7]

What they had not anticipated was the degree to which the civil rights movement was changing the national conversation about race, power, and democracy in America. As the public became increasingly aware—and intolerant—of the massive imbalances in representation, the Court couldn't continue to ignore the issue.

The first step into the thicket came in 1961, when the Court agreed to hear a case called *Baker v. Carr*.[8] *Baker* began with a lawsuit out of Tennessee, where state lawmakers had refused to redraw their legislative maps since the turn of the century, with a familiar outcome: in the more rural, eastern part of the state, one state lawmaker represented as few as 3,800 people; in the more urbanized western half, which included Nashville and Memphis, a single lawmaker represented as many as 70,000.

In case anyone thought these numbers were the result of innocent, unbiased mapmaking, consider the words of James H. Cummings, a lawmaker from rural Cannon County and one of the more influential politicians in the state. Cummings told a reporter, "I believe in collecting the taxes where the money is—in the cities—and spending it where it's needed—in the country."[9]

Cummings felt free to speak so openly about malapportionment because the Supreme Court had refused to intervene to stop it.

At the same time, the skews in favor of rural areas were only getting more extreme, and the justices knew the problem went far beyond Tennessee. Only five states apportioned their districts so that a legislative majority represented at least 40 percent of the population. In many others, less than 20 percent of the population could, and sometimes did, control the entire state legislature.[10]

Faced with increasing public pressure, the Court struggled intensely over whether to step in. It heard seven hours of oral arguments in the case during three separate sessions. The justices fought bitterly: Justice William Brennan led the charge in insisting that the Court had a role to play in stopping malapportionment; his main opponent, Justice Frankfurter, was best known for his conviction that the Court should stay out of politics entirely. The case took its toll on the Court's members. Just weeks before the ruling was issued, Justice Charles Whittaker, who was considered a swing vote, admitted himself to the hospital after a nervous breakdown. He would never return to the bench. A week after the ruling was issued, Justice Frankfurter had a massive stroke, and also never heard another case.

Despite the tumult, the pro-intervention side eventually prevailed. On March 26, 1962, by a vote of 6–2, the Court said what it had never been willing to say before: a state's legislative district lines can be drawn in such a way that they violate the Fourteenth Amendment's guarantee of equal protection. Significantly, the Court did not rule that Tennessee's maps were unconstitutional—that, for the time being, would be for the lower courts to decide. But simply by holding that this was a matter for the courts in the first place, it had changed the game.

The reverberations of the *Baker* ruling continued into early 1963, when the Court decided *Gray v. Sanders*, a case out of Georgia. The issue in *Gray* was an unusual primary election process known as the county unit system. Under this system, every Georgia county received a number of "unit votes"—the eight largest counties got six votes each, the 30 midsized counties got four votes each, and the least populous got two votes each. In the primaries, whichever Democratic candidate won the most popular votes in a county would receive all of that county's unit votes; the candidate with the most unit votes statewide won the nomination. Effectively, Georgia had created an electoral college at the state level.

It wasn't a matter of legislative districts, but while the device was different, the effect was the same: rural voters were massively overrepresented compared with urban voters. In Fulton County, which includes Atlanta, 550,000 residents, or 14 percent of the state's entire population, got just six of 410 county unit votes. Meanwhile, Echols County, a small plot in southern Georgia with fewer than 2,000 residents, had two unit votes. In other words, Echols County voters had about 100 times the voting power of those in Fulton County.

For the Supreme Court, the Georgia case was the first opportunity since the *Baker v. Carr* ruling to define a standard of representational equality. Justice William O. Douglas, writing for an 8–1 majority, landed on a memorable one.

"How can one person be given twice or ten times the voting power of another person in a statewide election merely because he lives in a rural area or because he lives in the smallest rural county?" Justice Douglas asked. For the first time, the Court answered that he can't.

"The concept of 'we the people' under the Constitution visualizes no preferred class of voters, but equality among those who meet the basic qualifications," Justice Douglas wrote—and those qualifications had changed dramatically since the nation's founding. The Fifteenth and Nineteenth Amendments had enfranchised blacks and women, respectively, while the Seventeenth Amendment gave citizens the right to vote directly for their senators. In light of these developments, the decision in *Gray v. Sanders* seemed only natural, the next step toward a democracy in which all were treated as equal. Justice Douglas's opinion concluded, "The conception of political equality from the Declaration of Independence, to Lincoln's Gettysburg Address, to the Fifteenth, Seventeenth, and Nineteenth Amendments can mean only one thing: one person, one vote."[11]

If it had been restricted to Georgia's primary election system, the one person, one vote principle would have been quickly forgotten. But once it was expressed, it couldn't be easily contained. It was like an expanding drill bit—as soon as it entered the body politic, the force of its logic kept pressing outward. Over the next 15 months, the Court would apply the one person, one vote requirement to virtually all elections in the country—federal, state, and local.

In February 1964 the Court decided *Wesberry v. Sanders*, another case out of Georgia, this time involving the state's hugely malapportioned congressional districts. Relying on the one person, one vote principle, the justices ruled that all U.S. House districts had to include roughly equal numbers of people. Unequal congressional districts didn't just violate the equal protection clause, they said, but ran against the clear intent of the framers. The Court wrote, "To say that a vote is worth more in one district than in another would not only run counter to our fundamental ideas of democratic government, it would cast aside the principle of a House of Representatives elected 'by the People,' a principle tenaciously fought for and established at the Constitutional Convention."[12]

A few months later came the coup de grâce: in a case called *Reynolds v. Sims*, the Court extended the principle of equal representation to all state legislative elections. Once again, the case came out of the former Confederacy—this time Alabama, where lawmakers had refused to redraw their district lines since 1901, even though the population had shifted heavily toward cities. As a result, political power in Alabama was among the most unrepresentative in the country. Lowndes County, with just over 15,000 residents, had a single state senator; so did Jefferson County, with a population of more than 600,000—a discrepancy of more than 40 to 1.

In an opinion by Chief Justice Earl Warren, the Court in *Reynolds* ruled that this violated the equal protection clause. "Legislators represent people, not trees or acres. Legislators are elected by voters, not farms or cities or economic interests," the chief justice wrote.[13]

"The complexions of societies and civilizations change, often with amazing rapidity," he continued. "A nation once primarily rural in character becomes predominantly urban. Representation schemes once fair and equitable become archaic and outdated. But the basic principle of representative government remains, and must remain, unchanged—the weight of a citizen's vote cannot be made to depend on where he lives."

The Court justified its new principle by repeatedly pointing to the broad arc of American democratization and highlighting the progress the country had made since its founding. But it also admitted that this principle was actually quite old, quoting the words of James Wilson—the founding father who had made the most insistent case for political equality two centuries earlier. "All elections ought to be equal," Wilson said. "Elections are equal when a given number of citizens in one part of the state choose as many representatives as are chosen by the same number of citizens in any other part of the state."[14]

Two hundred years later, Wilson's simple, intuitive formulation remained the only workable solution. All districts must include essentially equal numbers of people. States that had relied for decades on deeply skewed maps were now forced to redraw them. The result was a massive shift in political power toward the cities, and the racial and ethnic minorities who disproportionately lived there—that is, away from trees and acres and toward the people.

The resistance to the Court's malapportionment decisions was fast and fierce. Rural voters everywhere, but especially white southerners, claimed that the new standard would "make the urban parts and interests of this nation the unchallenged and total masters of our affairs."[15] That's not what was happening, but as the *New York Times* columnist Michelle Goldberg put it in another context years later, "When one is accustomed to privilege, equality feels like oppression."[16]

In California, opponents of reapportionment took out newspaper ads saying "You Are in Danger" and "Don't Be Squeezed Off the Map."[17] Others used the slogan "Let the

People Decide"—of course, the deciders in this case were a very specific subset of "the people." It's an indication of how ingrained modern democratic values had become by the 1960s that even opponents of the most fundamental reforms had to invoke the language of democracy itself to fight back.[18]

Resistance also came from leading conservative intellectuals. In a 1969 article in the *New York Times Magazine*, Irving Kristol and Paul Weaver criticized what they called an "obsession" with political equality and referred to one person, one vote as "abstract political dogma" that "vulgarized and trivialized" American democracy.[19] Our system of government, they argued, was based on a complex idea that had now been "debased into a simple-minded, arithmetical majoritarianism—government by adding machine."

Many critics of the one person, one vote rulings argued that the Court had improperly taken control of what was always meant to be a political process, and usurped the rightful power of lawmakers. Chief Justice Warren believed the Court had done the exact opposite. Reflecting on the rulings years later, he said, "If everyone in this country has an opportunity to participate in government on equal terms with everyone else, and can share in electing representatives who will be truly representative of the entire community and not some special interest, then most of the problems that we are confronted with would be solved through the political process rather than through the courts."[20]

In the end, what was most remarkable about the Court's one person, one vote decisions was the speed with which states fell into line. Despite the pushback, only three years after *Reynolds v. Sims* was decided, the legislative districts in every state represented more or less equal numbers of people.

∎∎∎

The one person, one vote rulings didn't just reshape the idea of what a democracy could be and who was represented in it; they also shined a new light on the most undemocratic elements of our political system—above all, the Electoral College. If "one person, one vote" was now the rule for congressional and state legislative elections, how was it fair to not hold the presidential election to the same standard?

The justices had anticipated this challenge, and they had a legally correct if unsatisfying response. It was true, they wrote in *Gray v. Sanders*, that the Electoral College treated some votes as worth more than others, just as malapportioned districts did. In this case, however, there was nothing they could do about it. After all, "specific historical concerns validated the collegiate principle despite its inherent numerical inequality." In other words, they were admitting that the Electoral College violates basic political equality, and yet it is constitutional . . . because it is literally in the Constitution.[21]

In a footnote to the ruling, the justices added an editorial aside. Whatever the original intent of the College, they suggested, there was no modern justification for it. The Fifteenth, Seventeenth, and Nineteenth Amendments showed that the framers' "conception of political equality belongs to a bygone day."

But that was as far as the justices could go. The Supreme Court has the power to interpret what's in the Constitution, but not to rewrite it. To do that, you need a constitutional amendment.

Amending the Electoral College wasn't a new idea. The first proposed fix had been introduced into Congress in 1797, less than a decade after the Constitution was ratified. By the early 1960s, there had been about 500 attempts to reform or abolish it, more—by a long shot—than for any other single provision of the Constitution. Of all these efforts, only one—the Twelfth Amendment—had succeeded.

There was a constant drumbeat of discontent with the College, but even the two split elections of 1876 and 1888 failed to trigger any sustained outcry for its reform. And while bills to amend or abolish it were introduced regularly in Congress, the general public was largely unaware of the surrounding debates, which seemed arcane and technical—the province of lawmakers, political scientists, and legal scholars. That's no surprise. By the middle of the twentieth century, only a handful of Americans had been alive the last time a popular vote loser was elected, in 1888. Any warning that it might happen again sounded less like a genuine threat than like a statistician's ghost story.

All that would change in the 1960s. American democracy was expanding faster than at nearly any point in history. None of those developments were directly related to the way Americans chose their president, but it was impossible not to hear the echoes. Within months of the Supreme Court's one person, one vote decisions, the Electoral College would become one of the most urgent political issues of the era.

I I I

Lyndon Johnson admired how skillfully Birch Bayh had navigated the Twenty-Fifth Amendment through Congress. Before that amendment was even ratified, Johnson asked Bayh to start on the Twenty-Sixth—reforming the Electoral College. At first, there were no grand visions of abolition, only tweaks to the system.

A persistent concern was the "faithless elector"—the one who pledges to vote for one candidate and then casts a ballot for another. Faithless electors have always been rare, and have never come close to altering the outcome of an election. Still, there had been a concerted campaign by disaffected southern Democrats in recent elections to convince electors to break their pledges in favor of third-party segregationist candidates like Harry Byrd. This had unnerved the leadership of both major parties, and especially President Lyndon Johnson, whose support depended on southern Democrats. He asked Bayh to take up the charge.

This small-bore approach suited Bayh, who was moderate by nature. In his opening statement at the hearings, on February 28, 1966, Bayh emphasized that the goal was to perform minor surgery to the Electoral College, not an amputation. Any changes to the existing presidential election process would be in the service of protecting America's federal system of government, which ensures that every state has a "guaranteed minimum voice" not only in the Senate but also in the selection of the president.[22]

Bayh acknowledged that a direct popular vote might seem like "the ideal solution, the natural answer for a democratic society." But it would be politically impossible to adopt because small states would never agree to give up the disproportionate power they got from their two extra electoral votes. "Putting it optimistically," Bayh said, the odds of passing a popular vote amendment were "extremely slim, if not hopeless."[23]

His proposal was known as the "automatic" plan: keep

electoral votes, which would preserve each state's relative power, but get rid of the electors themselves, and thus eliminate the risk that one or more of them could go rogue.

Bayh was reflecting the conventional wisdom of the day, which was that reform was desirable in small doses. Yes, the Electoral College had its flaws, but those could be fixed without dumping a system that had served the country well, more or less, for 200 years.

Bayh believed this too, at first. Then he sat through the hearings. For two months he listened to a parade of lawmakers, political scientists, constitutional scholars, legal experts, and even mathematicians. As witness after witness explained the problems with the Electoral College in its current form as well as with various reform proposals, Bayh listened closely and took notes.

Besides Bayh's automatic plan, there were two main proposals for amending the Constitution to ban winner-take-all allocations of electoral votes: the district system and the proportional system.

The district system—which many states used in the first decades of the nation's existence, and which two (Maine and Nebraska) still use today—awards electors by congressional district: whichever candidate wins the most popular votes in a district wins that district's elector. The two electors representing the state's senators are awarded to the candidate who wins the statewide vote. Versions of this system have been proposed in Congress numerous times over the years.

The proportional system awards electors based on the proportion of the statewide popular vote each candidate received. If a state has 10 electoral votes and the Republican candidate wins 60 percent of the vote, he or she gets six electors. No state has ever used this system, although in 1950 the Senate approved an amendment that would have adopted it nationwide. It was easily defeated in the House.

In theory, both the district and proportional systems sound sensible. As we'll see in the next chapter, however, neither lives up to the basic democratic ideals of political equality and majority rule. They both give some votes more weight than they give others based on where they are cast, and they both allow for the possibility that the person who wins more votes nationally could still lose the election.

As this fact dawned on Bayh, he realized he'd been aiming too low, getting trapped in the details of endless debates about ratios and percentages. He was missing the bigger picture.

"All of a sudden, you're in the weeds and people are saying, 'You're amending the Constitution for *this*?'" Jay Berman, Bayh's staffer, said to me about the feeling that emerged after months of hearings. "'Look, we have fundamental issues here. We've expended so much time and effort to expand the franchise. You've been involved in all these civil rights bills. What are the consequences for the present system if the person with the most votes doesn't win? What was all this about if it doesn't mean that every vote should count?"[24]

I I I

In the May 19, 1966, edition of the *Congressional Record*—sandwiched between an announcement of funding for a new Washington, D.C., museum and sculpture garden and the designation of National Halibut Week—there is a transcript of a speech delivered on the floor of the Senate the day before.[25]

The three-page speech, titled "Direct Popular Election of

the President," was the most emphatic argument for a popular vote in nearly two centuries.[26] Yet unlike the words of James Wilson, James Madison, and Gouverneur Morris, which were spoken in secret and hidden from the American people for nearly half a century, this speech, by Birch Bayh, was spoken in public and meant to be heard right away.

After "a great deal of study and reflection," Bayh said, he had changed his mind: the president of the United States should be chosen directly by the people.

This was a big deal coming from the chair of the subcommittee that had just succeeded in getting a constitutional amendment approved by Congress. But Bayh had come by his change of heart honestly, and he wanted everyone to understand his reasoning.

Bayh first reminded his listeners of the unique circumstances that led the Constitution's framers to adopt the College in 1787—circumstances that had ceased to exist long before 1966. Then he quoted the familiar refrain of the popular vote skeptics, among whom he'd counted himself only weeks earlier. "'It may be a fine idea, but it will never pass,'" he said in their voice. But things were different now. American democracy was expanding, becoming more inclusive—and moving closer to the nation's founding ideals. "Today, for the first time in our history, we have achieved the goal of universal suffrage regardless of race, religion or station in life," Bayh said. "Today, we are witnessing a political development in our states where for the first time in decades, legislatures fully represent people."

The partial reforms on the table, including the one he had been promoting himself, were simply not up to the task.

Adopting any one of them, Bayh said, "would be like shifting around the parts of a creaky and dangerous automobile engine, making it no less creaky and no less dangerous. What we may need is a new engine, because we are in a new age."

The new engine was a direct popular vote. It was the only way to ensure that all votes were treated as equal, and that the candidate who received the most votes would always become president. This was hardly a radical proposal, Bayh said. Echoing the Supreme Court's one person, one vote rulings, he framed it as the "logical, realistic and proper continuation of this nation's tradition and history—a tradition of continuous expansion of the franchise and equality in voting." It was also the way every other election in the country was run.

But hadn't Bayh just called the Electoral College an essential feature of American federalism, a way for the states to play a central role in electing the nation's leader? Yes, he had. And he had been wrong. "We elect our local official locally; our Congressmen by districts to protect district interests; our Governors and Senators statewide," Bayh said. "Why should we not elect the President and Vice President nationally? The President has no authority over state government. He cannot veto a bill enacted by a state legislature. Why then should he be elected by state-chosen electors? He should be elected directly by the people, for it is the people of the United States to whom he is responsible."

Bayh then took up the other common objection to a popular vote—that it would allow the big cities and states to dominate every election. Wrong again: the Electoral College already renders the small states irrelevant, Bayh said, because they don't have enough electoral votes to matter. Under a popular vote, however, "candidates would have to go where the votes are, and that is everywhere."

In closing, Bayh played his ace: the founding fathers, whose wisdom he invoked even as he hinted that they had made a mistake. "Direct popular election brings with it many virtues and no vices," he said, "If there was doubt about it in the early years of the Republic, there can be no doubt today. Let us echo Madison. Let us put our trust in the people."

I I I

The people, as it turned out, were more than ready to be trusted.

On May 18, the same day as Bayh's speech, Gallup released the first-ever national poll on a direct vote for president. Sixty-three percent of Americans said they favored dumping the Electoral College for a popular vote. Twenty percent opposed it, and 17 percent had no opinion.

In January 1966, the United States Chamber of Commerce released the results of a nationwide referendum of its members on the question of presidential selection—the first major national organization to do so publicly. By a margin of more than nine to one, they favored abolishing the winner-take-all Electoral College in favor of either a direct popular vote or the district system.[27] This was significant not only because the Chamber's membership was very large—representing 30,000 businesses and about four million people across the country—but because it tended to support conservative political positions, and the popular vote was an issue that had so far been identified primarily with liberals.

Soon the movement had support from across the political spectrum. The League of Women Voters came out in favor, as did organized labor. In February 1967, the American Bar Association—which had played a central role in generating public and legislative support for the Twenty-Fifth Amendment—put its stamp of approval on Bayh's amendment. In a report that would later be quoted in the *New York Times*, the ABA called the Electoral College "archaic, undemocratic, complex, ambiguous, indirect, and dangerous." The report compared the various alternative proposals before coming down strongly in favor of a direct, nationwide popular vote for president. No alternative to the College was perfect, it said, but a popular vote would "more accurately reflect the will of the people than any other system," and only it would eliminate the risk of electing a popular-vote-losing president.[28]

The range and depth of support for a popular vote gave Bayh the confidence that he was on the right track. Still, he moved cautiously. As the 1968 presidential race heated up, he pulled back on the popular vote campaign. Merits aside, any debate over how America might choose its president in the future would surely get tangled up in the politics of how America was choosing its president in 1968.

What Bayh couldn't know was how much that year's election—and the collective heart attack it gave the nation—would help his cause.

III

Birch Bayh had the job, he had a theory of the case, and he had the wind at his back. But it wasn't until the near-catastrophe of the 1968 election, a three-way race that almost ended up getting thrown into the House of Representatives, that the push for a national popular vote took on a life of its own.

The race that year featured Richard Nixon, the Republican former vice president, against Hubert Humphrey, the Democratic sitting vice president. It was tight to the end, but the real electoral angst was supplied by the third-party candidate, Alabama governor George Wallace.

Wallace was a traditional southern Democrat, which meant he was an ardent segregationist and a steadfast opponent of civil rights. That put him at odds with his national party, which had been taken over by Democrats in the North and was quickly moving in the opposite direction. For a while, the two Democratic camps coexisted uneasily, but by the late 1960s the divide had grown too wide to sustain. While earlier southern segregationists, like Strom Thurmond and Harry F. Byrd Jr., had run for president as Democrats or at least Dixiecrats, that wasn't possible in 1968. The party was going through a final fracture, and Wallace wanted to extract as much blood as he could before it was all over. He found a new home on the ticket of the far right American Independent Party.

Wallace's plan was not to get elected outright himself—he knew that would be impossible—but to peel off enough electoral votes from both Nixon and Humphrey to prevent either from winning a majority. If he managed that, it would trigger the Constitution's rarely used electoral backup plan: an election of the president by the House of Representatives, with each state delegation getting to cast a single vote. Dangling the mere threat of that scenario before both parties, Wallace could exert immense leverage over the final choice.

It nearly worked: Wallace won just shy of 10 million popular votes, most in the Deep South, and came in first in the balloting in five states: Georgia, Alabama, Mississippi, Arkansas, and Louisiana, good for a total of 46 electoral votes.

While Nixon ended up winning both the popular vote and the Electoral College, a switch of fewer than 78,000 votes in two states, Illinois and Missouri, would have dropped him below an electoral vote majority and forced the election into the House.

Wallace didn't succeed at his ultimate goal, but he did succeed at putting a massive scare into millions of Americans who had never before given much if any thought to the bizarre way our president gets chosen.

The main fear revolved around that backup plan, which hadn't been triggered in nearly 150 years, and which virtually everyone—including some of the Constitution's framers themselves—considered a disaster.

What's so bad about it? For starters, it's even more undemocratic than the Electoral College itself. In the College, at least, population matters for something—bigger states have more electors than smaller ones. In a House election, every state counts the same. Wyoming gets one vote and so does California, even though California today has almost 70 times as many people as Wyoming. And since a state will almost always vote for the candidate of the same party as a majority of its delegation, a House-decided presidency will have no relation at all to the popular vote, only to the happenstance of which party controls a majority of state delegations in the House. In 1968, that was the Democrats, who held a majority of representatives in 29 state delegations. So even though Richard Nixon won the popular vote, the House could have snatched the White House out of his hands.

But that's not the end of the story. Several of those states with Democratic majorities were in the South, so they would not have voted automatically for Humphrey. This raises the other major problem with the House election: the risk that candidates will have to cut backroom deals with members of Congress in order to secure enough votes to win the presidency. That's precisely what happened both times the presidency was decided by the House, in 1800 and 1824. And it would have happened in 1968, as either Humphrey or Nixon would have had to make all kinds of concessions to win over House delegations from the southern states. For millions of Americans, the prospect of an unreconstructed racist deciding who would be America's next president by extorting members of Congress was the last straw.

As the 1968 election played out, the debate over the Electoral College—which was already at a simmer thanks to the efforts of Birch Bayh—boiled over. It was no longer confined to dusty academic journals and congressional subcommittees. Newspaper editorials supported it. Columnists argued about it. Articles in favor of or opposed to it appeared everywhere from *Reader's Digest* to *Playboy*.[29] The country's best-known writers weighed in, with sentiments ranging from skeptical to panicked. Russell Baker, the hugely popular *New York Times* columnist, spun off a short novel imagining the 1968 election being deadlocked and thrown to the House of Representatives, which becomes paralyzed by politics, leaving the nation without a president as Inauguration Day approaches. When an unelected Robert Kennedy installs himself in the White House, the American people revolt. "In mid-January the mobs had begun assembling daily on the Capitol grounds," Baker wrote, "at first quarreling and fighting among themselves, then submerging their mutual antipathies in demonstrations against the House. It had become necessary to bring up Army and Marine units to maintain order at gunpoint."[30]

It didn't play out quite that way, but Baker's anxiety was an accurate reflection of the national mood. In the aftermath of the election, James Michener, the bestselling author of *Tales of the South Pacific* and *Hawaii*, wrote a brief, urgent polemic called "Presidential Lottery," in which he called America's presidential election system a "ridiculous and unnecessary anachronism." It contained "so many built in pitfalls that sooner or later it is bound to destroy us." It was, in short, a "time bomb lodged near the heart of the nation."[31]

The upshot was that the 1968 election, while it didn't end up in the House, injected the movement to abolish the Electoral College with a last big dose of momentum. The fix seemed clear: a national popular vote. It would eliminate the risk of an election decided by the House and guarantee that the candidate with the most votes becomes president— fulfilling the basic democratic principle of majority rule.

▌▌▌

By 1969 the popular vote movement seemed unstoppable. If all went according to plan, the American people could be voting directly for their president as early as 1972.

Support for Bayh's amendment came from all sides. There were the nation's most influential organizations, including the Chamber of Commerce, the AFL-CIO, the League of Women Voters, and the American Bar Association.

Top Democrats and Republicans came out in support of the popular vote, including Gerald Ford, then-senator Walter Mondale, and then-congressman George H. W. Bush, who called the switch to a popular vote a "drastic" reform, but supported it because it would solve the problems of the Electoral College while maintaining state control over elections, thus preserving "the basic nature of our federal system."[32]

In early September, the House of Representatives held a floor debate on abolishing the Electoral College. Emanuel Celler, the House Judiciary Committee chair, set the tone. Putting a popular vote loser in the White House, he said, would be "barbarous, unsporting, dangerous, and downright uncivilized."[33]

On September 18, for the first time in the nation's history, the House approved an amendment to the Constitution abolishing the College and adopting a direct popular vote for president. It wasn't close: 339–70, easily surpassing the needed two-thirds majority.

A few days later, President Nixon signed on to the cause. "Unless the Senate follows the lead of the House, all opportunity for reform will be lost this year and possibly for years to come," Nixon said.[34]

Even more important, the public was on board. All the sustained attention and advocacy was having an effect. After nearly two centuries, the American people were at last talking about the Electoral College—and, by an overwhelming margin, they wanted to get rid of it. According to a Gallup poll taken in November 1968, about 80 percent of the public now favored picking the president directly.

Faced with numbers like these, even the most ardent critics of a popular vote had to admit that things didn't look good for the Electoral College. In a 1969 essay in the *New York Times Magazine*, Irving Kristol and Paul Weaver warned that the American people were rushing headlong into a major constitutional reform without considering the potentially disastrous consequences, like the destruction of the two-party system. The Electoral College's winner-take-all rules prop up that system, they wrote, and a direct vote would "fragment our party system and diminish the legitimacy of the Presidential succession."[35]

Still, they saw the writing on the wall. The popular vote amendment, they wrote, had an "excellent chance" of Senate approval and a "better-than-even chance" in the states.

They were right on the second point. A *New York Times* survey of state legislatures published in October had found that 30 favored a direct vote for president—eight short of the 38 needed to adopt the amendment. Of the remaining states, six were undecided and six were somewhat opposed. Only eight states strongly opposed a direct vote.[36]

But what about that first prediction? Were the amendment's chances in the Senate really "excellent"?

Bayh had two hurdles to clear. First, the bill had to pass the full Judiciary Committee, which was chaired by James Eastland, the long-serving segregationist from Mississippi. If it succeeded there, it would move on to the floor of the Senate, where it would need to win a two-thirds majority in order to be sent on to the states, three-quarters of which would need to agree for it to be ratified.

Bayh was confident he had the votes in both the committee and the full Senate. He planned to use the same strategy that had worked in the House: hold a vote for every alternative reform, like the district and proportional plans, each of which had its backers but not enough support to pass. Once all the other options were voted down, only one would remain: a direct popular vote.

It was straightforward, it was clean, and it looked like it would work.

And then it collapsed. By September 1970, a year after the House vote, Bayh's amendment was dead. His four-year effort to bring the nation's presidential election process into line with modern democratic ideals was effectively over.

What killed it? The autopsy offered one possible explanation: a bitter Supreme Court nomination battle divided and distracted the Senate for months, as Democrats rejected President Nixon's first two picks to fill the seat vacated by Justice Abe Fortas. By the time the seat was filled, by Harry Blackmun in 1970, Bayh had spent most of the political capital he was planning to use on the amendment.

If you dug a little deeper, however, you'd find that the real force that ended any chance for a direct popular vote was the same in 1970 as it had been in 1787: the South's maintenance of disproportionate political power through racial subjugation.

This time, the popular vote was suffocated through a series of insidious parliamentary maneuvers employed by the descendants of slaveholders. Three powerful southern senators took the lead: Strom Thurmond, the long-lived South Carolina Dixiecrat who had run for president in 1948 on a segregationist platform and filibustered every major piece of civil rights legislation he could get his hands on; Sam Ervin, the sweet-talking North Carolinian who led the fight against school integration after the Supreme Court's ruling in *Brown v. Board of Education*; and James Eastland, who had given

Bayh the chairmanship of the amendments subcommittee years before, but whom Bayh later recalled as "a plantation owner, one step away from being a slave master."[37]

It is no surprise that men like Eastland, Ervin, and Thurmond were the modern saviors of the Electoral College. Slavery may have been gone for a century, but its ghost lived on, embedded in the structure of American politics—particularly in systems like the Electoral College, under which, as the southerners well knew, black people always counted for less, if they counted at all.

While the long-term effects of the civil rights movement weren't yet clear, black citizens were being encouraged to participate in elections, and now they were protected by federal law. Segregationists were trying to preserve a world in which blacks remained off the rolls, or at least out of the voting booth. In a popular vote, millions of black citizens across the South would suddenly start to count just as much as whites.

For the southerners, protecting the unearned benefits of the Electoral College became even more urgent as the North's population grew larger and concentrated more in cities. And yet this time there was an odd twist: the white segregationists were joined in their defense of the College by blacks and Jews in those northern cities.

If this seems strange, consider a basic truth about the Electoral College: its strongest defenders have never been those advocating some broader principle, but those who believe, rightly or wrongly, that the College advantages them politically. That is the case for Republicans today, and it was the case for big-city African Americans and Jews in the mid-twentieth century. At the time, New York was the country's most populous state and its biggest swing state—in other words, thanks to its closely divided electorate and the winner-take-all rule, it had more power than any other state to determine the outcome of the presidential election. And the voters who held the most power to swing New York one way or the other were racial and ethnic minorities in large urban areas.

In October 1969, K. Leroy Irvis, the majority leader of the Pennsylvania House of Representatives, admitted to the *New York Times* that it was "a very purely selfish reason" to support the Electoral College. "The Negro people are collected in the north and east in urban areas. The only way they can have any political clout is through their vote in presidential elections. If by being the balance of power they can swing an election, they have a leverage which popular election removes."[38]

It was an ironic side effect of the Great Migration, the decades-long shift of black Americans from southern farms to northern cities. While blacks remained effectively unrepresented in the South, they suddenly found themselves with unique leverage in big cities like New York and Chicago, which were often the decisive factor in swinging their entire states to the Democrats.

This advantage was not lost on southern white conservatives. Texas representative Ed Gossett, who in 1950 had cosponsored a constitutional amendment to require a proportional allocation of electoral votes for precisely this reason, explained his opposition to the winner-take-all rule during a House hearing on Electoral College reform in 1951:

> Now, please understand, I have no objection to the Negro in Harlem voting and to his vote being counted, but I do resent the fact that both parties

will spend a hundred times as much money to get his vote, and that his vote is worth a hundred times as much in the scale of national politics as is the vote of a white man in Texas. I have no objection to a million folks who cannot speak English voting, or to their votes being counted, but I do resent the fact that because they happen to live in Chicago, or Detroit, or New York, their vote is worth a hundred times as much as mine because I happen to live in Texas. Is it fair, is it honest, is it democratic, is it to the best interest of anyone in fact, to place such a premium on a few thousand labor votes, or Italian votes, or Irish votes, or Negro votes, or Jewish votes, or Polish votes, or Communist votes, or big-city-machine votes, simply because they happen to be located in two or three large, industrial pivotal States?[39]

Strom Thurmond took advantage of this demographic fact and sent personal telegrams to prominent black and Jewish leaders in 1970, warning them of the consequences of supporting a direct popular vote. In a 2009 interview, Bayh recalled the ploy:

He told these groups, "What you're going to do is, you're going to give up your advantage to have influence to sway these large electoral votes if you have a direct popular vote. It will just be confined to one person, one vote. You won't be able to sway that whole group of electors," which is true, of course.

A couple of these guys . . . came to my office and said, "You're going to have to back away from this."

I said, "What do you mean?"

They said, "Well, it would give us less power."

I finally said—the only time while I was there, in my eighteen years—I said, "Look, I busted my tail to see that each of you and your constituencies got one person, one vote. Now you're telling me that if you have 1.01, you want to keep it? Get your rear ends out of my office and don't come back."[40]

But Thurmond's ploy worked, and generated enough opposition to keep Bayh's amendment bottled up. Eastland slow-walked it through the Judiciary Committee at every step. What should have taken days or weeks took months.

"It was so galling and so aggravating to live through what they were doing to us," Jay Berman said. "And that put us back almost a year, from the day that Celler passed it to the time we got to the floor of the Senate."[41]

As soon as that happened, in September 1970, the southerners mounted their filibuster. Bayh thought he had the two-thirds of the Senate he needed to stop them. He counted 60 votes out of the gate, and figured he would round up the rest along the way. But after Thurmond's scaremongering campaign, Bayh found that the opposite happened: he not only failed to gain conservative votes, but he lost liberal ones. "I think we ended up with maybe fifty-two or fifty-three votes, fifty-five maybe," he recalled in a 2009 interview. "I didn't even have my sixty."[42]

I I I

Bayh didn't spend time mourning his loss. He reintroduced the Electoral College bill in every Congress for the next decade—in 1971, 1973, 1975, 1977, and 1979. All together, there were several more weeks of hearings, dozens more witnesses, and thousands of additional pages of committee records. By the end, Bayh had 38 cosponsors for the bill. Twenty-two represented states with nine or fewer electoral votes. And from start to finish, it was the southern senators who took the lead in blocking it.

There was some drama, but not of the electoral variety. During a committee hearing in 1977, one of the Electoral College's most stalwart defenders, a political scientist named Martin Diamond, finished giving his testimony, got up, and collapsed to the ground from a massive heart attack. Bayh and Orrin Hatch, his Republican colleague from Utah, tried in vain to resuscitate him.

Finally, in July 1979, Bayh managed to get a full Senate vote on the issue. Fifty-one Senators voted to abolish the Electoral College, a majority, but well short of the 67 needed to pass a constitutional amendment.

One year later, Ronald Reagan swept into the White House with almost 51 percent of the national popular vote, nine percentage points higher than Jimmy Carter. That landslide became an avalanche in the Electoral College. Thanks to the winner-take-all rule, Reagan, who won the popular vote in 44 states, saw his 51 percent translated into more than 90 percent of all electoral votes.

The year 1980 was a banner one across the board for Republicans, who picked up 12 seats in the Senate and took control of that chamber for the first time in a quarter century. Bayh, who was seeking a fourth term, was among the Democratic incumbents sent packing. He was beaten by a young congressman from Indiana's Fourth Congressional District named Dan Quayle.

With Bayh's departure, the Senate lost its best advocate for a national popular vote. "No one was a better legislator than he was and he couldn't get it done," Jay Berman said. "It's just such an empty feeling because it was so right to do. And we couldn't do it."[43]

III

The Electoral College is like a core sample drawn from the trunk of the tree of American history. You can trace its rings back through nearly all of the key periods in which the maintenance of racial subjugation was central to the nation's growth and development: from the morally abhorrent deals that preserved and protected chattel slavery to the collapse of Reconstruction and the legalized discrimination of the Jim Crow era; from the racist dog whistle of "states' rights" to the twentieth-century segregationists who resisted racial equality and reordered American politics; from the Electoral College–aided election of a man who declared that all human beings are equal even as he owned hundreds of them himself, to the Electoral College–aided election of a man who campaigned on an explicit platform of white resentment and racial exclusion . . . and who also happened to represent everything the College was ostensibly designed to protect us from.

In this way, the story of why Birch Bayh's amendment failed is a familiar one: the persistence of the ideology of white supremacy. And yet that narrative is complicated by the unexpected alliance of self-interest between the segregationists and black lawmakers in northern cities. For both groups, the defense of the College was less about principle than about protecting an institution that gave both a special, unearned benefit. That is, they both wanted it precisely because it did not represent one person, one vote.

Birch Bayh tossed people out of his office for making that argument because he could see what the desire for partisan advantage had blinded them to: the United States had entered the next era of its democratization, and from the new vantage point, the Electoral College seemed ever more out of step with modern democratic sensibilities. It was a 200-year-old relic defended almost exclusively by those who believed, rightly or wrongly, that it benefited them at the expense of true political equality. Bayh understood that getting rid of the College would be the final step in the country's constitutional evolution—an evolution that began with the declaration that all men are created equal.

6

SETTING THE RECORD STRAIGHT, PART ONE: COMMON ELECTORAL COLLEGE MYTHS

What Does "Mob Rule" Mean, Anyway?

Half a century after Birch Bayh nearly managed to get a nationwide, bipartisan coalition to adopt a popular vote for president, the debate over the Electoral College is as partisan as it has ever been. The divide is no longer regional, or even primarily ideological. It is a split between Democrats and Republicans, between the perceived interests of large and small states, of urban and rural populations.

The argument goes on every day in newspapers and on websites around the country. Those on the left (for the most part) are ready for a change; those on the right (nearly always) are dug in, some because they are skeptical of change, but most because their candidate came out on top in 2000 and 2016.

That's not a knock on Republicans. The Electoral College's survival has always depended on adherents of one party or the other, and sometimes both, believing that it gives them a systematic advantage. But because we're talking about a provision of the Constitution, defenders look for ways to justify it on a higher principle. So they reach into a grab bag of explanations about why the College was created and how it functions today. Some of these explanations may have once contained some truth. Others are based on misconceptions or straight-up mistakes. Most are what the *New York Times* columnist Jamelle Bouie calls "folk civics"—stories we tell over and over because they sound logical and are easy to repeat. That doesn't make them right.[1]

Consider the familiar claim that a popular vote would lead to "mob rule." Taken at face value, this implies that regular Americans, speaking directly for themselves, pose a threat to the order and stability of their government and that they require an intermediary to translate their vote—and, if necessary, override it. That's an odd argument to make in a country that has elected all its presidential electors by popular vote for nearly 150 years.

And when, as usual, this fear of "mob rule" is attributed to the founding fathers, it's misleading. Yes, many of the Constitution's framers were wary of the people, and they imposed various obstacles to popular participation in government. But when it came to electing the president, a major concern was that members of the public—most of whom had little access to news and rarely traveled far from home—wouldn't know enough about national candidates to make an informed decision. In our information-saturated world, that's not an issue, which leads to an obvious question: Who, exactly, is the mob in 2020? If it is the people voting for the president, then in the last election the mob voted for the dull centrist technocrat, who also happened to be one of the most qualified candidates in American history. The Electoral College, meanwhile, picked the person it was literally designed to keep out of office.

When we talk about the Electoral College—with friends or coworkers, at family gatherings or at cocktail parties, the conversation almost always gets hung up on one or another of these misconceptions. So I thought it would be useful to do some debunking.

In this chapter, I discuss three of the most irrepressible myths and misconceptions about the Electoral College itself. In Chapter 8, I do the same for the national popular vote. Of course there are many dozens more that I don't cover here. If you're interested in seeing them all compiled in one place and addressed thoroughly, I encourage you to pick up *Every Vote Equal,* by John Koza, whom you will learn much more about in the next chapter.

For now, consider this a sort of cheat sheet to read before Thanksgiving dinner, when the talk turns, as it invariably does in election years, to how we choose our president. To simulate real life, I've created a skeptical debater whose gut instinct is to support the Electoral College, but who hasn't given the matter all that much thought. Let's call this person popular-vote-curious. Of course, such discussions probably won't play out this smoothly in real life, which is what the wine is for.

Myth #1: The Electoral College forces candidates to campaign and win support all over the country.

One of the most common modern defenses of the Electoral College is that it forces candidates to earn support from—and thus pay attention to the concerns of—voters in all states and regions in order to win.

Paul LePage, the former governor of Maine, said in a 2019 radio interview that if the country switched to a popular vote for president, "all the small states—like Maine, New Hampshire, Vermont, Wyoming, Montana, Rhode Island—you'll never see a presidential candidate again. You'll never see anybody at the national stage come to our state. We're going to be forgotten people."[2]

> *Well, won't they? If the goal is simply to vacuum up the most votes, why would any candidate waste time running around stumping in low-population states?*

The problem with this argument is that it ignores the reality under our existing winner-take-all system. Right now most states, and the voters in them, are ignored by the candidates, and for a simple reason: they are not electorally competitive in the presidential race. Every four years, the major parties effectively write off around 40 states—big, small, and in between—because the vote in those states is clear in advance. Since the electors in those states are awarded on a winner-take-all basis, there's no point in trying to win by more, or lose by less. Everyone knows what the outcome will be.

A presidential campaign's two most valuable resources are time and money; they have to spend both wisely. So they focus on the small handful of battleground states where a switch of even a few hundred votes can swing all the state's electors from one column to the other. In those states, a couple extra visits or a few more dollars could make the difference. This isn't favoritism or selfishness; it's just smart campaigning. The last presidential candidate to visit all 50 states in a campaign was Richard Nixon in 1960, and he did it because he'd promised to.

That's the pernicious effect of winner-take-all: A candidate running in a state where his or her party is destined to lose by more than 10 percentage points could spend a billion dollars in that state and still lose. So they don't spend a dime, don't poll a single person, and don't hold a single campaign rally. Thirty-four states haven't drawn a single general-election campaign event focused on their state's voters from a major-party nominee for president or vice president since the 2000 election.

Okay, but the battleground states are always changing, so doesn't that give everyone a chance to get some attention over the long run?

It's true that states once considered safe for one party can become battlegrounds later on, as Colorado did recently; it's also true that states that were once hotly contested become easy pickups, as has happened in New York. But these transitions are relatively uncommon and take decades to play out. Meanwhile the underlying dynamic stays the same: a few lucky states duke it out in the ring while the rest of America sits up in the nosebleeds, passive spectators to the most consequential election in the world's oldest democracy. It's always good for the small percentage of the population living in the battleground states, but how is that fair for everyone else?

But a candidate who knows that he or she has to win electors in battleground states all over the country will make an extra effort to turn out the vote in those states. That's a good thing, right?

It is a good thing, and there is no reason that only battleground states should get that benefit.

Name one major-party presidential candidate in the last 50 years who did not have a decent amount of support in every single state. Most of the time, it's much more than decent. In the modern era, presidential candidates are known everywhere and have lots of voters everywhere. In 2016, no state gave Hillary Clinton or Donald Trump more than 68 percent, or less than 20 percent, of its popular vote. (The District of Columbia was the exception; it voted for Clinton over Trump by 91 percent to 4 percent.) Sure, Democrats have more support in some states and Republicans have more in others, but look at any county-level map of voting results: it's a sea of purple, in varying shades. Even if the increase in political polarization has resulted in more counties that vote heavily for one party or the other, the bottom line is that no state is "red" or "blue"—we only paint them that way because of the winner-take-all method.

The candidates' focus on battleground states is evident in how and where their campaigns spend their time. In 2012, 100 percent of general election campaign events and almost all campaign spending took place in just 12 closely contested states. Two-thirds of the events were held in just four states— Ohio, Virginia, Florida, and Iowa. The pattern repeated in 2016: 94 percent of all events were held in 12 states, and two-thirds were held in six states—Florida, North Carolina, Pennsylvania, Ohio, Virginia, and Michigan.[3]

The story is the same with money. In 2012, when spending on the presidential race topped $1 billion for the first time, about two-thirds of that amount—$670 million—was spent in just three states: Ohio, Virginia, and Florida, which together account for barely one in ten Americans. And in case the distortions of the winner-take-all rule aren't already clear, note that President Obama won all three of those states by a total margin of fewer than 400,000 votes, for which he was awarded 60 electoral votes. Mitt Romney won the state of Oklahoma by almost the same popular vote margin—giving him seven electoral votes.

The point is that candidates *already* ignore the overwhelming majority of American voters. They spend their time in places like Ohio, Florida, Virginia, and North Carolina for no other reason than that the electorate in those states happens to be closely divided between Democrats and Republicans.

In presidential elections, the true "flyover" states aren't just Nebraska, Idaho, and Tennessee but New York, Texas, California, and dozens of others. Rural or urban, northern or southern, small or large—if you're not a battleground state, you get essentially no attention.

Scott Walker, the former Wisconsin governor and 2016 Republican presidential contender, summed it up when he said, "The nation as a whole is not going to elect the next president. Twelve states are."[4]

Okay, the candidates focus on a few states that determine the outcome of the election. So what? If they're winning votes everywhere, why does it matter?

It matters because attention from major-party presidential candidates, and the national party networks that back them, comes with all sorts of benefits. States that are not competitive lose out on campaign resources, weakening state party operations, discouraging voter participation, and affecting the results in down-ballot races.

Jamie Raskin, now a member of Congress from Maryland, was a co-chair of Barack Obama's statewide campaign for president in 2008. Early that year it became clear that Maryland would be an easy win for Obama, but Virginia, its neighbor to the south, would be a fight.

"We were told very explicitly that any volunteers had to go to Virginia, any money goes to Virginia," Raskin told me. "So we were sending tens of thousands of Marylanders into Virginia to turn Virginia blue. There's a certain charm to that at the beginning, and in a strategic sense, it was the right thing to do. But then you realize you're helping organize someone else's state political party. The carryover effect of that is we're not building up big margins to win closer races in *our* state. We've got a Republican governor, for example. So from the standpoint of building Maryland's political culture and organization, it was an absurdity. But that's the logic of our presidential system. The more you're ignored, the worse your situation gets."[5]

The same thing happens in every other non-battleground state, as members of both the dominant party and the minority party in any of those states will attest. Why waste valuable resources going after votes that won't affect the outcome?

It's not only political party operations that suffer. Researchers have found a swing-state effect when it comes to presidential policy-making and discretionary grants. This happens even with disaster aid, which seems like it should be distributed without regard to its potential political benefits.[6]

Distortions like this should upset anyone who thinks it's bad for candidates for national office to pay attention to a small subset of voters in a few states. It certainly upset James Madison, who lived long enough to see all but one state adopt the winner-take-all method. He was so disturbed by it that he proposed a constitutional amendment barring the practice and requiring states to award their electors by district, which he claimed was the system most of the framers had envisioned.[7]

I still think the framers knew what they were doing.

In many ways they did! The Electoral College they designed was flexible, giving states full control over how to allocate their electors. That system was also designed to make it as likely as possible that the office was filled by the fittest and most broadly supported candidate. So let's consider the case of Donald Trump. Trump did win support everywhere, and yet from the moment he was sworn in he has governed like he is the president of Michigan, Wisconsin, and Pennsylvania, and treated the White House as though it were Republican campaign headquarters. He behaves less like the chief executive of a vast and sprawling republic than like a warrior for the 27 percent of eligible voters who voted for him. More than any president in history, he has factionalized the office, speaking almost exclusively to and for his base and showing disdain for the wishes of the majority of voters who did not choose him. The Electoral College didn't just fail to stop him from acting in this way; it's the one thing that made it possible.

Fair enough: the winner-take-all Electoral College may be broken, but at least candidates know how it works and how to campaign to win it. We have no idea what would happen under a national popular vote campaign.

In fact you can get a pretty good sense of how a popular vote campaign would play out right now—by paying attention to the two kinds of elections we already run that mimic it: battleground state elections and elections for governor.

For the first category, you can learn a lot by analyzing the distribution of presidential campaign events *within* battleground states rather than *between* them and non-battleground states.

Take Ohio, which in 2012 saw a greater share of general election campaign events than any other state. An analysis of the candidates' public rallies—which are usually followed by fundraisers and meetings with local political and community leaders—found that they tracked with remarkable precision the distribution of the state's population. Slightly more than half of Ohioans live in the state's four biggest metropolitan areas—Cleveland, Columbus, Cincinnati, and Toledo. Those four areas saw 52 percent of campaign events. Twenty-three percent of events took place in Ohio's seven medium-sized cities, which hold a combined 24 percent of the population. And in the state's rural areas, where 22 percent of Ohioans live, campaigns held 25 percent of their events.

The campaigns weren't just carefully targeted; they were evenly balanced. If you divide Ohio into four quadrants, each containing four of its 16 congressional districts (and thus one-quarter of the state's population), you find that the campaigns held a nearly identical number of events in each quadrant.

These patterns were repeated in other battleground states, including Florida, Virginia, Iowa, and Colorado. While results like these make sense, it's still striking how closely campaign activity maps onto population. It's "almost surgical," said John Koza, the popular-vote advocate who compiled the data. "They're not making this six-stop-per-day itinerary because they enjoy getting on and off planes. It's because they know it pays off, and if it stops paying off, they'll stop doing it. They do this because it works. This is very Darwinian."[8]

In other words, the people who run presidential campaigns aren't stupid. They have limited resources, and when they are faced with a close election in which every vote counts the same, as is the case in every battleground state, they behave rationally and spend those resources as efficiently as they can.

The lesson is not that campaigns favor big-city voters over those in rural areas. It's that when every vote matters, they treat voters as though they matter, and spend exactly as much time as they need to in order to maximize their chances of picking up as many votes as possible.

The same thing happens in governors' races—another statewide contest in which every vote counts equally and the person who gets the most votes wins. Akhil Reed Amar, the Yale constitutional law scholar, argues that this is the essential point. "When we're picking governors, we don't give a damn about any of this," he said. "Everyone gets a vote regardless of where he lives: the city, the suburbs, the country. If a popular vote were bad because it helps big-city folks, then every state, especially states with big cities, is picking its governor the wrong way. States should copy the Electoral College model for selecting their governors—and no state does."

Myth #2: The Electoral College protects the smaller and more rural states.

Consider this frequently quoted statistic: Wyoming, which has 577,000 residents, gets three electoral votes; California, with just under 40 million residents, gets 55. Do the math and you find that there are nearly 70 times as many people living in California as in Wyoming, but California gets just 18 times as many electoral votes. This means that in the presidential election, a Wyomingite counts nearly four times as much as a Californian.

That is insane. How can it be fair for the small states to have so much more power in choosing the president?

With numbers like that, it certainly seems unfair. For decades, the belief that small states are the main beneficiaries of the Electoral College has been one of the most common arguments put forward by the College's defenders, and also accepted wisdom by its opponents. It's still wrong.

The College has almost never worked to the small states' benefit—not at the founding, and not today. To the contrary, small states are some of the biggest losers under the Electoral College, for two reasons.

First, the statewide winner-take-all rule benefits larger states, which can offer candidates a much bigger jackpot. Would you rather net all of California's 55 electors or all of Wyoming's three?

Second, the smallest states are almost all noncompetitive in presidential elections. Of the 13 states with three or four electoral votes, 12 vote reliably Democratic or Republican, which means they get ignored by the campaigns, just like all the other "safe" states. The one battleground small state is New Hampshire. Even though it has only four electoral votes to give, it gets more attention from the major-party campaigns than the other 12 small states combined.[9]

Then why do I always hear that small states are the ones that will stop us from reforming the College?

Partly because people just keep saying it. In fact, small states have always held a wide range of views about the College. Some have fought to protect it, but others have understood that it is not their friend. In 1966, Delaware brought a federal lawsuit against New York and other large states, arguing that their use of the winner-take-all method of allocating electors violated the equal protection clause. Delaware was right about the effect of winner-take-all, but the Supreme Court didn't take the case.[10] By the end of Birch Bayh's push to abolish the Electoral College and replace it with a national popular vote, in the late 1970s, he had the support of 22 senators from smaller states.

If it's so obvious, why haven't they all come around?

Blame it on the Senate, and what I call the "plus-two fallacy." Remember, Congress is divided into two chambers: the House of Representatives, which is apportioned by population, and the Senate, which treats all states as equal, regardless of their size.

Within the Senate, those two extra votes make a big difference. They put the smaller states on an equal footing with larger states, giving them far more leverage over policy-making and presidential nominees than they would have in a proportional system.

Because the Electoral College reflects a state's congressional representation, it's natural to assume that the Senate advantage carries over to the Electoral College—the "plus-two fallacy."

And technically, it does. Those two extra votes give disproportionate power to each small-state voter. The presidential ballot of one Wyomingite does in fact weigh nearly four times as much as that of one Californian. But what is that extra weight actually worth? Almost nothing, because the winner-take-all rule—which gives a huge boost to larger states, and especially to large swing states like Florida and Pennsylvania—overwhelms the bump smaller states get from their two Senate-based electors.

According to one historian's calculations, the smaller states' bump has played a role in the outcome of only three elections—1876, 1916, and 2000.[11] In two of those elections, the presidency was won by the candidate who lost the national popular vote.

In short, the "plus-two fallacy" is the mistaken belief that because small states have a significant advantage in the Senate, they must have the same advantage in the Electoral College.

(You may have noticed that the ratio of representatives in California and Wyoming is 53 to one, but if California has 70 times more people than Wyoming, and the House of Representatives is apportioned by population, shouldn't that ratio be 70 to one? Yes, it should. The reason it's not is that the House is far smaller than it should be, which has a very real impact on Electoral College outcomes, as well as on the one person, one vote principle. See the next myth for details.)[12]

All right, I get it: the small states don't benefit from the Electoral College. But I'm sure I heard that the framers created the College specifically to protect the smaller states from being drowned out by the larger ones.

It's true, they did—but only in one specific and rarely used way. A provision in Article II, Section 1, slightly revised by the Twelfth Amendment, says that whenever the electors are deadlocked—that is, when no candidate wins a majority of electoral votes—the House of Representatives gets to choose the president. In that scenario, the representatives pick from among the top three electoral vote finishers, with each state getting a single vote. If a state delegation is evenly split between two candidates, it loses its vote.

Weird. How does that help the small states?

Think of it as a supercharged Senate: every state gets the same voting power, regardless of its population, but rather than just passing bills, the states are literally picking the president. So, to use the example above, Wyoming's single representative, who represents a little more than half a million people, would have just as much say in choosing the president as California's 53 representatives, who represent about 40 million people.

As some framers imagined it, this is how elections would usually go. There would be two rounds of voting for the president. The larger states would have the advantage in the first round, by the Electoral College, because they had so many more electors. The small states would get the upper hand in the second round, the House election, because they would be equal to the large states. George Mason, a Virginia delegate to the constitutional convention, assumed that 19 out of 20 elections would be decided this way.

What's so unfair about that?

For one, it creates massive political inequality, since states of wildly different sizes are given identical voting power. That leads to an even more perverse result, which is that the presidency will be decided based on a transient political quirk: whichever party happens to be in the majority in more House delegations on Election Day is essentially assured of installing its candidate in the White House—even if that candidate has lost the popular vote, and even if that party is in the House minority overall. So, for example, Barack Obama won the popular vote in 2012, but if the election had ended up in the House, Mitt Romney almost certainly would have become president, because Republicans controlled more state delegations than Democrats did.

Wait, it gets worse: the presidency is decided by the outgoing, lame-duck House, not the incoming one. Imagine that on Election Day, the Republican nominee wins the national popular vote, and Republicans in Congress regain control of a majority of state delegations from Democrats. No matter: the Democrats would still be in charge when the House voted for president, and thus could elevate their nominee, even though the American people had made clear by their votes that they wanted the opposite.

Wow. I thought the voting differential between Wyoming and California was bad enough, but that's bonkers.

I almost forgot: if no vice presidential candidate wins a majority of electoral votes, then under the Twelfth Amendment the Senate chooses between the top two vote-getters, with each senator getting a vote. Now imagine that the Senate is controlled by one party and the House is controlled by another; we could end up with a president and vice president of opposing parties.

In short, pretty much everyone since the founding has realized that this back-up process is a disaster. James Madison, in his later years, called for an amendment to remove the House election provision from the Constitution.[13] Today you would be hard-pressed to find anyone who defends it. The good news is that the House has only been called to decide two elections—in 1800 and 1824. (It played an indirect role in determining the outcome in 1876.) Each time, it has been a mess.

> *Now that I think about it, why should smaller states get any extra power in the first place?*

Good question. Everyone wants more power than they have, but a desire for power is not by itself a legitimate reason to demand a disproportionate amount of it.[14] At least the slave states were united by both geography and a common interest. Small states have no shared interests on account of being small—they didn't at the founding and they don't today. What do South Dakota and Delaware have in common other than similar populations?

Then, there's the common but mistaken assumption that small equals rural. In fact, some small states, like Rhode Island and Hawaii, are proportionally more urban than some large states, like Texas, Ohio, and North Carolina.[15]

In short, people base their political positions on many factors—their personal background, their political ideology, their community's leanings. But no one votes based on the *size* of the state they live in. As one political scientist put it, "If you are a Republican in one state, you are probably going to be pushing the same agenda as a Republican in another state, and the same is true for Democrats."[16] That's why it should not surprise you that in 2016, the 12 "safe" small states (those with three or four electoral votes) split down the middle—six went for Clinton (Rhode Island, Delaware, Hawaii, New Hampshire, Vermont, and Maine) and six went for Trump (Wyoming, North Dakota, South Dakota, Alaska, Montana, and Idaho). Clinton also won the District of Columbia, which has three electoral votes, and Trump picked up a single elector in Maine, which divides its electors by congressional district.

But isn't the Electoral College, like the Senate, necessary to preserve American federalism?

Let's talk about federalism for a moment—that careful balance of power between the national and state governments that is built into the design of our Constitution. By providing for state or local control in many areas of policy, our federalist system is key to the health of a large and diverse democracy.

But federalism already is protected and reinforced through a combination of structures and practices. States have their own laws, written by their own legislatures, enforced by their own executives, and interpreted by their own judiciaries. In Congress, the states wield enormous power—over the passage of federal laws, the confirmation of federal judges, the adoption of international treaties, and the decision whether to initiate impeachment proceedings. Any amendment to the Constitution must go through the states, three-quarters of which have to agree for it to be ratified. In short, American federalism is valuable, it's protected, and it's not going anywhere.

The presidency is, or should be, different. The head of the executive branch is the only elected officer whose job is to represent all the American people as a whole. That's why the title is President of the United States. And no matter which states are "red" and which are "blue," no candidate today can win the White House without nationwide support. That's what should matter, not the varying proclivities of a few thousand voters who happen to live in a few closely contested states. (And this isn't even getting into the complicated politics behind the creation of states and their boundaries in the first place, many of which exist solely because they helped increase the power of one party or the other at the time.[17])

Another key difference: Without the Senate, there would have been no Constitution. The small states would have walked away from the table. There's no evidence that was the case with the Electoral College. If the framers talked about federalism in the debate over how to elect the president, there's no record of it in the notes of the constitutional convention.

That said, it's true that the Electoral College is fundamentally a state-based institution, because it invests so much power in state legislatures. Those legislatures have used that power to enhance democracy by letting people vote directly for their electors. They've also used their power to suppress it by adopting the winner-take-all rule.

The framers understood this two centuries ago. Plenty

of other people have understood it since then, and it is more obvious than ever today. So it's useful to remember one of the most enduring features of our system of federalism: when state practices turn out not to work or prove to be harmful, the states can change them.

Myth #3: The Electoral College would work better if electors were allocated proportionally or by congressional district.

All right, so maybe a winner-take-all Electoral College is harmful to our democracy. But I'm not sure I'm ready for a wholesale switch to a national popular vote. Why not just allocate electors the way James Madison suggested, by congressional district?

It sounds fairer, doesn't it? Under the district system, as it's known, a state awards its electoral votes according to the popular vote result in each of its congressional districts. In addition, the candidate who wins the statewide popular vote gets two extra electors, representing the state's senators.

Take Maine, which uses this method today. The state has two congressional districts, giving it four electors overall—one for each district, plus two for its senators. In 2016, Hillary Clinton won the statewide vote, so she was awarded the two Senate-based electors. However, the state's two congressional districts split—the first district went for Clinton, while the second district went for Trump. Final result: three of Maine's electoral votes went to Clinton, and one went to Trump. Under a winner-take-all system, Clinton would've won all four of Maine's electors.

So the district system would seem to do a better job of reflecting the wishes of the American electorate. Rather than the electoral sledgehammer of winner-take-all, which delivers 100 percent of a state's electors to the candidate who wins the most popular votes in that state, this method allows for different regions in a state to make their voices heard and award electors to different candidates.

This is the system James Madison said most of the framers had in mind when they adopted the College; in 1823, he even advocated a constitutional amendment to require the states to use it.[18]

But on closer examination, allocating electors by congressional district may be even worse than the current winner-take-all system.

For starters, it doesn't eliminate the risk that the popular vote winner could lose in the Electoral College—a major drawback if you believe the president should be the person who wins the most votes. If the district system had been in use nationwide in 2012, Mitt Romney would have become president, despite losing to Barack Obama by about five million votes.

Then there's the problem of partisan gerrymandering—the drawing of legislative district lines to make those districts "safe" for one party or the other. It's an egregiously antidemocratic practice, but the Supreme Court has said it's entirely legal, and both parties do it when they can.

To see just how skewed partisan gerrymandering can get, look at North Carolina, where Republicans took control of the state legislature in 2010 and promptly redrew the state's 13 congressional districts to their extreme advantage. It worked: in a state where Democratic and Republican voters are closely divided, Democrats held a 7 to 6 advantage after the 2010 midterms—an accurate reflection of reality. But in 2012, under the new Republican-drawn maps, Republicans won 9 seats, and Democrats won 4. If North Carolina used the district system to allocate its electors, the Democratic nominee for president could theoretically win 51 percent of the statewide vote and still pick up just 6 of the state's 13 electors, one for winning each of the four Democratic-majority districts, plus two for winning the statewide vote. (After the United States Supreme Court refused to step in, a three-judge panel of a North Carolina state court struck down both the state and congressional district maps for violating the state constitution.[19])

At the moment, gerrymanders only affect the makeup of Congress and state legislatures. But if electoral votes are awarded by congressional district, the distortions of gerrymandering will be imported into the presidential race and could be the decisive factor.

That's bad. Still, partisan gerrymandering isn't the only reason, or even the most important reason, that more districts lean Republican, is it?

No, it's not. Even without intentional partisan gerrymandering, congressional districts are biased in favor of Republicans, who tend to be more evenly spread out across the country, while Democrats are more concentrated in cities. For example, in the 2000 presidential election, Al Gore won more than half a million more popular votes than George W. Bush nationwide, but Bush won more districts,

228 to 207, even though most of those districts had been drawn by Democratic-led state legislatures. Or consider 2008, when John McCain won more districts than Barack Obama across five states, but Obama won the popular vote in those states, and thus all their electors.[20]

Even though it's not intentional, this geographic clustering still weighs the votes of people differently depending on where they live.

> *It's almost as though the House of Representatives needs more members.*

Bingo! This may seem like a tangent, but stay with me. The House of Representatives is far too small to accurately represent the population of twenty-first-century America. Recall from Chapter 4 that its membership, 435, hasn't grown in more than a century. It last changed in 1911, when the country's population was one-third what it is today. There's no constitutional reason for this; prior to 1911, Congress expanded the House in every decade but one following the decennial census and reapportionment. (And here comes James Madison again, always tinkering with his creation: Madison drafted a constitutional amendment that would tie the House's membership directly to the nation's population—which today would mean a House of nearly 11,000 members. The amendment, which passed Congress and was submitted to the states along with the rest of the Bill of Rights, was the original First Amendment. It came one state shy of being ratified.)[21]

Anyway, back to the future: Congress could expand the

House by federal law tomorrow. But as long as the number of representatives stays the same, the House becomes increasingly unrepresentative, primarily to the detriment of bigger cities—and this has arguably had a direct impact on the outcome of presidential elections. In a 2003 study, two mathematicians found that if the House in 2000 had 830 members, Al Gore would have won the presidency. (They got to 830 by calculating how many representatives would be required to give each member the same number of constituents that House members had in 1941.) In fact, with one exception, Gore would have won any election in which the House had 597 members or more, while George W. Bush would have won all elections in which the House had 490 members or fewer.[22]

The bottom line is that even if all states allocated their electoral votes using the congressional district system, we'd have the same problems we do today—but instead of fighting over a few battleground states, candidates would be fighting over a few battleground districts. Most of the country would still be stuck on the sidelines.

There's another alternative, right? Proportional allocation of electors. That sounds the most intuitive, and seems like it would solve basically all our problems.

Under proportional allocation, a state awards its electoral votes according to the breakdown of its statewide popular vote. If a candidate wins 45 percent of a state's vote, he or she gets 45 percent of the state's electors. It sounds sensible, and even better than the district system at reflecting the actual vote totals. No state has ever tried it, but it's had enough appeal that the Senate passed a constitutional amendment in 1950 that would require states to use it in allocating their electors. The bill failed in the House.

But despite its surface appeal, proportional allocation has its own problems. First, like the district system, it doesn't guarantee that the popular vote winner will become president.

It wouldn't have helped Hillary Clinton in 2016. If all states had used proportional allocation that year, neither candidate would have won a majority of electoral votes, sending the election to the House, where the majority of state delegations were Republican-led, and almost surely would have chosen Trump anyway.

Second, while it is better than winner-take-all, proportional allocation still doesn't accurately reflect the will of the people, because you have to round off electoral votes to the nearest whole number. This becomes an issue especially in states with few electors.

Take Delaware, which has 3 electoral votes. If 67 percent of the vote went for the Democrat and 33 percent for the Republican, the Democrat would get 2 electors and the Republican would get 1. Easy enough. But what if Delawareans split their votes 50–50? A proportional system in which the popular vote is evenly divided but the electoral vote splits 2–1 is not a proportional system.

Another problem with this type of proportional allocation of electors is that any political activity in a state would swing at most one electoral vote, regardless of the state's size. This would put voters in big states at a huge disadvantage. Why would presidential campaigns spend time and money trying to swing that one vote in California or Texas when they could have the same impact in dozens of smaller states, and for a relative bargain?

If whole numbers are the issue, then why not just allocate electoral votes in fractions?

Because presidential electors are human beings, and human beings can't be cut into fractions. To do that you'd need to pass a constitutional amendment eliminating the electors and replacing them with disembodied electoral votes to be carved up and distributed however state lawmakers like.

By the way, the proportional system would also distribute some electors to third-party candidates, who currently struggle to win anything because of the winner-take-all rule. This increases the chance that no candidate wins a majority of electors, thus throwing the election to the House, with each state getting a single vote. That hasn't happened in nearly 200 years, and we can only hope it doesn't happen for 200 more.

Even if you stuck with whole-number proportional allocation, you'd still need all 50 states to adopt it for it to work, which they will never do on their own. States that made the switch would suddenly lose political influence in the presidential election relative to those that kept winner-take-all. The only reason states voluntarily switch how they allocate electors is to gain a partisan advantage, as California Republicans tried to do by pushing for the district system in 2007 and Colorado Democrats tried to do with the proportional system in 2004. Both failed. In other words, the only way to ensure the nationwide implementation of either the district or the proportional system would be by constitutional amendment.

Why is this so hard?

Both the district and proportional systems fail in the end because they are trying to graft some semblance of logic and fairness onto a fundamentally unfair, illogical system. Adopting either one would be like trying to retrofit a horse-drawn buggy with an internal-combustion engine. Sure, you might be able to get the thing moving a little faster, but wouldn't you rather have a car?

Isn't there a simple solution to this mess?

In fact there is. It's called a national popular vote. And we don't even need to amend the Constitution to adopt it.

Wait, so the national popular vote is the buggy, or the car?

Read the next chapter.

7

THE NATIONAL POPULAR VOTE INTERSTATE COMPACT

You Don't Need a Constitutional Amendment

Ray Haynes was stuck in rush-hour traffic outside Los Angeles one morning in the fall of 2010, talk radio droning in the background, when it hit him: we need to elect the president by a national popular vote, and we can do it without laying a finger on the Constitution.

Haynes, a staunch conservative, is not someone you would expect to have this particular revelation at this particular political moment. He had served eight years as a Republican state senator and one term as the national chair of the American Legislative Exchange Council, known as ALEC, a pro-business group that works with state lawmakers to draft and pass conservative policies around the country.

Haynes was also on record as a defender of the Electoral College. In 2006 he'd spoken before the California Assembly as lawmakers were considering whether to join a new agreement among several states that would change the way those states award their presidential electors: instead of giving them to the winner of the statewide vote, as California and 47 other states do, they would give them to the winner of the national popular vote. Once states representing a majority of electoral votes sign on, the agreement kicks in and the president is guaranteed to be the popular vote winner.

Haynes thought this was a terrible idea. The Electoral College was part of the framers' careful design, and junking it would invite disaster.

"What the Electoral College actually does is require presidential candidates, instead of just running around and raising monies and buying commercials in large urban areas, it makes them go to Iowa and shake hands of people in Iowa; makes them go to Ohio and makes them shake hands with people in Ohio. In Tennessee and in Kentucky," Haynes said in the speech, a clip of which was posted to YouTube. "And that is actually a good thing! . . . Having them actually go and touch real people makes them a better president, and the Electoral College makes sure that that's what occurs."[1] Haynes considered these truths to be self-evident.

A couple of years after the speech, he was making the rounds of the booths at ALEC's annual meeting in San Diego when he came across a group promoting the state-level agreement he'd spoken out against. It was called the National Popular Vote Interstate Compact. Around the corner was another booth opposing it.

"I hit the pro booth, and talked to them for a little while. Then I hit the anti booth and talked to them for a bit," Haynes recalled. He bounced back and forth like that all morning, asking questions and listening. To his surprise, he found that the popular vote advocates seemed to have all the right answers. After several hours, he realized that he had been wrong. His support for the Electoral College was based on a misunderstanding of how the system actually worked. It did not ensure, in fact, that candidates visit voters in states all over the country; it encouraged the exact opposite—a narrow, targeted campaign aimed only at voters in a few critical battleground states.

Haynes thought back to his days as a state senator. "I knew from my own experience, if every single vote counts, you pay attention to every single voter." He told the popular vote advocates that they had convinced him. But when they asked him to join their team and help get the compact passed in California, he balked. "I told them I thought they had the better argument. I didn't say I thought it was a good idea."[2]

His main doubt involved the compact's constitutionality. Didn't the Constitution set out clear rules for the presidential election? And didn't any change to those rules require an amendment? He was not interested in amending the Constitution, and he was definitely not going to support a law that he believed would subvert the amendment process itself.

The popular vote advocates had heard these arguments often—so often that they had published a book addressing all of them. They gave Haynes a copy to take home with him that day. The book, called *Every Vote Equal*, explained in 800 pages of excruciating detail the legal and constitutional justifications for the compact.[3] It laid out the history of the Electoral College and of the hundreds of attempts to reform it over the years. And it responded to every counterargument that Haynes could come up with.

Months passed. Each evening, Haynes read a little more of the book, then he went back and reread the *Federalist Papers*, James Madison's notes on the constitutional convention, and Supreme Court opinions involving the Electoral College. The more Haynes read and thought, the harder it became for him to reject the logic of the popular vote compact.

That's where he was on that November morning, trapped in his car on the clogged freeway, when the months of reading and processing came together in a moment. The Interstate Compact wasn't just constitutional; it was the best possible way to get to a popular vote. And Haynes felt sure that the founding fathers themselves would have blessed it.

❙❙❙

Many Americans, perhaps most, assume that the way the Electoral College works today—presidential electors chosen directly by the people of each state and awarded on a statewide winner-take-all basis—is part of the Constitution. It's not. Under Article II, Section 1, each state's electors are appointed "in such manner as the legislature thereof may direct."

In other words, states can award their electors in almost any way they like. We, the people, have no constitutional right to be involved at all in the election of our president. Not only can't we cast a direct vote for any of the candidates, we can't even vote for our state's electors if our lawmakers don't want us to. They can pick the electors themselves, as many did at the nation's founding. They can give the job to the governor. They can draw the winner's name out of a hat.

Not that they would. Imagine a state informing its citizens in 2020 that they might as well stay home on Election Day because they won't be voting for the president. The last time this happened was in 1876, when lawmakers from the brand-new, sparsely populated state of Colorado decided they didn't have time to organize a statewide popular vote and so chose their three electors themselves.

What stops the states from doing this today is not the law; it is our universally held belief about the people's proper role in American democracy. We all expect to be able to vote for our president, and we would never tolerate being told that we can't.

But if the question of *who* votes for electors is long settled, *how* those electors are awarded by each state is much more controversial, and it's at the heart of the Popular Vote Interstate Compact.

The compact asks a simple question: If a state has the constitutional authority to award all of its electors to the candidate who wins the most votes within its own borders, what's to stop it from awarding them to the candidate who wins the most votes in the whole country? The answer is nothing. The power to allocate electors is exclusive to the states, as Supreme Court decisions going back more than a century have reaffirmed. The only limit on the power comes from the other parts of the Constitution. A state, for instance, can't award its electors based only on how its white voters vote because that would violate (among other things) the equal protection clause.

For constitutional conservatives like Ray Haynes, this faithfulness to the nation's charter is the key to the popular vote compact. It relies on the explicit words of the Constitution itself rather than attempting to alter that language by amendment.

"The words are clear," Haynes said. "And if the words are clear, there is no outside evidence that can change the meaning of the words."

After his 2010 freeway conversion, Haynes became part of a group of conservatives who spend their days crisscrossing the country from California to Massachusetts to Missouri to Georgia, pressing the case for the Popular Vote Compact to Republican lawmakers. They're used to encountering a lot of skepticism, if not outright resistance. Some legislators have done their research and respond by throwing the old You-Tube clip of Haynes defending the Electoral College in his face. His rejoinder: "It is still the best speech I've ever heard in opposition to the compact. But I can say today that I had all my facts wrong."[4]

In the 14 years since it was introduced in 2006, the compact has become a national phenomenon. Maryland passed it first, in 2007. California passed it, with Haynes's help, in 2011. Four states signed on in 2019 alone, and two more came very close. It now has a total of 15 member states and the District of Columbia, together representing 196 electoral votes. With 74 more, the compact takes effect.

The problem lies in getting those last 74 votes. To date, all the states that have passed the compact did so under a Democratic-led legislature and, with the exception of Hawaii, a Democratic governor. That's no surprise: Democrats have been burned twice in the past two decades by the Electoral College and are most eager to see it changed, with one interesting exception we'll get to shortly. Even so, the National

Popular Vote Interstate Compact is the closest America has come to changing the way it elects the president since Birch Bayh nearly did it in 1970.

I I I

The man who designed the Popular Vote Interstate Compact is John Koza, a 76-year-old inventor and computer scientist living in northern California. Koza has a polite yet distant manner, an affection for old-fashioned video games, and is no one's image of a democratic revolutionary.

Growing up in suburban Detroit in the 1940s and 1950s, he showed an early knack for understanding the new technology of computers. By 15 he was designing and building his own rudimentary computers out of parts he scrounged at war surplus stores and winning first place in local science fairs. He didn't pay much attention to politics until his twenties, when he first learned of the Electoral College and became fixated on its bizarre and convoluted math. In 1966, as a graduate student in computer science at the University of Michigan, Koza invented a board game, *Consensus*, in which players were presidential candidates strategizing to win as many electoral votes as possible by appealing to various political groups in different states—Catholics, blacks, Bible Belters, and so on. The game enjoyed cult status among a small community of computer geeks and political junkies, but it never found commercial success.

That would come a few years later, when Koza co-designed the scratch-off lottery ticket and sold it to statewide lottery systems, making him wealthy and, in the process, teaching him about the workings of interstate compacts, which states joined as a way to combine their smaller individual jackpots into a larger combined one that would draw more gamblers.

For the last several decades, Koza has lived by himself on a hillside in Silicon Valley, surrounded by thousands of books on genetic programming, artificial intelligence, complex systems analysis—and, filling several whole bookcases, American government and political theory. He taught at Stanford until 2013, when he turned all of his energy to implementing one of the biggest transformations of American politics in history.

Koza came up with the Popular Vote Compact in the summer of 2004 after watching a news report about a citizen-led ballot measure in Colorado that was trying to change the way the state allocated its electoral votes.

Since 1920, Colorado had given its electors to the Republican nominee in all but five elections. But by 2004 its Democratic minority was growing fast, especially in and around Denver. Many of these voters were still angry about Al Gore's loss in 2000, and about the pointlessness of casting their presidential ballot in Colorado, which used the winner-take-all method for its electors.

The initiative, known as Amendment 36, would switch Colorado from winner-take-all to the proportional system. Instead of all nine of the state's electors going to the Republican candidate, they would be divvied up according to each candidate's share of the popular vote—winner-take-some. If, say, two-thirds of voters chose the Republican and one-third chose the Democrat, the Republican would get six electors, and the Democrat would get three—not a huge difference, until you consider that a swing of three electoral votes would have made Al Gore president.

The measure faced fierce pushback. The main opposition group was called Coloradans Against a Really Stupid Idea, and included some Democrats who had lost their appetite for reform when they saw that the state was moving closer to becoming a true battleground. As they saw it, if Colorado switched to the proportional system and then their nominee, John Kerry, won the statewide vote, Democrats would be giving away five or six electoral votes. One volunteer told the *New York Times*, "Originally, I thought, gee, this sounds like it's not a bad idea. But speaking as a Democrat, if Kerry does win in Colorado—or when he wins—he should have all of the electoral votes."[5] Winner-take-some is only appealing when you're not the winner.

In the November election, Amendment 36 went down in flames. Colorado voters chose to keep winner-take-all by a nearly two-to-one margin. They also chose President George W. Bush over John Kerry, 52 percent to 47 percent, giving Bush all nine of the state's electoral votes.

John Koza agreed that Amendment 36 was stupid, but not because of its partisan implications. Rather, he knew that the reason states cling to the winner-take-all rule is that it gives them far more clout in the presidential election than they would otherwise have. Why would any state voluntarily and unilaterally relinquish that clout?

Even if every state were to adopt the proportional method, it wouldn't eliminate the two major flaws of the winner-take-all Electoral College system—the risk of a popular vote loser becoming president and the incentive for candidates to concentrate their campaigns in a small number of battleground states.

Koza understood what Birch Bayh had understood decades earlier: the only true fix was a national popular vote. The problem was that a constitutional amendment was out of the question. Bayh had tried and failed at a time when Republicans and Democrats were far less polarized than they were in 2004. That's when Koza realized: Why not make the Electoral College the vehicle to a popular vote rather than an obstacle to it?

▪▪▪

Koza wasn't the first person to hit on this idea. An early version appeared in a 1976 law review article titled "Direct Election of the President Without a Constitutional Amendment: A Call for State Action."[6] The article's author, a lawyer named Dale Read Jr., called on states to change their laws in order to award their electors to the national popular vote winner. He admitted that his idea "departs radically from current thinking on electoral reform," but said that the hundreds of unsuccessful efforts to reform the Electoral College by constitutional amendment showed that that approach was "misplaced."

Read's article got no public attention at the time. Another quarter century would pass before the idea came up again, this time in the wake of the 2000 election debacle. In a 2001 article in *Green Bag*, an online legal journal, Robert Bennett, a law professor at Northwestern University, proposed his own version of Read's plan.[7] Like Read, he said that the plan would work best if states representing a majority of electors signed on, but he pointed out that if just one or two hotly contested states chose to use this method—at the time that meant places like Wisconsin, Minnesota, and Missouri—they could by themselves force a national popular vote. That's because candidates from both parties would know they needed to win those states to win the Electoral College.

Later in 2001, constitutional law scholar Akhil Reed Amar suggested a similar approach in an article cowritten with his brother, Vikram Amar, also a law professor.[8] They pushed it one step further, by recognizing that states would need to have some assurance that they wouldn't be unilaterally disarming. Imagine if New Jersey decided to give its 15 electoral votes to the national popular vote winner, they wrote, but not enough other states joined in. New Jersey would be hurt in two ways: first, it would be telling both presidential candidates that they should feel free to ignore campaigning in New Jersey; second, it wouldn't be assured that the national popular vote winner would become president.

To solve this problem, the Amars proposed a model law that would give all of a state's electors to the national popular vote winner, if and only if other states representing a majority of electoral votes in the country did the same. In that way, the presidency would be guaranteed to the candidate who won the most votes in the country.

If that failed to work, the Amars had another plan. In an elaborate (and, really, outlandish) scenario worthy of a Tom Clancy novel, the presidential candidates of both major parties would pledge, in advance of the election, to honor the results of the national popular vote. If the winner of that vote—call her Jones—wound up losing in the Electoral College, it would trigger a series of agreed-upon steps. First, on Inauguration Day, immediately after the oaths of office were administered to the Electoral College winner, call him Smith, and his running mate, the running mate would resign; Smith would then replace the running mate with Jones, making Jones vice president; finally, Smith would step down pursuant to the terms of the Twenty-Fifth Amendment, and Jones, the newly minted vice president (who was also the national popular vote winner), would assume the presidency. Voila!

"Some will doubtless dismiss all this as mere academic daydreaming," the Amar brothers wrote. "But the daydreams are useful in illustrating how much constitutional creativity is possible within the existing constitutional framework, short of formal amendment."

They were right: the sheer difficulty of passing a constitutional amendment is the mother of invention. And John Koza is above all an inventor. As Koza saw it, the earlier proposals were moving in the right direction, but the only way for the plan to work in practice was if there was a binding agreement—an interstate compact—among the participating states.

Interstate compacts help two or more states work together to solve problems they couldn't solve alone, such as resolving a boundary dispute or promoting regional economic development. These agreements have been around longer than the Constitution. The Continental Congress approved one, involving fishing and navigation on the Chesapeake Bay and Potomac River, that remained in effect until 1958.[9] Interstate compacts function as contracts, and the states that join them are bound by their terms, just as people who sign a contract are bound to it by law. Once a state joins a compact, it cannot unilaterally withdraw except under the terms of the compact.

For these reasons, Koza saw the interstate compact as the perfect mechanism to achieve a national popular vote for president. Every member state would have to adopt the identical bill agreeing to award its electors to the winner of the popular vote, and all would be bound by its terms, which include a prohibition on dropping out of the compact between July 20 of election year and Inauguration Day. The compact would only go into effect once states containing a majority of electoral votes, 270, joined. That way, no one state would have to risk going it alone, no state could drop out at the last minute for partisan reasons, and the national popular vote winner would be guaranteed the presidency.

With the outlines of the plan in hand, Koza flew to Washington, D.C., with Barry Fadem, a lawyer who specialized in interstate compacts and had worked with him during the state lottery days. The first person Koza and Fadem met with was Birch Bayh, who was working in a D.C. law firm at the time. Bayh expressed immediate enthusiasm and offered to do what he could to help. He wasn't the only one. As Koza and Fadem made the rounds of the capital, they discovered there was enough interest in the project that they hired a team of lawyers to draft model language for a state statute. They founded a nonprofit organization, National Popular Vote, funded almost entirely out of Koza's pocket. On February 23, 2006, they officially introduced the compact at the National Press Club in Washington, D.C. Joining them at the podium were Bayh and a string of Republican former lawmakers, including John Anderson, who represented Illinois in Congress before running for president in 1980 as an independent.

It was, in the words of Hendrik Hertzberg, a correspondent for the *New Yorker* who was one of the few journalists sitting in the National Press Club that day, "an ad-hoc bunch of amateurs, once-weres, might-bes, and goo-goos"—and he loved the idea.[10]

Hertzberg, a longtime advocate of democratic electoral reforms, was only exaggerating a little. And yet over the last dozen years, this band of might-bes and goo-goos has managed to transform the national debate over how America elects its president.

▮▮▮

One of the first things Koza understood was that if he was going to sell an interstate compact, all the support in the world from people like Birch Bayh wouldn't matter. He had to convince the potential buyers—state lawmakers.

So he wrote a book. *Every Vote Equal*, which Koza self-published, was released along with the launch of the compact. Today he still ships it out himself from enormous pallets stored in his garage. The cover includes an illustration of the original Constitution and the framers deliberating at the Philadelphia convention—images intended to soothe conservatives like Ray Haynes, whose first impulse is to see this as another harebrained liberal scheme.

The book is carefully argued, meticulously annotated, and impressively heavy. The writing style is deliberately non-bestseller. "There are no adverbs," Koza said. "Our style is to be very factual and logical. All the people we're talking to, they're the recipients of constant bullshit, every day. So we're trying to be something different. When we present something, you can read and disagree, but you're not going to get the feeling that someone's beating you over the head with a truncheon."[11]

The first edition of *Every Vote Equal* ran to about 500 pages. It's now in its fourth edition, which checks in at 1,117 pages. More than a third of the book is taken up by a single chapter that serves as a methodical dismantling of every imaginable myth and misconception about the College and a popular vote, and then some.

There are basic, first-order myths about presidential elections ("Myth 9.1.1: A federal constitutional amendment is necessary for changing the current method of electing the President"); there are myths about the Constitution ("Myth 9.1.16: The Privileges and Immunities Clause of the Fourteenth Amendment precludes the National Popular Vote compact"); myths about small states and myths about big cities ("Myth 9.4.4: The small states oppose a national popular vote for President"; "Myth 9.5.3: Candidates would only campaign in media markets, while ignoring the rest of the country"); myths about mob rule ("Myth 9.17.2: The Electoral College acts as a buffer against popular passions"); about recounts ("Myth 9.15.4: Conducting a recount would be a logistical impossibility under a national popular vote"); about campaign spending ("Myth 9.12.1: Campaign spending would skyrocket if candidates had to campaign in all 50 states"); and about the weather ("Myth 9.36.1: The state-by-state winner-take-all rule minimizes the effects of hurricanes and bad weather").

Koza's heard them all. The book currently addresses 131 different myths, and the list is only getting longer as the debate goes on, old myths evolve or die off, and new ones pop up. Koza has already compiled a list of several dozen new entries to be included in the next edition, which he hopes to publish in later 2020. For example, there is now a "California Myth," a 2016 relative of the big-cities myth, contending that Hillary Clinton's three-million-vote margin came entirely from California.

Koza had an early list of myths ready to publish in the book's first edition, but he decided against it out of a concern that he would be providing an easy blueprint for his opponents. As the list got longer, it became harder to justify leaving it out. By the third edition, in 2011, it had become obvious that the opponents had all their arguments in hand anyway, so he put the myths chapter in. Koza now considers it to be the most important part of *Every Vote Equal*. "The myths are the way legislators work," he told me. "They're used to being in a battle with arguments thrown at them, and throwing arguments back."[12]

Koza realized that the more time he had to make his case to legislators, the more successful he was at bringing them to his side. He started running two-day seminars for lawmakers around the country, at which he and his colleagues hand out thick blue folders filled with charts, graphs, and shaded maps of the United States, then tag team to deliver what amounts to a five-hour summary of the book.

"We convert people when we can sit down with them and talk about it as a policy issue and not a shouting match about ending civilization," Koza told me. "Usually we convert almost everybody. Because the facts support it. Of all those myths, there isn't one you can say is convincingly true. Most are factually and demonstrably false."

After more than a decade of running these seminars, Koza

said he respects the job the lawmakers have to do. "Most of them are really hard working and genuine. Almost every legislator brings up a certain group of issues, and it's a question of working through them. If they're truly engaged, and not just being courteous, you can sell this. This is not a difficult thing to sell.

"The nice thing for us is that our strongest argument, which is that under the current Electoral College most states are politically irrelevant, is particularly salient to state legislators, who are involved with politics 24 hours a day."

But his audiences aren't always so welcoming.

|||

Early one Saturday morning in March 2019, Koza sat for an interview on a C-SPAN call-in show.[13] At the time, several state legislatures were on the verge of passing the compact, and the topic was in the news every day. As he does before every public appearance, Koza reread the myths chapter, as well as the shorter, targeted handouts that he and his team distribute at seminars.

It was just after 6:30 a.m. in California, but callers on both sides of the issue were wide awake and ready for battle. Reed, from Washington State, started out calmly. The Electoral College was there to protect people like him, he said, and he couldn't tolerate the idea of it being taken away. Then he got heated. "If I'm no longer counted, essentially because I'm trumped by the mob in the cities, I stop paying taxes. The revolution just might begin!"

The producers moved to cut him off, but Koza wanted to respond. Putting aside the threat of violence, it was a familiar charge—essentially a mashup of the big-cities myth (9.18.2) and the mob rule myth (9.17.1).

"First of all," Koza said in his usual measured tone, "the voters in 100 percent of the states vote for presidential electors, so you may want to call the voters a 'mob.' I don't. But if you want to use that term, we already have selection by 'the mob.' The issue presented by the National Popular Vote bill is whether you want the mob in five or six states to determine who is president versus the mob in all 50 states and the District of Columbia."

Koza remains almost inhumanly polite, if not quite warm, through exchanges like these, answering the same tendentious myths again and again. He sounds as though he's explaining a simple logic problem—maybe because in his mind, he is. When I asked him what compelled him to take on his nearly two-decade crusade to change the way Americans choose their leader, he seemed nonplussed. He expressed no deep philosophical commitment to popular sovereignty, as James Wilson did. He did not see his effort as the culmination of two centuries of American democratization, as Birch Bayh did. Rather, I got the sense that he was offended as much as anything by the Electoral College's violation of basic rules of math and logic. That's not surprising coming from a computer scientist, but it's a strikingly dispassionate attitude toward what is for most people an intensely emotional subject.

Scott Drexel, who has been working as a senior advisor to National Popular Vote since 2009, recalled a conversation he and Koza had a few years ago. "I asked him at some point, 'What do you think you'll do when this is all done?' He said, 'I'll probably just go back to inventing things.'"[14]

III

After Koza finished taping the C-SPAN program, he told me that he suspected the anti–popular vote callers had been coached. "Their questions were just too well structured. You can smell these things." It fit with a trend he had been noticing in his travels around the country—the opposition to the national popular vote was becoming more organized, better trained, more on-message. It was evident during floor debates in many state legislatures, where opponents of the compact, who used to be more or less solo fliers, were now racing one another to the podium to unleash suspiciously similar arguments.

Koza has heard most of the arguments countless times and can refute them from memory. But one in particular resists an easy answer.

It's what Koza refers to as the "red-blue" issue. This is the hypothetical scenario in which a state joins the compact and then gives more of its own popular votes to the candidate who loses the national popular vote. Imagine, for example, that Utah had joined the compact, and that the compact was in effect in 2016. Utah voters overwhelmingly chose Donald Trump, but because Hillary Clinton won the popular vote, Utah would have been bound by the compact to award all six of its electoral votes to her, and none to Trump.

Under the compact's logic, this should not matter. People don't care which candidate wins their state; they care who becomes president. And yet the sense of betrayal is real—*we* voted for Candidate X, but we're being forced to give *our* electoral votes to Candidate Y?

When Colorado lawmakers were debating whether to join the compact in 2019, one Republican senator, Bob Gardner, cast it as something close to usurpation. "Let's let other states decide for us," he said. "That's what this entire bill is about!" The compact would take each Coloradan's vote and "essentially surrender the power of that vote, dilute the power of the vote of the citizen of Colorado by mixing it in with the votes of the rest of the country."[15]

Another Republican senator, Rob Woodward, said, "Is it any wonder that Illinois, New York, and California want to do this plan? They want to buy our votes and add them to their own."[16]

Koza is well aware that this feeling isn't limited to Republicans. There are plenty of Democrats in states that have already joined the compact, like Massachusetts and New York, who would be horrified at the prospect that their state would vote strongly in favor of the Democratic candidate but send its electors to a national popular-vote-winning Republican.

Unlike virtually every other myth or misconception dealt with in *Every Vote Equal*, there is no silver-bullet answer to the red-blue issue. "It's absolutely true that there's a mismatch," Koza told me.[17] The solution, he believes, is to change how people think about their vote, to persuade them that when they vote for president, they are voting not as a resident of their state but as a citizen of the United States.

The other argument for which there's no simple rejoinder is a constitutional one. Under Article I, all interstate compacts must get Congress's consent before they can take effect. For more than a century, the Supreme Court has understood that the purpose of this provision is to prevent states from joining together to increase their power at the expense of the federal government. As a result, the Court has required consent only for those compacts that interfere in some way with the federal government's supremacy.

Koza sees this as an open-and-shut case. States have exclusive authority to decide how to appoint their electors, and so there is no encroachment on federal power. No congressional consent is necessary. Still, he knows that if enough states join the compact to make it effective, the issue is certain to be litigated. To be safe, he's working to get support in Congress. "It wouldn't shock me if the Supreme Court did rule against this," Koza said. "It *seems* like a federal matter. It involves the presidency. It seems like something that ought to go to Congress."[18]

∎∎∎

At first, it was far from clear that the National Popular Vote Interstate Compact would get any traction anywhere.

The first effort to pass it came in Maryland in 2007, less than a year after it was announced. The bill was introduced by Jamie Raskin, a first-term state senator who made the compact his first stab at sponsoring legislation. Working closely with FairVote, a nonpartisan electoral reform group that had helped Koza develop and promote the compact, Raskin knew he had the facts on his side. But facts wouldn't be enough.

"When I first decided to do it, everyone told me I was crazy," Raskin recalled. "Many people said, you do not want this to be the first bill you introduce. It's way too complicated, nobody's going to understand it. It's going to be hopeless."[19]

Part of the problem was the arcane subject matter: debating how we elect the president is exciting, but it requires knowledge of American history and a degree of fluency in constitutional law and theory. Many state lawmakers are more comfortable dealing with local issues, like budgets, schools, or transportation. There's also the inherent electoral conservatism of legislators, who tend to prefer the systems that got them elected and are wary of any big changes.

Neither of these were an issue for Raskin. Before entering politics, he had been a professor of constitutional law and a longtime critic of the Electoral College. He also knew that politicians don't like to see their state get the short end of the stick—which is what happens every four years in uncompetitive states like Maryland. So in addition to arguing for the basic principles of political equality and majority rule, Raskin emphasized the distortions caused by the winner-take-all method. It worked.

"What I discovered immediately was everyone on both sides of the aisle understood in a profound way how much Maryland is ignored in presidential elections because we're a safe blue state. They immediately perceived how safe states are overlooked and sidelined," he said.[20]

Raskin's Republican colleagues were particularly sensitive to this issue. There are more than a million registered Republicans in Maryland, but because the national party considers the state a lost cause, it gets pushed to the back of the line when it comes to funding and other resources.

"The more you're ignored, the worse your situation gets," Raskin told me. "That's the situation of political minorities all across the land."[21]

Using these arguments, Raskin was able to win over his fellow legislators. Within three months, the Popular Vote Compact bill passed both houses of the state legislature and was signed by Governor Martin O'Malley. John Koza had his first 10 electoral votes.

Over the next eight years, he'd get about 150 more, from 11 states and the District of Columbia. In less than a decade, the compact had gotten more than halfway to its goal. It was a remarkable accomplishment in a short period of time. There was just one problem: all of the member states were controlled by Democrats.

As a practical matter it is very hard to get to 270 electoral votes by relying on Democratic-led states alone. But more important, the one-sided nature of the early adopters made it difficult for Koza to sell the plan as a bipartisan effort aimed at making all Americans' votes matter. To Republicans, it looked like a Democratic plot to steal the White House.

Koza had been aware of this issue from the beginning, but solving it was another matter. Early on, there were glimmers of Republican interest. In 2008, 19 of 39 Michigan Republicans joined a Democratic majority in the state House of Representatives to pass the bill.

But in most states, the compact ran into a wall of partisan opposition. Several Republican-led legislatures refused to consider it at all. In some places where it passed, as in the North Carolina senate in 2007, it didn't get a single Republican vote.

Koza, a lifelong Democrat, realized that he needed to find a better way to communicate the compact's benefits to conservative lawmakers. And that meant speaking their language.

III

He found three translators: Ray Haynes, the former California legislator; Saul Anuzis, a former chair of the Michigan

Republican Party; and Pat Rosenstiel, a Republican consultant who had worked on George W. Bush's first presidential campaign. Together, the men developed their sales pitch for the compact—that it is a fundamentally conservative way to reform how we elect our president, a process the founders left to the states in the first place, and which currently benefits almost no one. They took it on the road in the hopes of engaging Republican lawmakers, just as Koza and the other Democrats on the team were meeting with their Democratic counterparts.

But unlike Koza's group, the conservatives faced unique hurdles, starting with the political temperament of their audience.

"Our biggest challenge is we're asking for a really big change, and we're trying to persuade people who, by definition, don't like change," Haynes told me. "We hold the burden of proof. So we have to meet that burden in a way that persuades this very large jury that this is a good idea. And the jury in many ways is prejudiced against us to start."[22]

Another hurdle was the amount of time it took to explain the compact and prove that it was constitutional. Ray Haynes spent months reaching that conclusion for himself; now he and his colleagues were trying to push people to the same revelation in a few hours. As Anuzis said, "It's not an elevator pitch. It's a deep dive."[23]

They were confident that they could succeed if they had enough time and were able to steer the conversation away from strictly partisan concerns. "We don't have a hard time winning them over on philosophical grounds," Anuzis told me. "The underlying reason people support this is that it's good public policy. If you did this purely on partisan standpoint, you never win. There has to be a higher purpose. If we make it quintessentially fair, if every voter has an equal voice, then I'm okay winning or losing."[24]

Pat Rosenstiel said, "We've never viewed this as anything other than a bipartisan coalition to address a nonpartisan problem to find a better way to elect the president."[25]

For those who believe, as Ray Haynes once did, that a constitutional amendment is the only appropriate way to make changes to how we elect the president, there is a straightforward response: virtually every other electoral reform—from the popular election of electors to enfranchising blacks and women to the popular election of senators to letting 18-year-olds vote—has originated at the state level. Most of these reforms have ultimately led to formal constitutional amendments, but they don't have to.

The one area the national popular vote team stays away from is the role of slavery in the Electoral College's adoption. "You're arguing about what the founders intended," Koza said. "It's a rabbit hole. You start talking, 30 minutes later you're exhausted, and so what? You haven't moved anybody any closer to favoring the national popular vote, even when you win all the arguments."[26]

Slowly, all the work began to pay off. Throughout the Obama presidency, and particularly after his 2012 reelection in which he again carried the Electoral College with ease, Republican lawmakers grew more open to the idea of a national popular vote.

Perhaps the most unexpected push came in New York, that modern-day bastion of liberalism, where five Republicans in the state assembly introduced a bill to join the compact within three months of its announcement. It passed the

Republican-led state senate twice, in 2010 and 2011, but the Democratic-led state assembly refused to bring it to a vote until 2013. What happened?

Remember from Chapter 5 that Birch Bayh's constitutional amendment abolishing the Electoral College was thwarted with the help of African Americans living in big cities such as New York, where they and other minority groups wielded extra electoral leverage under the existing system.

By the 2000s, of course, New York had not been a swing state for decades. It was a Democratic stronghold, and Republicans knew that under the winner-take-all rule, they would remain electorally invisible. But several older black Democrats had entered politics at a time when black voters in the city held the electoral fate of New York State, and sometimes the presidency, in their hands. Current reality aside, the memory was powerful, and they were not prepared to let it go.

Jeff Dinowitz, the Democrat who sponsored the bill in the assembly, said, "There were some African American legislators whose opinion was, 'We finally got this system working for us. Why do we want to change that?' I can understand that." But, he added, "those just weren't the facts anymore. New York is so overwhelmingly Democratic, the real issue is no one is paying attention to us. I don't like to be ignored."[27]

It took several years, but the popular-vote compact finally passed both houses of the New York legislature, and was signed into law by Governor Andrew Cuomo in April 2014.

In 2015 the Republican-dominated Oklahoma senate passed the bill. In 2016 it passed Arizona's Republican-led House, with support from two-thirds of Republicans. In Georgia and Missouri it passed Republican-led committees unanimously. By later 2016 the compact had 315 sponsors in state legislatures around the country: 162 Democrats and 153 Republicans.

Then came the 2016 election. In an instant, conservative support for the compact vanished, as Republicans rallied for the second time in two decades to defend the legitimacy of the system that had awarded the White House to their candidate. Lawmakers who had come out strongly in favor of the principle of political equality ran for the hills, at least in public. It was a devastating blow.

"If Trump had won popular vote and lost the Electoral College, this would've passed," Saul Anuzis told me. "We had seven Republican states on the verge of passing it."[28]

Instead, many Republicans quickly came to see the compact as nothing more than Democratic sour grapes, an effort to undermine President Trump. This infuriates Koza. "It makes no sense. The people who are actually being helped by this bill are the ones who are opposing it. It's that simple: Republicans in blue states. Theirs is the vote that's being canceled out."[29]

■■■

Meanwhile, Trump's victory was having the opposite effect on Democratic-led states. In May 2018, Connecticut passed the compact, becoming the twelfth state to join. In a matter of months in 2019, the compact was adopted in Delaware, Colorado, New Mexico, and Oregon, and it passed one legislative chamber in Maine and Minnesota.

In Nevada, the bill passed both houses of the legislature and seemed on track to be signed until the state's governor, Steve Sisolak, vetoed it. Sisolak explained that he did so because Nevada is a small state, and a popular vote would decrease its influence in presidential campaigns. He might have discovered his error if he'd read Myth 9.4.1 ("The small states would be disadvantaged by a national popular vote"). But it didn't matter; Sisolak became the first Democratic governor to reject the compact.

Meanwhile in Colorado, opponents mounted a campaign to put the question of whether to join the compact directly to the voters. "People feel that giving away your electoral votes without a vote of the people is overstepping," one of the campaign's organizers told the *Denver Post*.[30]

The bill's opponents got far more than the required number of signatures, which means that in November 2020 Colorado's voters are going to have a popular vote in the state on whether they want to help elect the president by a popular vote of the country.[31] It will be the first test of the compact's appeal to regular voters, and because Colorado is the closest to a purple state to have signed on so far, it may provide a sign of the compact's odds of success in other more conservative states over the coming years.

The compact's conservative team is continuing to reach out to lawmakers in those states, regaining their trust and rebuilding support day by day. It's been slow, but Pat Rosenstiel is convinced that he has a winning argument in the end, because he sees the United States as a fundamentally center-right country. "As a conservative American, I'm not afraid of my ideas," he told me as we sat in the lobby of a hotel in midtown Manhattan. "I absolutely, fundamentally believe there are more of us than there are of them."

Then there's the problem of popular vote losers winning

the White House, which Rosenstiel said "calls into question the legitimacy of American presidents—including my president, Donald Trump, who I supported, who's got to wake up every morning trying to defend himself to the *New York Times* and other people about whether he's the legitimately elected president of the United States, even though he won under the system as it was defined. That's a big deal."

Most people who hear about the National Popular Vote Compact assume that it's something only a liberal could love, but people like Ray Haynes, Saul Anuzis, and Pat Rosenstiel are fighting against that impression.

"Our opponents start from a very dishonest proposition, which is that the current system has worked well for over 200 years," Rosenstiel said. "Four out of five American voters feel as if they do not matter when electing the president of the United States. That's not a system working well. There is not a single redeeming quality to the current system."

He paused, then looked at a stack of Popular Vote Compact materials in front of him. "This genie's never going back in the bottle," he said.

8

SETTING THE RECORD STRAIGHT, PART TWO: COMMON POPULAR VOTE MYTHS

Big Cities, Two Parties, and a Democratic Plot

Now that we've learned about the National Popular Vote Interstate Compact, let's return to the Thanksgiving conversation with our skeptical Electoral College supporter, and debunk the most common myths and misconceptions surrounding the popular vote.

Myth #1: Big cities will dominate a national popular vote.

Seriously, they will, right? Without the Electoral College, everyone in the flyover states might as well stay home on Election Day, because New York City, Los Angeles, San Francisco, and a few other metropolises will be the only ones whose voices matter.

Let's get something out of the way: In an election where every vote counts the same—that is, in every election in the country except the one for president—it does not matter where you live. City, suburb, small town, countryside . . . we are all Americans, and we are all equal. If cities gain power relative to other parts of the country as a result of a national popular vote, it is only because more people live in cities. This shouldn't be so controversial.

But it is! The whole point of the Constitution was to design a republic in which bigger states can't just wipe the smaller states off the map.

You hear this a lot these days. In 2019, after some Democratic lawmakers called for abolishing the Electoral College, Iowa senator Chuck Grassley said the following:

> The U.S. system of government is based on the idea of creating checks and balances so that no one person, branch of government, political party or geographic region of the country gets too powerful, infringing upon the rights of others. America's Founding Fathers established the Electoral College to make sure smaller, more rural states like Iowa get as much attention from the federal government as bigger, more urban states like New York. Abolishing the Electoral College would be bad news for Iowa and for the Midwest generally. It would mean vital sectors of the economy, regional cultures and entire ways of life wouldn't have as much of a say in Washington. The voices of farmers, factory workers and so many others

in rural America would be drowned out by city dwellers on the coasts.[1]

With the exception of the first sentence, every word of this statement is either misleading or flat-out wrong.

First, there were no "urban states" or big cities in 1787 when the Constitution was drafted. There weren't even medium-sized cities. Ninety-five percent of Americans lived in towns of 2,500 people or fewer. The biggest city, New York, had about 33,000 residents—a little more than half the capacity of Yankee Stadium.

In other words, the framers weren't imagining big cities at all, let alone worrying about their influence on a presidential vote.

It's true that delegates from smaller states expressed the fear that larger states would dominate a popular vote election. But their problem wasn't with a popular vote itself; after all, the same delegates approved direct election for members of the House of Representatives, which they expected to be the most powerful branch of the federal government. The main issue was that most Americans had little knowledge of politics and even less of national candidates. With no mass communication or developed transportation network, voters would be left to choose the candidate they knew best—the one from their own state or region—and the state with the biggest voting population would prevail every time.

The framers couldn't possibly have anticipated our world today, in which, for a few hundred dollars, a person can go from one end of the continent to the other in six hours and every American with a television or internet connection knows as much as (and sometimes far more than) he or she could ever want to know about every major presidential candidate.

Local favoritism still gives candidates a little boost— Bill Clinton won Arkansas twice—but in the end a state is much more likely to be won by the candidate of its dominant party than by a native son or daughter. Hillary Clinton won New York not because it was her home state (it was Donald Trump's, too) but because more New Yorkers vote for Democrats than for Republicans. Barack Obama won Illinois, but Mitt Romney didn't win Massachusetts. George W. Bush won Texas, but Al Gore didn't win Tennessee. And so on.

Then there's Grassley's claim that without the Electoral College, "vital sectors of the economy, regional cultures and entire ways of life wouldn't have as much of a say in Washington," and "the voices of farmers, factory workers and so many others in rural America would be drowned out by city dwellers on the coasts."

This is a curious complaint coming from an Iowa senator. Like senators from other smaller states, Chuck Grassley wields his disproportionate power to the benefit of the very "regional cultures" and "sectors of the economy" that he claims are drowned out by "city dwellers." The Senate has always skewed in favor of rural America, and it always will.

Fine, so the framers didn't anticipate big cities, Chuck Grassley is inconsistent, and the Senate isn't going anywhere. Still, America's biggest cities are very big, and they would still dominate a popular vote election, right?

This is a very old argument. In 1961 former president Herbert Hoover provided testimony to the Senate warning that any change to the Electoral College "confronts the same difficulties as were met by the Founding Fathers—that is, to prevent domination by a few large states." That argument was echoed by former president Harry Truman, who feared "the emergence of the big cities into political overbalance, with the threat of imposing their choices on the rest of the country."[2]

Today, the big-cities argument may be the most common one offered against a national popular vote. You see it repeated across social media, usually accompanied by a cartoon map portraying California, New York, Texas, and Florida as making up about 80 percent of the country, or more than 260 million people. In reality, those four states together held about 109 million people in 2018—or one-third of the total United States population.[3]

Cartoons like these reflect a tendency among Americans to vastly overestimate just how big our cities are. The five most populous American cities—New York, Los Angeles, Chicago, Houston, and Phoenix—together hold a little more than 19 million people, or just under 6 percent of the country. In other words, 94 percent of the American people do not live in the cities that would supposedly dominate a popular vote election.

Expand the circle to include the 50 biggest cities—those with populations larger than 350,000—and you get to about 50 million people, or 15 percent of the United States. And remember that all those city voters are not voting for the same person. On average, big cities give about 60 percent of their votes to Democrats and 40 percent to Republicans.

John Koza often asks audiences how Democratic they

believe California is, then what proportion of the country's population the state represents. "The consensus is that California is about a third of the country's population and that it's 90 percent Democratic," he said.[4]

In reality, California holds about 12 percent of the country's population, and about 62 percent of its voters chose the Democrat in 2016. Put another way, about 1 in 10 American voters are from California, and a third of those voters are Republican. So it's not clear how California would be the deciding factor in favor of either party.

And yet this belief only became more widespread after the 2016 election. Donald Trump, the argument went, actually won the popular vote . . . if you took away Hillary Clinton's four-million-plus-vote advantage in California. Putting aside the notion that we can simply lop off entire states to suit our political preferences, this is a meaningless statistic.

As *New York Times* correspondent Nate Cohn pointed out shortly after the election, it's true that Clinton won California, a state with nearly 40 million people, with about 61 percent of the vote—or about 4.3 million more votes than Trump.[5] It's also true that Trump won about 61 percent of the vote in a cluster of states from West Virginia to Wyoming—a swath that covers about 38 million people, and that Cohn dubbed "Appalachafornia." In other words, Democrats win more support in some parts of the country, and Republicans win an almost equal amount of support in other parts. Right now, millions of votes for both candidates in these regions are effectively wasted.

We don't just overestimate the size of big cities, we underestimate the size of rural areas, which can be defined as places with a population under 50,000—the ones that would supposedly be overwhelmed in a national popular vote. In fact, the same percentage of Americans, roughly 15 percent, live in rural areas as live in the nation's 50 largest cities. And just as big-city dwellers vote Democratic by a margin of about 60 to 40 percent, rural Americans vote Republican by the same margin.

> *Granted, cartoon maps are imprecise. Still, you're defining "cities" awfully narrowly, aren't you? Wouldn't it be more accurate to say, as the United States census does, that America is roughly 80 percent urban—and that the sprawling metropolitan areas surrounding big cities often share the cities' politics?*

There are all kinds of ways to draw the lines. That 80 percent statistic counts towns with as few as 2,500 residents as "urban." If you reclassified all places with 20,000 people or fewer as small towns, which most people probably would, then 80 percent of that 80 percent of "urban America" consists of small towns.[6] But define the categories however you wish; the bottom line is that America's 50 biggest cities and its rural countryside almost exactly mirror each other in both population and voting margin. The remainder of the country, the 70 percent of Americans who live in suburbs, exurbs, and small towns, are much more narrowly divided politically, and for this reason they tend to be the people who decide who becomes president.

Here's another way to think about it: If the desires of big-city voters would inevitably dominate presidential elections, how did George W. Bush win the national popular vote in 2004 by three million votes—and without winning California, New York, Illinois, Massachusetts, New Jersey, or any other heavily Democratic states with big cities?

That's a tough one.

It's generally not expressed in public these days, although our friend Paul LePage, the former Maine governor, was more than happy to oblige. "If they do what they say they're gonna do," he said of the movement for a national popular vote, "white people will not have anything to say. It's only going to be the minorities who would elect. It would be California, Texas, Florida."[7]

LePage does the popular vote debate a service here, by explicitly tying the common miscalculation of the size of big cities and states to an underlying racism.

You heard versions of it during the 1960s debates over the Supreme Court's one person, one vote rulings, which had an explicit racial component—the growing cities that were seeking fairer representation were racially diverse, while the shrinking countryside was overwhelmingly white. When an Alabama newspaper columnist wrote that the one person, one vote rule would "make the urban parts and interests of this nation the unchallenged and total masters of our affairs," everyone knew what he was really saying.[8]

Thankfully, the Supreme Court rejected this reasoning. And though the rule still only applies to legislative elections, it's hard to see how it shouldn't also apply to the election of the one official who represents all Americans equally.

It sure sounds like you're saying that everyone's vote for president should count the same, no matter where they live.

That's about the size of it.

Myth #2: A national popular vote would mean the end of our two-party system.

I believe in majority rule, and I'm on board with trying to guarantee that the candidate who wins the most votes becomes president. But if we switched to a popular vote election, wouldn't there be so many candidates splitting the electorate that the "winner" would end up with say, 30 percent of the vote? We'd become Denmark.

What's wrong with Denmark? But seriously, the specter of a presidential free-for-all has been invoked as a warning against a popular vote for decades. Whatever the Electoral College's shortcomings, the argument goes, it protects America's two-party system by discouraging minor-party candidates from jumping into the race and producing a winner with a clear national mandate. This creates political stability and makes it easier for the president to govern.

In particular, the state winner-take-all rule discourages participation by candidates who don't have a good shot at winning a state's popular vote. Even those with the nerve (or the money) to dive in often come up empty.

Take Ross Perot, the self-assured Texas businessman who ran as an independent in 1992 and won 19 percent of the popular vote. That's a lot of votes, the best third-party showing in decades. But in the end Perot didn't have a single elector to show for it. That's because his support was wide but not deep, so even though he won nearly 20 million votes, they were spread too thin to add up to a victory in any one state.

In fact, no third-party candidate has won even one electoral vote since George Wallace in 1968. He won 46, but that was only because the Democratic Party was in the process of fracturing over the issue of segregation and civil rights, and five southern states were in revolt.

The lesson from Wallace's success and Perot's failure is that third-party candidates can make a dent in the current system if their support is regional, but not if it's dispersed across the country.

Under a popular vote, on the other hand, third-party candidates would have every incentive to run and try to draw support away from the major-party candidates—after all, every vote counts. If that were to happen, the person with the most votes nationwide could end up with 35 percent, or 30, or possibly even less.

Do you really think Americans would be willing to accept a president who doesn't win a majority?

I don't think; I know. As of 2020, fully one-third of our chief executives, 15 out of 45, have become president not by winning a majority of the popular vote (that is, with more than 50 percent of the votes cast), but simply by winning more votes than any other candidate—also known as a plurality. They include, among others, Donald Trump, George W. Bush (in 2000), Bill Clinton, Richard Nixon, John F. Kennedy,

Harry Truman, Woodrow Wilson, and Abraham Lincoln. (Lincoln won just under 40 percent of the vote in 1860, the lowest popular vote percentage in history—although he was kept off the ballot entirely in the southern states, which were on the verge of seceding from the union.)

When you consider that the American electorate today usually consists of roughly half of all eligible voters, no president ever wins the support of a popular majority.

Even more to the point, five of our presidents, including the current one, didn't just get less than a majority; they got less than their main opponent. If we are willing to live with a system that lets a popular vote loser sit in the White House, we can live with a popular vote winner who gets less than a majority.

Americans seem to be fine with non-majority-winners at the state level too. No state requires a presidential candidate to win a majority of the statewide popular vote in order to get all of its electors. Nor does any state require its candidates for governor to win a majority.

Speaking of governors, they provide a useful point of comparison. Governors are elected by a statewide vote in which all votes count the same—that is, the state equivalent of a national popular vote. So if the critics are right, we should expect to see this free-for-all effect playing out in state gubernatorial elections.

But we don't. Of the nearly 1,000 governor's races held around the country between 1948 and 2011, not a single winning candidate won less than 35 percent of the vote. Ninety-eight percent of the winning candidates won 45 percent of the vote or more, and 90 percent won a straight-up majority.[9]

These results can be explained by Duverger's law, an electoral phenomenon named after Maurice Duverger, a mid-twentieth-century French sociologist who observed a clear pattern repeating itself in elections around the world. Two-party systems are supported, not undermined, by plurality elections. This happens for two reasons: first, parties with similar interests tend to form alliances to improve their chances of winning; and second, voters ultimately realize that they are harming their own interests by "wasting" their vote on their preferred minor-party candidate—or worse, helping the majority-party candidate whom they most oppose. Think of Ralph Nader voters in 2000, who may have been instrumental in handing the White House to George W. Bush.

In short, America's two-party system is protected and preserved not by the Electoral College but by the type of plurality elections we hold in all 50 states today.[10]

Now I'm confused. Haven't we been talking about majority rule this whole time? Aren't you concerned that a candidate could win with few enough votes that his or her administration is politically hamstrung?

It's a fair point. The risk of a low-percentage winner is small, but it's there. One solution is to hold a runoff—a second election between the top two finishers from the first election. The details of a runoff—whether to have one at all, and at what percentage it would kick in—were debated intensely during the late-1960s push for a national popular vote.

The upside of a runoff would be that it would give us a majority (or near-majority) winner. The downside would be everything else: the cost and time of running another national election, the drop-off in turnout as voters grow exhausted, and a repeat of all the other risks that go along with any major electoral process.

Either way, there's no public clamor for runoff elections today, even though presidential candidates regularly win less than a majority of the statewide popular vote. In 1992, only one state gave a candidate a popular vote majority (Arkansas, to its hometown boy, Bill Clinton)—and yet, as John Koza points out, no one argued that any of the other 49 states should hold a runoff.[11]

There is a variation on runoffs, however, that would lead to a broadly acceptable winner without having to go through the time, expense, and uncertainty of a second election. It's known as ranked-choice voting, also called instant-runoff voting.

Here's how it works: In elections featuring multiple candidates, voters rank their candidates by preference. So, in 2000, a Ralph Nader fan might have picked Nader first, Gore second, and Bush third. Once the ballots are in, all first-place votes are tallied; if any candidate has a majority of first-place votes, he or she wins. If not, the candidate with the fewest first-place votes is eliminated. Then all the ballots listing that candidate first get a second life. They are recounted, this time for the candidate they listed second. Assuming Nader is eliminated after the first round of counting, all ballots that listed Nader first are then redistributed. Those listing Al Gore second would be transferred to Gore's vote total, and those that listed Bush second would go to Bush's vote total. The process keeps repeating itself until one candidate winds up with a majority of votes.

It's an elegant solution to a vexing electoral problem: the binary nature of our single-vote, first-past-the-post system often fails to reflect the scope of voters' political preferences. Under ranked-choice voting, voters can better express those preferences—by, say, listing a favorite minor-party candidate first without worrying about "wasting" that vote or helping elect someone they really dislike.

This sounds complicated. I don't like it.

It's not so hard in practice! As the law professor Vikram Amar wrote, "When Americans go to the grocery store, they understand the second-choice concept: Get Ruffles, but if they are sold out, get Pringles. If Americans can handle this level of complexity as shoppers, why not as voters?"[12]

Dozens of cities and towns around the country are already using ranked-choice voting to decide their local elections— including for the city council in Cambridge, Massachusetts; for the mayor in San Francisco; and for races in states from Colorado to New Mexico to Minnesota to Maine, which has become a national leader on ranked-choice voting. In 2018, Maine was the first state to use the system statewide, for its primaries, and it went well enough that the state decided to adopt it for the 2020 presidential election.[13]

Nearly everywhere, voters report being happy with the system and no more confused than they are by standard single-vote elections. Studies of ranked-choice voting have found that it increases voter participation, reduces polarization, and elects leaders who better reflect what a majority of voters want. It also leads to campaigns that are more civil and less negative, because candidates realize that it's not a zero-sum game anymore. They can do better by appealing to voters beyond their base, and possibly getting listed higher on those voters' ballots.

States can pass their own ranked-choice voting law to use in presidential elections, as Maine did in 2018 for its state-wide primary elections. If used in conjunction with a national popular vote, ranked-choice voting would effectively elimi-nate the risk of the 30-percent winner and thus preserve our two-party system.

Interesting! Now remind me again why we care so much about preserving the two-party system?

Well, since you asked, and since we're already on the topic of major electoral reforms, it's worth questioning the value of our traditional two-party, winner-take-all system.

Yes, it has provided clarity and stability to our politics. It helps resolve intraparty debates, it presents voters with a choice of clear policy alternatives, and—in theory at least—it promotes the ascendance of moderate leaders with broad na-tional appeal. But in the twenty-first century, the shortcom-ings of this system are obvious.

For one thing, the dominance of the two major parties has suffocated the development of alternative parties that might rise up and appeal to more people. As a result, voters are stuck choosing between what they see as the lesser of two evils—and that can drive down voter participation, because people feel they aren't well represented by any of the available options. It's not hard to imagine those alternative parties.

In 2019, Damon Linker, a political columnist, identified six proto-parties lurking behind the two major parties. On the right is the populist-nationalist party, which is anti-immigrant and skeptical of free trade; the internationalist conservative party, which likes immigration and free trade but not taxes; and the religious right party, which cares mostly about abortion and other hot-button cultural issues. On the left is the social democratic party, with politicians like Bernie Sanders and Alexandria Ocasio-Cortez, who favor a strong safety net and higher taxes on the rich; the internationalist progressive party, represented by liberal technocrats in the mold of Barack Obama; and the centrist working-class party, based in the post-industrial Midwest—older, whiter, and more conservative than the other parties on the left, but still supportive of Social Security and Medicare.[14] Whether or not you agree with Linker's list, it's an interesting thought experiment. More parties equal more opportunities for voters to find a political home and feel heard, which can in turn increase participation and lead the way toward a more genuinely representative democracy.

One 2017 study found more consensus and less divisiveness among citizens of parliamentary democracies with multiparty coalition governments, like those in Scandinavian countries, than in winner-take-all, majoritarian democracies like ours.[15]

The most immediate problem, of course, is that our electoral system isn't built to accommodate more than two parties. We don't have proportional representation like, say, Israel or Denmark, where multiple parties, some with support in the single digits, jostle for power, build temporary coalitions, and struggle to get things done.

In short, there are plenty of problems with multiparty

systems too, but are they really worse than what we're living with right now?

Myth #3: A national popular vote would benefit Democrats.

Admit it, you just want a national popular vote because you know the Democrats will always win.

Before I respond to this, let's return to a story I started to tell in the introduction.

In the weeks leading up to the 2000 presidential election, several polls suggested that America might be on the verge of electing its first popular-vote-losing president in more than a century—Vice President Al Gore. According to multiple news reports, there were discussions inside the Bush campaign about a public-relations push to persuade Democratic electors to vote for the national popular vote winner. There would be ads on TV and in the newspapers. There would be appeals to business leaders and clergy members, interviews with conservative talk-radio hosts and the mainstream press.

The plan, according to a story in the New York *Daily News*, was to take advantage of the expected "popular uprising" against the "Electoral College's essential unfairness." "I think you can count on the media to fuel the thing big-time," an unnamed Bush aide was quoted as saying. "Even papers that supported Gore might turn against him because the will of the people will have been thwarted."

The Gore campaign's response was, essentially, good luck with that. If the vice president were to get fewer popular votes than Bush but still win the Electoral College, Gore's team said, "then we win." As one staffer told the *Daily News*, "You play by the rules in force at the time. If the nation were really outraged by the possibility, then the system would have been changed long ago."[16]

Jeff Greenfield, a CNN correspondent at the time, reported that he had heard of the Bush team's plans from "at least two conservative commentators" who were briefed by the campaign on what to say publicly. Kenneth Duberstein, President Ronald Reagan's former chief of staff, told Greenfield that "it was part of the talking points."[17]

Karl Rove, George W. Bush's chief campaign strategist in 2000, strongly denied that there were ever any official plans to appeal to electors in the case of an Electoral College loss. "There was no discussion that I was aware of, and I would've been aware of it," he told me. If it ever came up, he said, it might have been over drinks among lawyers, but not as a serious campaign strategy. "Bush would never have stood for that," he said, adding that Kenneth Duberstein had no role in the campaign.[18]

Either way, the popular vote loser in 2000 did end up becoming president. Of course, it wasn't Al Gore. As a result, Americans never got to see Republicans coming out en masse to fight for the popular vote winner.

That's a shame, because it would have illustrated a couple of things that seem hard to imagine in 2020. First, the moment people on the right realize how the Electoral College could hurt their side, they feel just as strongly about its "essential unfairness" as those on the left. Second, Republicans recently believed it was possible, even likely, that their candidate would win the popular vote.

In fact, through much of the twentieth century and into the twenty-first, self-identified Republicans supported a popular vote for president at only slightly lower rates than Democrats. That support took a hit after the 2000 election, when many conservatives felt that attacks on the Electoral College were attacks on the legitimacy of President Bush. Still, as recently as 2011, polls showed that a majority of Republicans favored a national popular vote.

By contrast, today's debate over the popular vote is always and immediately politicized, most often as a plot hatched by Democrats who think it will help them waltz to electoral victory every time. Many Democrats and Republicans buy into this idea, as well as its corollary: that the Electoral College is systematically biased in favor of Republicans.

Both are wrong. Start with the College: throughout the 1970s and 1980s, it was widely accepted that Republicans had an Electoral College "lock" that made it all but impossible for them to lose the White House. The facts seemed to bear this out: between 1968 and 1988, Republicans won every election but one, in 1976, and even that was a squeaker. Then Bill Clinton won easily in 1992 and 1996, and Barack Obama did the same in 2008 and 2012. Suddenly it was the Democrats who had the built-in advantage: the so-called "blue wall" that couldn't be breached—until, in 2016, it was.

"Almost the whole Democratic hierarchy was convinced that the system was rigged for the Democrats," John Koza told me, speaking of the resistance he faced when trying to sell his popular vote compact to blue states during the Obama years. "This bill didn't move in Connecticut and Minnesota and Oregon and a couple of other Democratic places, like

Delaware, because of this mindset that was floating around. It's the same mindset that defeated Clinton."

At the same time, and despite what happened in 2000 and 2016, there is no good evidence that Republicans have any systematic advantage in the Electoral College.[19] And don't forget that in 2004, George W. Bush won the popular vote by more than three million votes.

There is one caveat to this general observation: a working paper released in 2019 by researchers at the University of Texas at Austin found not only that the chance of the popular-vote loser winning the Electoral College has always been higher than most people think—at least one-in-three when the popular-vote margin is less than 2 percent—but that for the past several decades, the Republican candidate has been at least twice as likely as the Democratic candidate to win under those circumstances.[20] The researchers found that Democrats had a similar advantage in the late nineteenth century, but that their current tendency to win high-population states by big margins and lose them by small ones makes it more likely that they will wind up on the short end of a split between the Electoral College and the popular vote.

Of course, it's always possible to determine *after* an election whether the College gave Democrats or Republicans a slight edge, but that's only retrospective—and, as the statistician Nate Silver has shown, there is no correlation between which party has an edge in one election and which party has an edge in the next.[21]

Zoom out and the picture becomes even clearer. In the 20 presidential elections between 1932 and 2008, Americans cast 1.5 billion votes for president. Democrats won 700,000 more of those votes than Republicans—an amount roughly equal to the current population of Alaska. In other words, over the long term popular vote, the parties are essentially tied.[22]

But you're ignoring the demographic direction of the country. As it becomes more diverse, doesn't that spell electoral doom for Republicans?

It's true that America's white population is aging and its nonwhite population is getting younger. Since younger people and minorities both lean left, the logic goes, a popular vote is likely to help Democrats.[23]

But demography doesn't necessarily equal destiny, as a 2013 Republican task force asserted when it warned that the party was "marginalizing itself," appearing to voters as "a party of 'stuffy old men.'"[24] The solution, according to the report, could be found in embracing immigration reform and increasing outreach to natural minority constituencies, like socially conservative black voters, Catholic Latinos, and business-friendly Indians and Asians.

Republicans have so far rejected that approach, but they can't reject it forever. If they continue to pursue a Trumpian agenda, stoking racial divisions and encouraging white resentment, then they are not going to expand their electorate any time soon. Eventually, they will hit a breaking point.

"Parties do what it takes to win," one political scientist told the *New York Times* in 2018, shortly before the midterm elections. "If Latino turnout in Texas was as high as white turnout in Texas, I think the campaign strategies of both Ted Cruz and Beto O'Rourke would be quite different."[25]

On the state level, there are plenty of examples of Republicans doing well in the popular vote. Since 2002, 47 states, including California, New York, Massachusetts, Illinois, and New Jersey, have elected a Republican governor.

And in 2016, Donald Trump won the popular vote by about 800,000 votes in the states where he actually campaigned.[26]

In short, the GOP has plenty of things to worry about, but winning a popular vote isn't one of them.

So why do they seem to have such a hard time doing it?

There are a few answers to that. First, the recency bias: our tendency to give extra weight to what has happened recently as opposed to that in the more distant past. People like to point out that Democrats have won the popular vote in six of the last seven presidential elections. But they never seem to remember that Republicans won it in five of the six before that. No matter the facts, it's hard to get people—and politicians—to think beyond what they've just experienced.

Second, it's a natural follow-on to the big-cities myth. If you believe cities would dominate a popular vote election, it makes sense to assume that such elections would be won by Democrats, who are favored by about 60–40 in cities. As we just saw, however, the biggest cities don't dominate; not even close. And remember that millions of Republicans live and vote in places like New York City, Boston, Chicago, Los Angeles, and San Francisco. Right now, they might as well not exist. Under a popular vote, their votes would count just as much as their Democratic neighbors' votes.

In fact, there's only one group of people who would lose representation in a national popular vote: noncitizens. There are nearly 23 million of them in the United States, most either legal residents or undocumented immigrants.[27] But they can't vote, so how are they represented in the first place? Because the census, which is the basis of apportioning congressional districts, is required by the Constitution to count all "persons," no matter their citizenship status. Remember that states get as many presidential electors as they have senators and members of Congress. So if a state has more people in it, citizens or not, it gets more seats, and thus more electors. By the same measure, if noncitizens move out of state, they can reduce its congressional representation.

After the 2010 census, five states gained between one and five electoral votes because of their noncitizen populations. Ten states lost a vote because noncitizens moved away. According to one calculation, Democrats currently enjoy a net gain of 10 electoral votes thanks to the presence (or absence) of noncitizens, a number that is expected to increase to between 12 and 18 after the 2020 census.[28] In a popular vote election, these noncitizens would not count at all.

Won't they just vote illegally?

Sigh. This has been a frustratingly familiar claim in right-wing conspiracy circles for a long time, but it was turbocharged when it got picked up by Donald Trump.[29] A few weeks after the 2016 election, as the magnitude of his popular vote loss became clear, Trump tweeted, "In addition to winning the Electoral College in a landslide, I won the popular vote if you deduct the millions of people who voted illegally."[30]

There is simply no evidence that noncitizens voted illegally on even a small scale, let alone at a rate that would have given Clinton a multimillion-vote margin.[31] Anyway, to the extent that voter fraud of any kind is a concern, it's more likely to affect the outcome under the Electoral College than it would in a popular vote election. That's because of the winner-take-all method, which makes it possible to swing all of a state's electors by changing a small handful of votes—say, 537 in Florida in 2000. In that election, one of the closest in decades, the national margin was more than 500,000. If you wanted to illegally influence the outcome of an election, would you rather target 537 votes in one state or half a million nationwide?

If either side can truly win a popular vote, then why are only Democrats pushing for it?

First, let's be clear about who's pushing for what. Almost as long as the issue of the Electoral College has been polled, which is nearly 80 years, a majority of both Democrats and Republicans have said they favor replacing it with the popular vote. Those numbers shifted dramatically after Trump's election, as Republicans grew defensive of the College and their president's legitimacy. In late 2016, Republican support for the popular vote had dropped to 19 percent.[32] Still, if the past is any guide, expect that support to rise again— especially if a traditionally Republican-dominated state like Texas or Georgia turns blue.

It's understandable that people struggle to think of this

issue in nonpartisan terms. More than any professed principle, the desire for partisan advantage has always been at the core of the defense of the Electoral College. Partisanship is not going away, but there is no reason it can't coexist with support for the fundamental democratic principles of political equality and majority rule. Most people, whatever their politics, instinctively believe in these principles.

Jamie Raskin, the Maryland congressman, recalled the reaction he got in 2007 when, as a state senator, he introduced the National Popular Vote Interstate Compact bill in the Maryland legislature.

"Inevitably people would approach me and ask, is this going to help Democrats or Republicans? And I said, think about it: it helps whoever gets the most votes! If you get the most votes, you win. If you don't get the most votes, you lose."[33]

Raskin, a former professor of constitutional law, has been pushing for electoral reform and voting rights throughout his political career, and he's familiar with the course of these debates. "In every one of these tussles to expand the franchise, you get a clash between the high-minded principle of universal voting rights and people fighting beneath that about what the partisan implications will be," he said. "And then, there's a surrender: let's just do it and see how it goes."[34]

Of course Jamie Raskin would say that. He's probably a socialist.

And Donald Trump called the Electoral College a disaster for democracy. Remember, we're all in this together.

9

IMAGINING A NATIONAL POPULAR VOTE

The Campaign Experts Speak

"Let's just do it and see how it goes."

Okay, so how *would* it go? It's easy to argue about the Electoral College in the abstract, but what would a presidential election actually look like if we changed the rules and let the people pick the president? Would the candidates alter their campaign strategies? Would more Americans register to vote and show up at the polls? Would our laws and policies be different? Would our political parties be remade, or even destroyed?

These are the questions that everyone asks and no one can answer—not with anything approaching certainty.

For many people, this uncertainty is enough to stick with the Electoral College. It may be a devil, but at least it's the devil we know. That's not a crazy instinct. It's human nature to be wary of big, untested changes. "The" greatest myth in

American politics is that people want change," Jennifer Palmieri, who served as the communications director for Hillary Clinton's 2016 campaign, told me. "They are much more likely to believe they're going to lose something than gain something under a change."[1]

Of course, the same thing could be said about the reaction to every major democratic advance in American history. And yet over the past two centuries, our political system has evolved again and again to be more expansive, inclusive, and egalitarian than any of the framers, save perhaps James Wilson, could have imagined. From the removal of property qualifications, to the enfranchisement of black people, women, and younger Americans, to the switch to popular election of electors and senators, we have inched closer to our founding creed.

Each time, skeptics and detractors pushed back, issuing dire warnings, invoking everyone from the founding fathers to God and defending the status quo with the pen and the sword, all in an attempt to preserve their own power and prevent others from having an equal share.

Each time, democracy has won—except when it comes to the Electoral College.

❙❙❙

In the course of writing this book I reached out to dozens of campaign managers, field directors, ground-game coordinators, and other top officials from Republican and Democratic presidential campaigns of the last few decades. If anyone could give me a good perspective on what a national popular vote might look like, it would be the people who have devoted their professional lives to winning national elections.

I asked them, first, how the Electoral College had defined their approach to campaigning and, second, what they would have done differently if the goal were to win the most popular votes in the whole country.

Answering Question One was easy.

"The first thing you do is eliminate states completely," said Jeremy Bird, the deputy national field director for Barack Obama's 2008 campaign and the national field director in 2012. "Which states are so blue, which are so red—they're not going to be an impact. You do that, and automatically, 100 million Americans are out of the conversation."

That point was echoed by Matthew Dowd, who served as chief strategist for George W. Bush's 2004 reelection bid. "I was running all the polling, and I said to myself, Why are we doing all these national polls? Why are we talking to voters in 40 states that we're not even competing in? We didn't run a single national poll in the year of the reelection campaign. What difference does it make?" he said. "Practically, what that does is, whatever the national dialogue is doesn't matter. And that one thing—basically saying no more national polls, and only polls in five or six or seven states—is really detrimental to democracy."

The process plays out in a straightforward way. In the year or two before an election, long before most Americans have started thinking about it, campaigns are watching the polls and identifying the states they expect will be battlegrounds. These days it's a dozen, give or take. In each of these states, the campaigns determine which precincts present the biggest opportunities for increased registration and turnout. They set up field offices in those precincts, hire staff, build a party organization, and identify what policies will sell best in that region.

They start buying ad time on local television and radio. They begin social media pushes aimed at the voters in those states. They visit the major media markets in order to establish a presence on local news.

By around Labor Day of election year, the campaigns reassess their positions and cut the number of battleground states roughly in half. They direct all their time and money to those states, and limit their social media advertising to very narrowly targeted demographics of likely voters.

Once October rolls around—a time when Americans are most engaged in the political process—the presidential campaigns and their candidates are spending all of their time and money in just three or four states, and even there, it's all about getting out the vote in a small number of pivotal precincts.

"This is how the game is played," Reed Hundt, the former chairman of the Federal Communications Commission in the Clinton administration, told me. "The people who control the outcome of the current process are a tiny fraction of citizens—at most a few hundred thousand in a handful of states—who are fairly uninterested and uninformed about the candidates, and are in no way representative of the interests or demographics of the rest of the country."

Today Hundt runs Making Every Vote Count, a nonprofit dedicated to electing the president by a popular vote. He was driven to the cause by his realization, developed over a lifetime in electoral politics, that because of the Electoral College, 100 million American voters—all those who don't live in one of the battleground states—might as well be invisible when it comes to choosing their leader. Forget fly-over country; these voters live in what Hundt calls "the land of the ignored."

"This is as far from what Madison and the framers thought was the right idea as you could possibly imagine," Hundt said. "It's not that people have lost their minds or are overwhelmingly selfish or shortsighted. The way you can get elected in the U.S. is what shapes the campaigns. The campaigns are what shape the candidates. And the candidates are what shape the presidency."

And that has profound effects on how the president governs. As Stuart Stevens, the senior strategist for Mitt Romney's 2012 presidential run, put it, "It is absurd that you have someone who is elected by not campaigning in all the country who then has to govern the entire country."

Question Two—how would you run a national popular vote campaign?—generated a range of opinions.

For starters, "it would expand the map dramatically," Matthew Dowd said. "Instead of having five, six, or seven key states in 2020, you'd have a concerted campaign in at least 40. You'd still campaign in Ohio, and in Michigan, and in Wisconsin, but also in Texas, California, New York, New Jersey, and Louisiana. You'd add red states and blue states to the mix that both candidates would have to campaign in."

Campaigning isn't just about where candidates show up to eat corn dogs and kiss babies. When campaigns have to put their resources toward winning a state, they draw attention to the needs of that state, which can have concrete benefits. Right now, a disproportionate amount of those benefits go to the swing states.

That discrepancy gets compounded by presidents themselves, whether they are running for reelection or trying to help their party hold power after they depart. John Hudak, a senior fellow at the Brookings Institution, has found that presidents consistently direct more federal grants and dollars to battleground states than to safe states.[2]

While Congress controls the bulk of federal spending, presidents have far more power to direct the flow of money than most people realize, through discretionary grants and other tools. These grants are "an ideal electoral tool," Hudak writes, because they allow presidents to engage directly in their version of pork barrel politics, providing money to key electoral states and localities and generating free publicity for the White House. Thanks to the Electoral College, a president can target his or her spending in a way that has a big impact. Specifically, "presidents will direct the most funds to swing states, where the ultimate electoral payoff will be at its highest."[3]

Hudak examined nearly $1 trillion in presidentially controlled federal grants between 1996 and 2008 and found that swing states received 7.6 percent more grants than other states and about 5.7 percent more grant money. Both of these numbers go up when a presidential election is approaching.

It's not just the federal funding, but the broader impact on presidential policy-making, which is distorted by the need to win over voters in key battleground states. Federal policies are influenced by multiple factors, of course, and it's not always possible to determine exact causation, but it's hard not to notice patterns. John Koza sees the Electoral College effect playing out now, for example, in Donald Trump's steel tariffs. Protectionism isn't popular among free-trade Republicans, but it is in the

Midwest industrial states that pushed Trump over the top in 2016 and hold the key to his 2020 victory. Similarly, George W. Bush passed the Medicare prescription drug benefit, originally a Democratic proposal and a massive government entitlement program—which would normally be opposed by Republican politicians, but was a key issue for one voting bloc: elderly voters, of whom there are a disproportionate number in Florida.

A recent example on the Democratic side is President Obama's 2009 automaker bailout, which was unpopular in most of the country, but not in the upper Midwest—and especially in states like Ohio and Michigan—where many of the more than one million jobs the bailout saved were based. During his 2012 reelection bid, Obama also made sure to remind Ohioans that he had steered more than $125 million in alternative-energy grants to companies in the state, almost four times the national average per state.[4]

A national popular vote would begin to unwarp these incentives. Presidents could use discretionary grants and funds to address the needs of people and states everywhere, including those that currently get ignored. In effect, dozens of states would be turned into battleground states, and money would flow in greater proportion to where it is needed. And policies would begin to reflect the interests and demands of people across the country.

Of course, both parties would work to rack up votes in places where they know they will do well—cities and inner-ring suburbs for Democrats; outer-ring suburbs, exurbs, and rural areas for Republicans—but both would work to get out the vote everywhere, if not to win outright, at least to lose by less.

When this plays out at a national level, it would mean

more national advertising and national branding of candidates. Right now, the overwhelming majority of campaign ads on TV run locally. "Why?" asks Reed Hundt. "Because you're wasting your money on national ads, and 85 percent of your audience is irrelevant." In a national popular vote election, he said, candidates would advertise on the Olympics broadcast, the World Series, the Super Bowl—"whatever gets a huge audience. . . . And if you have to nationally brand, your candidate can't be the same as one who'd be locally branded."

A popular vote election could influence the types of candidates who emerge in other ways too. "If you don't have a swing state strategy, you don't put the guy from Virginia on your ticket to lock up that region," Hundt said, referring to Hillary Clinton's choice of Tim Kaine as her running mate in 2016. "The political mistake of Al Gore in 2000 that mattered most was not putting Bob Graham on the ticket. They thought that what they wanted as a complement was someone who'd stood up and criticized Clinton. What they needed was the guy who would carry Florida."

Campaign managers and other staffers point to at least three major benefits that would flow from a national popular vote: more public participation, more political moderation, and more presidential legitimacy.

Voter Participation

When every vote counts the same and every vote matters, more people vote. This isn't a theory; it happens in every presidential election. In 2016, 10 of the 14 highest-turnout states were battleground states.[5]

According to FairVote, an electoral reform group, battle-ground state turnout averaged 66 percent in 2012, nine points higher than in safe states.[6] If candidates treated most or all states as battlegrounds, and if the national turnout average rose to match that of the current battleground states, as many as 17 million more Americans would go to the polls on Election Day.

Adding that many people to the electorate across the country would also drive the buildup of state-level party organizations. As Matthew Dowd explained, "If one vote in Mississippi matters as much as a vote in Oregon, or one in Iowa as much as one in Kentucky, Democrats would have to have a campaign organization in Texas and Republicans would have to have a campaign organization in California. You're basically thinking, if this thing's going to be won by ten or fifteen thousand votes, you're not going to want to leave any place unorganized."

This extra attention can have downstream effects beyond presidential elections. "If we're running campaigns like this every four years, then we should be competing in these states every two years," Dowd said. "I better start doing these statewide offices, even if I'm only doing it to prepare for the presidential. And that would cause states that are more red or more blue to begin to become more competitive in off-year elections."

David Plouffe, who ran Barack Obama's 2008 campaign, estimated that about one million swing state voters are persuadable by either party in 2020. "But if you open it up to the whole country, then you're probably talking about five to seven million" voters.

Plouffe had a warning, though. "A progressive should be careful to think that this is some panacea." His point was that once both parties start appealing to voters everywhere, it scrambles the standard political calculus in ways that are hard to predict.

One other potential benefit of an increase in public participation is a decrease in the impact of outside spending on elections. "Big money, able to spend at will thanks to Citizens United, loves the current system," Reed Hundt argues. "It gets to pay the smallest amount of money for the biggest impact, because so few people tilt the election." But if it's harder to figure out where the money would make the most difference, the overall impact of that money could be reduced.

Political Moderation

Under the winner-take-all Electoral College, candidates have little incentive to appeal to a broad cross-section of Americans, because the path to victory runs through a few key regions in a few battleground states. This undermines the framers' ideas of how republican government would work.

"The Constitution fundamentally was designed so that multiple factions would actually have to come together and compromise to pass legislation," said Chris Lehane, the political director for Bill Clinton's 1992 campaign. "The idea was to seek a genuine balance out there. The current electoral system—between money, redistricting, the Electoral College—is really creating a political dynamic where it's in your electoral interest to go to the extremes. In fact, you get punished if you go to the middle."

On the other hand, when candidates know they need the most votes to win, they will be more responsive to the needs of a majority of voters everywhere, rather than playing to a small base of voters in key battleground states. And that could create more space for policies that better address the most difficult and divisive issues facing the nation, like immigration reform, health care, the economy, the environment, and more.

"If every vote counted equally at the end of the day, you'd have candidates who couldn't write off any group of states or group of people completely," said Joel Benenson, a Democratic consultant who worked on both Obama campaigns and Hillary Clinton's 2016 run. "Think about what it would really mean to have a Republican party that suddenly had to compete for votes of Latinos and African Americans and LGBTQ voters and suburban women. How about Democratic candidates having an economic revival plan for rural America? People in coal country know coal isn't coming back, so how about a real economic plan for those communities so they can raise their kids there?

"If you have to communicate with a broader swath of Americans, how could that possibly be bad for the country?" Benenson asked. "You know what voters really hate? This is the lesson of the last election: they hate being ignored."

Jeremy Bird, the Obama staffer, pointed out how many constituencies are out there waiting to be tapped. "There are a lot of Democrats, or persuadable voters, in Salt Lake City. You don't talk to them at all. There are a lot of Republicans in New York City. Even though they're a small percentage of the population, there's still a large number of them."

Reed Hundt added to the list. "You'd find Democrats campaigning for African American votes in the old Confederacy. That hasn't happened in generations. By the same token, Republicans would go to the Central Valley of California and Buffalo, New York."

Stuart Stevens, the Romney strategist, believes that this process could be salutary for Republicans, in particular, who have grown increasingly reliant on older, whiter voters at the expense of a big-tent coalition. "I think it would help Republicans if they knew they had to campaign all over the country," he said. Right now, the Republican Party "can exist and flourish as basically a whites-only party. And I think that's incredibly corrosive. Once you're elected president, you're not just president of the Electoral College states; you're president of the whole country.

"Would it be painful? Sure. I can't tell you it'd be good for the Republican Party in the next election. But if it's going to be a national party in 10 years, it'll be good. If you really like cheeseburgers and you only eat cheeseburgers, and someone says you're gonna die if you eat more cheeseburgers, is it hard to quit? Yes. Will it mean you live longer? Yes."

More moderation by the major parties could lead to less polarization among the electorate, as candidates would aim for every possible voter, appealing to them based on what they want rather than on where they live. This could reduce the influence of the extremes on both the left and the right, and also encourage third-party candidates who appeal to voters who currently feel unrepresented by the major parties.

Right now, Matthew Dowd says, "One party has a demographic advantage, the other party has a geographic advantage, and both need to figure out how to come together. The best forcing mechanism would be a national popular vote. It forces Democrats to have to compete for rural voters in the South and for other places which have been reliably red. It forces Republicans to have to compete for Latino voters, so they figure out how to talk to them to cut the margin."

Reed Hundt is even more optimistic about the moderating influence of a popular vote. "It is inconceivable that the winner could be anything other than a moderate on most issues, someone who is responsive to the wishes of most people on most topics," he said. "The law of large numbers gives us cheeseburgers everywhere, gas stations at intersections, and moderate presidential campaigns. If you want radicals and radicalized partisan politics, then you like the presidential selection system we have."

Presidential Legitimacy

Finally, a national popular vote provides legitimacy to the winner, which is critical to the long-term health of any democracy. Democrats may be the ones talking about legitimacy now, but Republicans will be just as upset, and rightfully so, if their candidate wins the popular vote and loses the White House.

Mitch Stewart, a state-based field director in the 2008 Obama campaign and President Obama's battleground states director in 2012, acknowledged this. "As a Democrat, you always look to 2000. The Democrats don't point to 2004, and they should. We were 60,000 votes away from John Kerry winning the Electoral College but losing the popular vote by three million votes. That's inherently unfair."

"It's much more destructive than people realize," Stuart Stevens said of the most common campaign strategies used under the existing Electoral College. "I've sat in these rooms. It is really antithetical to the notion of getting elected president of the United States when you're a Republican and you automatically write off one out of every nine voters. You don't even think about them except using them as an ATM in California. Think about that! That's a really bad concept. The two great wealth engines of America, California and New York, you're just going to write off? What does that do to your public policy? What does that do to how you see yourself?"

Stevens recalled the days after the 2000 election, when George W. Bush was clinging to a four-vote Electoral College lead even as he trailed in the national popular vote by more than 500,000 votes. "We used to joke, and it seemed sort of funny at the time, anybody can win an election when you get more votes. It takes professionals to win when you lose by half a million."

For that reason, Matthew Dowd told me, Bush's 2004 re-election team did something unusual, if not unprecedented: it aimed to win the popular vote as well as the Electoral College. In the American system, that could qualify as political malpractice. For the Bush team, it was essential. "Some of us were exceedingly sensitive to it because of questions of legitimacy in the aftermath of 2000," Dowd said. "President Bush was sensitive to it as well. Many of us thought, we had to win both [the Electoral College and the popular vote] to preserve our legitimacy as national leader."

❚❚❚

Not all campaign managers I spoke to were fans of the popular vote.

Take Karl Rove, chief strategist for George W. Bush's 2000 campaign and a longtime GOP consultant. Rove dismissed the idea that political minorities in states feel disenfranchised by the Electoral College. And he argued that getting rid of the College would "blow up the two-party system and give us the same problems that are affecting western European democracies, where trust and confidence in the government declines dramatically because nobody can be held responsible. You want to be Italy? Everybody feels good because everybody can organize their own party and run their own candidates for leader, and there's no institutional framework that points things toward a two-party system and points people toward something that confirms the democratic choice of the people."

Rove disagreed that the Electoral College was a driver of extremism in American politics. On the contrary, the two-party framework protected by the College is what "causes the political parties to hew generally to the center. Where parties have most suffered defeat is when they have gotten out of the great American center and, for good or for ill, been out there on the flanks of their respective parties."

I was more surprised by the other campaign staffer who stood up for the Electoral College—Jennifer Palmieri, from Hillary Clinton's campaign. If anyone had reason to abhor the College, I thought, it would be the members of the Clinton team. But Palmieri took the long view.

"American democracy is very frustrating and moves at a slow pace," she said. "There's a reason why we have survived as long as we have. America's staying power is related to having to work out agreements with a really large number of people who have different views. I happen to think, even though it can be frustrating, that's preferable to some of the less stable democracies."

Palmieri told me she values the Electoral College not only because of how it affects campaigning but because of how it affects voters' perceptions of their place in the larger citizenry. In that light, campaign strategy is only one part of the equation. "The other is, How do people feel? Do they feel like they matter? Do they feel like they don't have a stake in the democracy? That's why I'm not like, like a lot of Democrats, hell yeah, get rid of the Electoral College!"

I I I

Over the past decade, and especially since 2016, there has been a stream of books, articles, and academic papers arguing, more or less, that democracy is doomed. Throughout the twentieth century, democratic governments spread across the world, a seemingly unstoppable force for freedom and equality. And yet today, from Europe to Central and South America to Asia to the United States, democratic governments are under attack, as real or would-be autocrats come into power, stripping away basic democratic rights and structures and replacing them with an illusory populism.

The challenges facing democracy in the twenty-first century are very real, which is why it is all the more urgent that we do everything we can to strengthen the oldest continuously functioning one in the world. A presidential election system that ignores 100 million voters and lets the loser win is not the way to do that. A democracy that doesn't simply tolerate minority rule but encourages it is not a true democracy, and it cannot survive for long.

That was the overriding message I got from my interviews with campaign managers and other staffers. "It's so fundamentally basic that you're running to govern the country and you don't have to campaign in the whole country," Stuart Stevens said. "It just seems so antithetical to one person, one vote. Why should my vote in Indiana, which went for Obama and then Romney, mean more than my vote in Mississippi? It shouldn't! I mean, I could move to Indiana and vote there. I'm the same person."

As long as our system for choosing the president remains unchanged, it distorts our nation's politics and culture. It deforms our relationship to one another, creating a false picture of a country divided into bright red and blue blocks when in fact we are purple from coast to coast.

It warps how presidential candidates campaign, focusing virtually all their efforts on battleground states and ignoring the rest of the country. It undercuts policies with broad public support.

It increases mistrust of government and decreases voter turnout.

It ignores tens of millions of Americans, whose votes are effectively erased because they happen to live in a state where the majority-party candidate they preferred came in second. In 2016, this was the fate of 55 million people, or 42 percent of the electorate—and that's not counting the seven million plus who voted for third-party candidates or wrote in their own choice.[7]

In short, the winner-take-all Electoral College is a key driver of the dysfunction in the American political system. The fix is, and always has been, staring us in the face.

"It's not complicated," Mitch Stewart said. "As soon as we did a national popular vote, people would be saying, Why haven't we done this for the last 100 years?"

ACKNOWLEDGMENTS

One of the best things about writing a book on the Electoral College is that everyone—and I mean everyone—has an opinion about it. For the past couple of years, I have been listening to those opinions daily, whether I was interviewing a constitutional scholar, sitting in a bar with friends, checking in to a hotel, or standing in line to pick up the drycleaning. More than once, someone came at me with the very misconception about the Electoral College or popular vote that I was writing about that day, which gave me the opportunity to work out the best response in real time.

The tone of these conversations ranged from passionate to perplexed, but through them all ran one constant: people care deeply about the way we elect our president. I knew that before I wrote the book, of course, but I had never experienced it so directly. It has been a gift to talk with fellow Americans about something so fundamental to our sense of who and what we are as a nation.

Another gift was the generosity of so many incisive, thoughtful scholars of American politics, political science, democracy, law, statistics, and history. In sharing their time and wisdom, they gave me an education as good as any I could have paid for. Without them this book would be a shadow of itself.

These include: John Banzhaf, Mary Sarah Bilder, Walter Dellinger, Garrett Epps, Noah Feldman, Paul Finkelman, Woody Holton, Sam Isaacharoff, Michael Klarman, Sandy Levinson, Rob Mickey, Trevor Morrison, Rick Pildes, Andy Pincus, Richard Primus, Jed Purdy, Jack Rakove, Leonard Richards, Jeffrey Rosen, Shlomo Slonim, Larry Tribe, Sam Wang, and Adam Winkler.

Special thanks are due to Akhil Amar, Barry Friedman, and Michael Waldman, each of whom spent hours talking to me, reading early chapter drafts, and edifying me. Bill Ewald, the nation's foremost scholar on James Wilson, was endlessly responsive and helpful in walking me through the complexities of one of America's least-known but most important founders.

I am grateful to the electoral reformers and democratic visionaries of past and present who have worked so tirelessly and so long on behalf of fairness and equality in voting, and who gave me so much of their time and attention: the late Senator Birch Bayh, who sat with me for an afternoon during what turned out to be the final stages of his life; his wife, Kitty, who welcomed me so kindly into their home; his former staff members Jay Berman and Kevin Faley; John Koza and the rest of the team at National Popular Vote, including Saul Anuzis, Scott Drexel, Ray Haynes, Chris Pearson, Pat Rosenstiel, Craig Barratt, Ari Savitsky, and Drew Wilson.

I relied heavily on the wisdom and assistance of Rob Richie and the remarkable staff at FairVote; Dean John Feerick and John Rogan at Fordham University School of Law; and Kathleen Cruikshank at Indiana University.

For the inside story of the aftermath of the 2016 election, I thank Micheal Baca, Bret Chiafalo, Larry Lessig, and Michael Signer. For the insights into modern campaign strategy that make up most of Chapter 9, I am grateful to the campaign managers, field directors, and other staff members named in that chapter. I also learned a great deal about how modern politics work from federal and state politicians on the left and right, including Rep. Jamie Raskin, of Maryland; New York Assemblyman Jeff Dinowitz; Delaware state senator Anthony Delcollo; and Delaware state representative Jeff Spiegelman.

At the *New York Times*, I am surrounded by colleagues who make me a better thinker and writer every day. First, I have to thank Arthur G. Sulzberger and Arthur Sulzberger Jr., whose multigenerational stewardship allows the paper to remain the greatest news organization in the world. Andy Rosenthal and Terry Tang took a chance on me when they didn't have to. Bob Semple, Frank Clines, Brent Staples, Carol Giacomo, Dorothy Samuels, Phil Boffey, Teresa Tritch, Eleanor Randolph, Vikas Bajaj, Linda Cohn, Snigdha Koirala, Eileen Lepping, Maureen Muenster, Juliet Lapidos—and especially David Firestone and Lawrence Downes—welcomed me into the fold. A lot has changed in the last seven years, but I am still surrounded by the best colleagues I could ask for in Binyamin Applebaum, Michelle Cottle, Mara Gay, Jeneen Interlandi, Serge Schmemann, Emma Goldberg, Phoebe Lett, John Broder, Nick Fox, Lauren Kelley, Alex Kingsbury, Katie Kingsbury—and James Bennet, the best news editor I have ever worked for.

A profound thanks to others at the *Times*, including Linda Greenhouse, Adam Liptak, Nick Kristof, Michelle Goldberg, Clyde Haberman, Clay Risen, Jen Senior, Bari Weiss, Elfie Engl, David McCraw, Alain Delaqueriere, and Cristian Farias.

Outside of the *Times*, I have been grateful for the insights of some of the best journalists and writers I know, including John Avlon, Joan Biskupic, Jess Bravin, Alexis Coe, Hendrik Hertzberg, Dahlia Lithwick, Jay Michaelson, Ian Millhiser, Mike Sacks, J. Douglas Smith, and Jeff Toobin.

A very precise thank-you to my indefatigable fact checkers, who saved me from myself so many times I cannot count—although I am sure they can, and most likely have: Adam Rubenstein, Andrea

Katz, and Priscilla Jensen. Thanks also to Elijah Fox, who took on all manner of bizarre archival research tasks with gusto.

I am grateful to the dear friends who provided support, encouragement and insight along the way: Mehrsa Baradaran, Ian Bassin, Adam Frankel, Jesse Green, Matt Hand, Dave Isay and Jen Gonnerman, Micah Kelber and Tracy Perrizo, Terra Lawson-Remer, Anya McMurray, Alex Podulke and Jei Olson, Margaret Quinn and David Kriebel, Evan Ratliff, Fred Sperounis and Jane Leavy, Reuben Teague, Zachary Thacher, Kate Wenner, and Katherine Zoepf.

Finally, I want to thank those without whom this book literally would not have happened:

Reed Hundt, who walked in to the *Times* a few years ago, sat down, and proceeded to argue with me for several hours about the critical importance of a national popular vote. I started out a skeptic and ended a convert. After reading our editorial calling for the end of the Electoral College, Reed called and said, "You should write a book about this!"

I took that idea to my agent, David Kuhn at Aevitas Creative Management, who had for four years showed endless patience as I sent him one half-baked book idea after the next. David was right to hold out. Nate Muscato at Aevitas was also an enormous help throughout the proposal process.

I can't imagine a better first-book experience than the one I got from the dogged, devoted team at St. Martin's Press, including George Witte, Alan Bradshaw, Martin Quinn, Gabrielle Gantz, Kevin Reilly, and, most of all, Adam Bellow, who seized on the promise of this idea, encouraged and challenged me at every step, gently educated me in American politics and intellectual history, and reminded me, through the profound care he takes in speaking, of the importance of finding exactly the right word.

Medical emergencies don't often find their way into book acknowledgments, but I will be forever indebted to the amazing doctors and surgeons at New York Eye and Ear Infirmary, who literally saved my vision in the middle of the night, and several times after. They are directly responsible for my ability to see the screen on which I'm writing these words: Gennady Landa, Richard Rosen, and Brittany Powell. James Fowler, my physical therapist, works modern-day miracles. If you don't know him, you should.

I have been buoyed by the support of my family all over the world. I particularly thank those who were instrumental in helping get this project finished, whether through childcare or draft comments or both: David and Carolyn, Marya, Ruth and Lynda, Steve, Diane and Frank, and Sheryl.

I am grateful to my beautiful girls, Sami and Natalya, whose patience I tested far too often, and who filled my mornings and evenings with a pure and simple beauty that is easy to lose sight of during the day; and above all, to Kyra—her undying enthusiasm boosted my spirits and her moral clarity lighted my way. Her presence echoes on every page of this book, and in every moment of my life.

NOTES

Introduction: A More Perfect Union

1. Alexander Hamilton, *Federalist* No. 68, in *The Federalist*, ed. Robert Scigliano (New York: Random House, 2000), p. 437.
2. "Electoral College: Make Hillary Clinton President," Change.org petition. https://www.change.org/p/electoral-college-make-hillary-clinton -president-on-december-19-2017. Accessed September 21, 2019.
3. Michael Signer, "The Electoral College Was Created to Stop Demagogues Like Trump," *Time Magazine*, November 17, 2016. https://time.com /4575119/electoral-college-demagogues/. Accessed September 21, 2019.
4. Kyle Cheney, "Lessig: 20 Trump Electors Could Flip," *Politico*, December 13, 2016. https://www.politico.com/story/2016/12/donald-trump -electors-lessig-232598. Accessed September 21, 2019.
5. "A Message for Electors to Unite for America," YouTube video, December 14, 2016. https://www.youtube.com/watch?v=0z0iuWh3sek. Accessed September 21, 2019.
6. Kyle Cheney, "The People Who Pick the President," *Politico*, 2016. https://www.politico.com/magazine/thepeoplewhopickthepresident /2016. Accessed September 21, 2019.
7. Lisa Hagen, "Kasich to Electors: Don't Vote for Me," *The Hill*, December 6, 2016. https://thehill.com/homenews/campaign/309042-kasich-to -electors-dont-vote-for-me. Accessed September 21, 2019.
8. Interview with author, July 25, 2019.

9. Ed Kilgore, "Trying to Deny Trump the Presidency in the Electoral College Is a Really Bad Idea," *New York Magazine*, November 30, 2016. http://nymag.com/intelligencer/2016/11/electoral-college-plot-against -trump-will-fail-and-backfire.html. Accessed September 21, 2019.

10. Megan McArdle, "Let Trump's Election Stand," Bloomberg Opinion, December 13, 2016. https://www.bloomberg.com/opinion/articles/2016 -12-13/let-trump-s-election-stand. Accessed September 21, 2019.

11. Jonathan Bernstein, "Mischief by Democratic Electors Needs to Stop," Bloomberg Opinion, December 6, 2016. https://www.bloomberg.com /opinion/articles/2016-12-06/mischief-by-democratic-electors-needs -to-stop. Accessed September 21, 2019.

12. Kyle Cheney and Gabriel Debenedetti, "Electors Demand Intelligence Briefing Before Electoral College Vote," *Politico*, December 12, 2016. https://www.politico.com/story/2016/12/electors-intelligence-briefing -trump-russia-232498. Accessed September 21, 2019.

13. Kyle Cheney, "California elector files suit, joins anti-Trump Electoral College push," *Politico*, December 10, 2016. https://www.politico.com/story /2016/12/california-elector-files-suit-joins-anti-trump-electoral-college -push-232472. Accessed November 2, 2019.

14. Interview with author, July 25, 2019.

15. Reena Flores, "Obama Press Conference: The President Calls Electoral College a 'Vestige,'" CBS News, December 16, 2016. https://www .cbsnews.com/news/obama-press-conference-the-president-electoral -college-debate/. Accessed September 21, 2019.

16. YouTube. https://www.youtube.com/watch?v=SkOLtBWfz1g&feature =youtu.be. Accessed September 30, 2019.

17. Michael Kramer, "Bush Set to Fight an Electoral College Loss," New York *Daily News*, November 1, 2000. https://www.nydailynews.com/archives /news/bush-set-fight-electoral-college-loss-article-1.881690. Accessed September 21, 2019.

18. Arthur Schlesinger Jr., "Fixing the Electoral College," *Washington Post*, December 19, 2000. https://www.washingtonpost.com/archive/opinions /2000/12/19/fixing-the-electoral-college/1326d431-966a-4d7d-af37 -6b77e742162e/. Accessed September 25, 2019.

19. Staff, "Sunshine, Sand and Stony Partisan Silences. Painful Splits in Florida Likely to Last Long After Election Is Finally Settled," *The Baltimore Sun*, December 7, 2000, p. 19A.

20. Kevin Merida, "So Close, So Far: A Texas Democrat's Day Without Sunshine," *Washington Post*, January 21, 2001. http://www.washingtonpost .com/wp-dyn/articles/A24413-2001Jan20.html. Accessed September 21, 2019.

21. Robert C. Turner, "The Contemporary Presidency: Do Nebraska and Maine Have the Right Idea? The Political and Partisan Implications of the District System," *Presidential Studies Quarterly*, Vol. 35, No. 1 (February 8, 2005), p. 117. https://doi.org/10.1111/j.1741-5705.2004.00238.x.

22. Erica Chenoweth and Jeremy Pressman, "This Is What We Learned by Counting the Women's Marches," *Washington Post*, February 7, 2017. https://www.washingtonpost.com/news/monkey-cage/wp/2017/02/07/this-is-what-we-learned-by-counting-the-womens-marches/. Accessed September 21, 2019.

23. Lesley Stahl, "President-Elect Trump Speaks to a Divided Country," *60 Minutes*, November 13, 2016. https://www.cbsnews.com/news/60-minutes-donald-trump-family-melania-ivanka-lesley-stahl/. Accessed September 21, 2019.

24. Donald Trump, Twitter post, November 15, 2016. https://twitter.com/realDonaldTrump/status/798521053551140864. Accessed September 21, 2019.

25. Paul Waldman, "The Electoral College Is an Abomination, and Democrats Should Keep Talking About It," *Washington Post*, March 20, 2019. https://www.washingtonpost.com/opinions/2019/03/20/electoral-college-is-an-abomination-democrats-should-keep-talking-about-it/. Accessed September 21, 2019.

26. Paul Finkelman, "Original Sin: The Electoral College as a Pro-Slavery Tool," *Los Angeles Review of Books*, December 19, 2016. https://lareviewofbooks.org/article/original-sin-electoral-college-proslavery-tool/. Accessed September 21, 2019.

27. Noah Zucker, "A Colorado Law Aims to Have U.S. President Elected by Popular Vote. Republicans Are Organizing to Stop This," *Colorado Times Recorder*, June 21, 2019. https://coloradotimesrecorder.com/2019/06/a-colorado-law-aims-to-have-u-s-president-elected-by-popular-vote-republicans-are-organizing-to-stop-this/16307/. Accessed September 21, 2019.

28. Ned Jilton II, "Doing Away with the Electoral College Is a Bad Idea," *Times News*, June 19, 2019. http://www.timesnews.net/Blog/2019/06/19/Doing-away-with-the-Electoral-College-is-a-bad-idea.html. Accessed September 21, 2019.

29. Rob Natelson, "National Popular Vote Would Impose Third World Election System on U.S.," *The Complete Colorado*, May 5, 2019. https://pagetwo.completecolorado.com/2019/06/24/video-national-popular-vote-a-third-world-system/. Accessed September 21, 2019.

30. Allen C. Guelzo and James H. Hulme, "Our Turn: Electoral College Gave Us Abraham Lincoln," *Providence Journal*, June 22, 2019. https://www.providencejournal.com/opinion/20190622/our-turn-allen-c-guelzo-and-james-h-hulme-electoral-college-gave-us-abraham-lincoln. Accessed September 21, 2019.

31. Richard E. Berg-Andersson, "By Whom U.S. Presidential Electors Were 'Appointed,'" *The Green Papers*, October 13, 2009. https://www.thegreenpapers.com/Hx/ByWhomElectorsWereAppointed.phtml. Accessed September 21, 2019.

32. *Reynolds v. Sims*, 377 U.S. 533, 562 (1964).

33. *Gray v. Sanders*, 372 U.S. 368, 381 (1963).

34. Jack Rakove, "Here's Hoping for Chaos on Tuesday," *Los Angeles Times*, October 31, 2004. https://www.latimes.com/archives/la-xpm-2004-oct-31-op-rakove31-story.html. Accessed September 21, 2019.

35. Jonathan Bernstein, "You Say Democracy, I Say Republic," Bloomberg Opinion, April 11, 2019. https://www.bloomberg.com/opinion/articles/2019-04-11/is-u-s-republic-or-democracy-why-some-conservatives-pick-a-side. Accessed September 22, 2019.

36. Michael Gastner, Cosma Shalizi, and Mark Newman, "Maps and Cartograms of the 2004 US Presidential Election Results," 2004, updated October 31, 2008. http://www-personal.umich.edu/~mejn/election/2004/. Accessed September 21, 2019.

37. Donald Trump, Twitter post, November 6, 2012. https://twitter.com/realdonaldtrump/status/266038556504494082. Accessed September 21, 2019.

38. Katie Glueck, "Trump Throws Fit on Twitter," *Politico*, November 7, 2012. https://www.politico.com/story/2012/11/trump-throws-fit-on-twitter-083450. Accessed September 21, 2019.

39. Nomination and Election of President and Vice President: *Hearings Before the Subcommittee on Constitutional Amendments*, Senate, 88th Cong. (1963) (Testimony of James MacGregor Burns), pp. 19–20.

40. Michael Geruso, Dean Spears, and Ishaana Talesara, "Inversions in US Presidential Elections: 1836–2016," NBER Working Paper No. 26247, September 2019. https://www.nber.org/papers/w26247. Accessed September 25, 2019; Vinod Bakthavachalam and Jake Fuentes, "The Impact of Close Races on Electoral College and Popular Vote Conflicts in US Presidential Elections," unpublished paper, October 8, 2017. http://election.princeton.edu/wp-content/uploads/2017/10/bakthavachalam_fuentes17_MEVC_popular-electoral-split-model-8oct2017.pdf. Accessed September 25, 2019.

41. Nate Cohn, "One Year From Election, Trump Trails Biden but Leads Warren in Battlegrounds," *New York Times*, November 4, 2019. https://www.nytimes.com/2019/11/04/upshot/one-year-from-election-trump-trails-biden-but-leads-warren-in-battlegrounds.html. Accessed November 4, 2019.

42. Dana Blanton, "Fox News Poll: High Interest in Election, Democrats Top Trump in Matchups," FoxNews.com, September 18, 2019. https://www.foxnews.com/politics/fox-news-poll-high-interest-in-election-democrats-top-trump-in-matchups. Accessed November 4, 2019.

43. Interview with author, July 25, 2019.

44. Trip Gabriel, "Electoral College Members Can Defy Voters' Wishes, Court Rules," *New York Times*, August 22, 2019. https://www.nytimes.com/2019/08/22/us/politics/electoral-college-faithless-elector.html. Accessed November 3, 2019.

45. Noah Feldman, "Appeals Court Opens the Door to Electoral College Chaos," Bloomberg Opinion, August 25, 2019. https://www.bloomberg.com/opinion/articles/2019-08-25/electoral-college-chaos-is-possible

-over-faithless-elector-ruling. Accessed November 3, 2019; Pete Williams, "Faithless Elector: A Court Ruling Just Changed How We Pick Our President," NBCNews.com, August 21, 2019. https://www.nbcnews.com /politics/elections/faithless-elector-court-ruling-just-changed-how-we -pick-our-n1044961. Accessed November 3, 2019.

1 Did the Founders Fear Democracy?

1. My recounting of the Fort Wilson Riot is drawn from three very thorough histories of the incident: C. Page Smith, "The Attack on Fort Wilson," *Pennsylvania Magazine of History and Biography*, Vol. 78, No. 2 (April 1954), pp. 177–88. https://www.jstor.org/stable/20088567; John K. Alexander, "The Fort Wilson Incident of 1779: A Case Study of the Revolutionary Crowd," *William and Mary Quarterly*, Vol. 31, No. 4 (October 1974), pp. 589–612. doi:10.2307/1921605; William Ewald, "James Wilson and the Drafting of the Constitution," *University of Pennsylvania Journal of Constitutional Law*, Vol. 10, No. 5 (2008), pp. 901–1009. https:// scholarship.law.upenn.edu/jcl/vol10/iss5/1.

2. Alexander, "The Fort Wilson Incident of 1779," p. 596.

3. Smith, "The Attack on Fort Wilson," p. 182.

4. Benjamin Rush to John Adams, October 12, 1779. https://founders .archives.gov/documents/Adams/06-08-02-0138. Accessed September 21, 2019.

5. Cited in Alexander, "The Fort Wilson Incident of 1779," p. 589.

6. Clinton Rossiter, *1787: The Grand Convention* (New York: W. W. Norton, 1987), pp. 23–40.

7. Michael J. Klarman, *The Framers' Coup: The Making of the United States Constitution* (New York: Oxford University Press, 2016), pp. 162–63.

8. *Notes of the Debates in the Federal Convention of 1787*, Reported by James Madison, Introduction by Adrienne Koch (Athens: Ohio University Press, 1966; reprint edition 1985), p. 39.

9. *Notes of the Debates in the Federal Convention of 1787*, p. 39.

10. Gordon S. Wood, *The Creation of the American Republic, 1776–1787* (Chapel Hill: University of North Carolina Press, 1998; originally published 1969), p. 626.

11. Andrew C. McLaughlin, "The Lost Founder: James Wilson in the Philadelphia Convention," *Political Science Quarterly*, Vol. 12, No. 1 (March 1897), p. 15. https://www.jstor.org/stable/2140026.

12. Nicholas Pedersen, "The Lost Founder: James Wilson in American Memory," *Yale Journal of Law & The Humanities*, Vol. 22, No. 2, Article 3 (2010), p. 276. https://digitalcommons.law.yale.edu/yjlh/vol22/iss2/3.

13. For this brief background sketch of James Wilson and my broader understanding of his significance to the Constitution and the founding era, I am deeply indebted to the work of William Ewald at the University of Pennsylvania Law School and his two comprehensive articles on Wilson: "James Wilson and the Drafting of the Constitution," and "James Wilson

and the Scottish Enlightenment," *University of Pennsylvania Journal of Constitutional Law*, Vol. 12, No. 4 (2010), pp. 1053–1114. https://scholarship.law.upenn.edu/faculty_scholarship/989.

14. James Wilson, "Considerations on the Nature and Extent of the Legislative Authority of the British Parliament" (1774). https://oll.libertyfund.org/titles/wilson-collected-works-of-james-wilson-vol-1#lf4140_head_013. Accessed September 21, 2019.

15. James Wilson, *Collected Works of James Wilson*, ed. Kermit L. Hall and Mark David Hall, with an Introduction by Kermit L. Hall, and a Bibliographical Essay by Mark David Hall, collected by Maynard Garrison (Indianapolis: Liberty Fund, 2007). Vol. 1. https://oll.libertyfund.org/titles/2072#Wilson_4140_85. Accessed September 21, 2019.

16. Ewald, "James Wilson and the Drafting of the Constitution," p. 905 FN10; Garry Wills, *Inventing America: Jefferson's Declaration of Independence* (New York: Doubleday, 1978), pp. 248–55.

17. Thomas Jefferson, *Notes of Proceedings in the Continental Congress*, June 7–August 1, 1776. https://founders.archives.gov/documents/Jefferson/01-01-02-0160. Accessed September 21, 2019.

18. Ewald, "James Wilson and the Drafting of the Constitution," p. 903.

19. *Notes of the Debates in the Federal Convention of 1787*, p. 40.

20. John Bakeless and Katherine Bakeless, *Signers of the Declaration* (Boston: Houghton Mifflin, 1969), p. 153.

21. John P. Kaminski, ed., *The Founders on the Founders: Word Portraits from the American Revolutionary Era* (Charlottesville: University of Virginia Press, 2008), p. 535.

22. *Notes of the Debates in the Federal Convention of 1787*, p. 189.

23. Max Farrand, ed., *The Records of the Federal Convention of 1787*, Vol. 1 (New Haven: Yale University Press, 1911), p. 183.

24. Jack Heyburn, "Gouverneur Morris and James Wilson at the Constitutional Convention," *University of Pennsylvania Journal of Constitutional Law*, Vol. 20, No. 1 (2017), p. 182. https://scholarship.law.upenn.edu/jcl/vol20/iss1/5.

25. Transcript of Northwest Ordinance (1787). https://www.ourdocuments.gov/doc.php?flash=false&doc=8&page=transcript. Accessed September 21, 2019.

26. *Notes of the Debates in the Federal Convention of 1787*, p. 287.

27. Pedersen, "The Lost Founder: James Wilson in American Memory," p. 275.

28. William Ewald, personal correspondence, December 10, 2018.

29. *Notes of the Debates in the Federal Convention of 1787*, p. 275.

30. Heyburn, "Gouverneur Morris and James Wilson at the Constitutional Convention," p. 188.

31. James Wilson, October 6, 1787, in *Collected Works of James Wilson*.

32. My description of the last years of Wilson's life is drawn from Ewald, "James Wilson and the Drafting of the Constitution," and Pedersen, "The Lost Founder: James Wilson in American Memory."

33. Cited in Robert A. Dahl, *How Democratic Is the American Constitution?* (New Haven: Yale University Press, 2003), p. 34.

34. Dahl, *How Democratic Is the American Constitution?*, pp. 34–35.

35. Dahl, *How Democratic Is the American Constitution?*, p. 37.

36. Thomas Jefferson to George Washington, December 4, 1788. https:// founders.archives.gov/documents/Jefferson/01-14-02-0111. Accessed September 22, 2019.

37. Thomas Jefferson, "Notes on John Adams and the French Revolution," January 15, 1793. https://founders.archives.gov/documents/Jefferson /01-25-02-0073. Accessed September 22, 2019.

38. Thomas Jefferson to "Henry Tompkinson" (Samuel Kercheval), July 12, 1816. https://founders.archives.gov/documents/Jefferson/03-10-02 -0128-0002. Accessed September 21, 2019.

2 The Fraught Origins of the Electoral College

1. Max Farrand, ed., *The Records of the Federal Convention of 1787*, Vol. 3 (New Haven: Yale University Press, 1911), p. 166

2. From James Madison to George Hay, August 23, 1823. https://founders .archives.gov/documents/Madison/04-03-02-0109. Accessed September 21, 2019.

3. Jeffrey Rosen, *Constitutional* podcast, Episode 1 ("Framed"), July 24, 2017. https://www.washingtonpost.com/news/on-leadership/wp/2017 /07/24/constitutional-podcast-is-here-episode-01-framed/. Transcript accessed September 21, 2019.

4. *Notes of the Debates in the Federal Convention of 1787,* Reported by James Madison, Introduction by Adrienne Koch (Athens: Ohio University Press, 1966; reprint edition 1985), p. 240.

5. A Federalist, "A Dangerous Plan of Benefit only to the 'Aristocratick Combination,'" *Boston Gazette and Country Journal*, November 26, 1787. https://www.constitution.org/afp/borden01.htm. Accessed September 21, 2019.

6. *Notes of the Debates in the Federal Convention of 1787*, Reported by James Madison, Introduction by Adrienne Koch (Athens: Ohio University Press, 1966; reprint edition 1985), p. 46.

7. *Notes of the Debates in the Federal Convention of 1787*, pp. 47–48.

8. *Notes of the Debates in the Federal Convention of 1787*, p. 49.

9. Farrand, *The Records of the Federal Convention of 1787*, Vol. 3, p. 391.

10. Madison Debates, Friday, June 15, 1787, FN4. The Avalon Project at Yale Law School. https://avalon.law.yale.edu/18th_century/debates_615.asp. Accessed September 21, 2019.

11. *Notes of the Debates in the Federal Convention of 1787*, p. 230.

12. Mary Sarah Bilder, *Madison's Hand: Revising the Constitutional Convention* (Cambridge: Harvard University Press, 2015), p. 195. The standard versions of Madison's notes do not include "the states" in this sentence; Bilder's examination of the original notes found that Madison had originally transcribed

those words, but subsequently deleted them, making Morris's dramatic statement "considerably more ambiguous."

13. *Notes of the Debates in the Federal Convention of 1787*, p. 255.
14. *Notes of the Debates in the Federal Convention of 1787*, p. 215.
15. Notes of the Secret Debates of the Federal Convention of 1787, Taken by the Late Hon. Robert Yates, Chief Justice of the State of New York, and One of the Delegates from That State to the Said Convention, Friday, June 29, 1787. The Avalon Project at Yale Law School. https://avalon.law.yale.edu/18th_century/yates.asp. Accessed September 21, 2019.
16. *Notes of the Debates in the Federal Convention of 1787*, p. 224.
17. *Notes of the Debates in the Federal Convention of 1787*, p. 295.
18. See, e.g., Leonard L. Richards, *The Slave Power: The Free North and Southern Domination, 1780–1860* (Baton Rouge: Louisiana State University Press, 2000), pp. 1–10; Garry Wills, *"Negro President": Jefferson and the Slave Power* (Boston: Houghton Mifflin, 2003).
19. David Ramsay, "Address to the Freemen of South Carolina on the Subject of the Federal Constitution," *The Federalist and Other Constitutional Papers*, ed. E. H. Scott (Chicago: Scott, Foresman and Co., 1902), p. 922.
20. *Notes of the Debates in the Federal Convention of 1787*, p. 306.
21. *Notes of the Debates in the Federal Convention of 1787*, p. 307.
22. Paul Finkelman, "The Proslavery Origins of the Electoral College," *Cardozo Law Review*, Vol. 23, No. 4 (2002), p. 1154. https://ssrn.com/abstract=1447478.
23. *Notes of the Debates in the Federal Convention of 1787*, p. 309.
24. *Notes of the Debates in the Federal Convention of 1787*, pp. 322–24.
25. *Notes of the Debates in the Federal Convention of 1787*, p. 327.
26. Christopher S. Yoo, "James Wilson as the Architect of the American Presidency" (2018). *Faculty Scholarship at Penn Law*. 2017. https://scholarship.law.upenn.edu/faculty_scholarship/2017/. Accessed September 21, 2019.
27. *Notes of the Debates in the Federal Convention of 1787*, p. 327.
28. For some educated guesses, see Richard E. Berg-Andersson, "What Are They All Doing, Anyway? An Historical Analysis of the Electoral College," *The Green Papers: History*, September 17, 2000. https://www.thegreenpapers.com/Hx/ElectoralCollege.html. Accessed September 21, 2019.
29. William Ewald, personal correspondence, December 10, 2018.
30. *Notes of the Debates in the Federal Convention of 1787*, pp. 365–66.
31. *Notes of the Debates in the Federal Convention of 1787*, p. 266.
32. *Notes of the Debates in the Federal Convention of 1787*, p. 411.
33. *Notes of the Debates in the Federal Convention of 1787*, p. 411.
34. *Notes of the Debates in the Federal Convention of 1787*, p. 412.
35. *Notes of the Debates in the Federal Convention of 1787*, p. 505.
36. *Notes of the Debates in the Federal Convention of 1787*, p. 505.

37. Sean Wilentz, "The Electoral College Was Not a Pro-Slavery Ploy," *New York Times*, April 4, 2019. https://www.nytimes.com/2019/04/04/opinion/the-electoral-college-slavery-myth.html. Accessed September 25, 2019.

38. Akhil Reed Amar, "Actually, the Electoral College Was a Pro-Slavery Ploy," *New York Times*, April 6, 2019. https://www.nytimes.com/2019/04/06/opinion/electoral-college-slavery.html. Accessed September 25, 2019.

39. See, e.g., Richard Beeman, *Plain, Honest Men: The Making of the American Constitution* (New York: Random House, 2010), p. xii ("Few among [the delegates] had much confidence that their attempt to harmonize [their] differences of opinion—through the creation of an electoral college— would prove a durable and workable solution").

40. Pauline Maier, *Ratification: The People Debate the Constitution, 1787– 1788* (New York: Simon & Schuster, 2010), p. 286.

41. Alexander Hamilton, *Federalist* No. 68, in *The Federalist*, ed. Robert Scigliano (New York: Random House, 2000), p. 434.

42. *Notes of the Debates in the Federal Convention of 1787*, p. 578.

43. Maier, *Ratification*, p. 114.

44. James Wilson, "Remarks of James Wilson in the Pennsylvania Convention to Ratify the Constitution of the United States, 1787," in James Wilson, *Collected Works of James Wilson*, ed. Kermit L. Hall and Mark David Hall, with an Introduction by Kermit L. Hall, and a Bibliographical Essay by Mark David Hall, collected by Maynard Garrison (Indianapolis: Liberty Fund, 2007), Vol. 1. https://oll.libertyfund.org/titles/2072#Wilson _4140_1402. Accessed September 21, 2019.

45. Michael J. Klarman, *The Framers' Coup: The Making of the United States Constitution* (New York: Oxford University Press, 2016), p. 367.

46. Cited in Paul Finkelman, "The Founders and Slavery: Little Ventured, Little Gained," *Yale Journal of Law & the Humanities*, Vol. 13, No. 2, Article 3 (2001), p. 445. https://digitalcommons.law.yale.edu/yjlh/vol13/iss2/3/.

3 Did the Electoral College Ever Really Work?

1. Samuel Miles, "Auto-Biographical Sketch of Samuel Miles," *The American Historical Record, and Repertory of Notes and Queries*, Vol. 2, ed. Benson J. Lossing (Philadelphia: Samuel P. Town, 1873), p. 118. https://archive.org /details/pottersamericanm02lossuoft/page/118. Accessed September 21, 2019.

2. Cited in George C. Edwards III, *Why the Electoral College Is Bad for America* (New Haven: Yale University Press, 2004), p. 53.

3. None did, although one Gore elector in the District of Columbia abstained from voting as a protest against the district's lack of representation in Congress.

4. Transcript of President George Washington's Farewell Address (1796). https://www.ourdocuments.gov/doc.php?flash=false&doc=15&page =transcript. Accessed on September 21, 2019.

5. Cited in Philip Kurland and Ralph Lerner, eds., *The Founders' Constitution*, Vol. 3 (Chicago: University of Chicago Press, 1987), p. 552.

6. *Annals of Congress*, House of Representatives, 4th Congress, 2nd Session (January 1797). http://memory.loc.gov/cgi-bin/ampage?collId=llac&fileName=006/llac006.db&recNum=154. Accessed September 21, 2019.
7. Tadahisa Kuroda, *The Origins of the Twelfth Amendment: The Electoral College in the Early Republic, 1787–1804* (Westport, Conn.: Greenwood Press, 1994), pp. 102–3.
8. Kuroda, *The Origins of the Twelfth Amendment*, p. 104.
9. Kuroda, *The Origins of the Twelfth Amendment*, pp. 113–14 (italics in original).
10. Akhil Reed Amar, *America's Constitution: A Biography* (New York: Random House, 2005), pp. 342–47; Joshua D. Hawley, "The Transformative 12th Amendment," *William & Mary Law Review*, Vol. 55, No. 4 (2014). https://scholarship.law.wm.edu/wmlr/vol55/iss4/5.
11. Thomas Jefferson to James Monroe, January 12, 1800. https://founders.archives.gov/documents/Jefferson/01-31-02-0256. Accessed September 21, 2019.
12. From James Madison to George Hay, August 23, 1823. https://founders.archives.gov/documents/Madison/04-03-02-0109. Accessed on September 21, 2019.
13. Annals of Congress, Senate, 18th Congress, 1st Session (February 1824), p. 170. https://memory.loc.gov/cgi-bin/ampage?collId=llac&fileName=041/llac041.db&recNum=2. Accessed on September 21, 2019.
14. Annals of Congress, Senate, 14th Congress, 1st Session (March 1816), p. 220. https://memory.loc.gov/cgi-bin/ampage?collId=llac&fileName=029/llac029.db&recNum=107. Accessed on September 21, 2019.
15. *McPherson v. Blacker*, 146 U.S. 1, 35 (1892).
16. Daniel Seligson, "Electoral College Reform Falls Flat," *Pew Stateline*, March 28, 2001. https://www.pewtrusts.org/en/research-and-analysis/blogs/stateline/2001/03/28/electoral-college-reform-falls-flat. Accessed September 21, 2019.
17. From James Madison to George Hay, August 23, 1823.
18. From Thomas Jefferson to George Hay, August 17, 1823. https://founders.archives.gov/documents/Jefferson/98-01-02-3707. Accessed December 3, 2019.
19. Andrew Jackson, December 8, 1829: First Annual Message to Congress. https://millercenter.org/the-presidency/presidential-speeches/december-8-1829-first-annual-message-congress. Accessed September 21, 2019.
20. Specifically, Jackson said, "I would therefore recommend such an amendment of the Constitution as may remove all intermediate agency in the election of the President and Vice President. The mode may be so regulated as to preserve to each state its present relative weight in the election . . ."
21. John Quincy Adams, *Memoirs of John Quincy Adams*, Vol. 10, ed. Charles Francis Adams (Philadelphia: J. B. Lippincott & Co., 1876), entry of April 28, 1841, p. 468.

4 The Second Founding

1. "The Colored Member Admitted to His Seat in the Senate," *New York Times*, February 26, 1870, p. 1. https://archive.nytimes.com/www.nytimes.com/learning/general/onthisday/big/0225.html. Accessed on September 21, 2019.
2. 1790 Census. https://www.nationalgeographic.org/media/us-census-1790/. Accessed September 21, 2019.
3. William W. Freehling, *The Road to Disunion: Secessionists at Bay, 1776–1854* (New York: Oxford University Press, 1990), p. 147.
4. Garry Wills, *"Negro President": Jefferson and the Slave Power* (Boston: Houghton Mifflin, 2003), p. 2.
5. Leonard L. Richards, *The Slave Power: The Free North and Southern Domination, 1780–1860* (Baton Rouge: Louisiana State University Press, 2000), p. 42.
6. Wills, *"Negro President,"* p. 1.
7. *Annals of Congress*, Senate, 14th Congress, 1st Session (March 1816), p. 226. https://memory.loc.gov/cgi-bin/ampage?collId=llac&fileName=029/llac029.db&recNum=110. Accessed September 21, 2019.
8. William W. Wiecek, "The Witch at the Christening: Slavery and the Constitution's Origins," in *The Framing and Ratification of the Constitution*, ed. Leonard W. Levy and Dennis J. Mahoney (New York: Macmillan, 1987), p. 180.
9. The 1790 census calculated the slave population in the southern states at 654,121; in 1860, the population had increased to more than 3.95 million. See, e.g., Jenny Bourne, "Slavery in the United States," EH.Net Encyclopedia, ed. Robert Whaples. March 26, 2008. http://eh.net/encyclopedia/slavery-in-the-united-states.
10. Richards, *The Slave Power*, p. 9.
11. Richards, *The Slave Power*, pp. 9, 42.
12. U.S. Constitution, Amendment XIV, Section 2.
13. "Wade Hampton's Canvass," *New York Times*, October 13, 1876, p. 1. https://timesmachine.nytimes.com/timesmachine/1876/10/13/80633067.pdf. Accessed on September 21, 2019.
14. Eric Foner, *A Short History of Reconstruction: 1863–1877* (New York: Harper Perennial, 1990), p. 189.
15. "Wade Hampton's Canvass."
16. Congressman George H. White's Farewell Address to Congress, January 1901. Blackpast, January 28, 2007. https://www.blackpast.org/african-american-history/1901-george-h-whites-farewell-address-congress/. Accessed September 21, 2019.
17. Edward B. Foley, *Ballot Battles: The History of Disputed Elections in the United States* (New York: Oxford University Press, 2016), p. 120.
18. Foley, *Ballot Battles*, pp. 140, 142.
19. Foley, *Ballot Battles*, pp. 142–44.
20. *Population of States and Counties of the United States: 1790–1990,*

Department of Commerce, U.S. Bureau of the Census, Population Division, compiled and edited by Richard L. Forstall, March 1996. https:// www.census.gov/population/www/censusdata/PopulationofStatesan dCountiesoftheUnitedStates1790-1990.pdf. Accessed September 21, 2019.

21. Michael F. Holt, *By One Vote: The Disputed Presidential Election of 1876* (Lawrence: University Press of Kansas, 2008), pp. 28–32.

22. National Archives and Records Administration, Historical Election Results, *Electoral College Box Scores 1789–1996*. https://www.archives.gov /federal-register/electoral-college/scores.html#1880. Accessed on September 21, 2019.

23. Foley, *Ballot Battles*, pp. 152–53.

24. Foley, *Ballot Battles*, pp. 159–60.

25. Neil R. McMillen, *Dark Journey: Black Mississippians in the Age of Jim Crow* (Urbana: University of Illinois Press, 1990), p. 41.

26. C. Vann Woodward, "The Anachronistic Electoral System," *New Republic*, June 1, 1968, pp. 44–45.

27. Patrick Rael, "Did Disenfranchisement Give the South an Electoral Advantage?" *Journal of the Civil War Era*, December 13, 2016. https://www .journalofthecivilwarera.org/2016/12/disenfranchisement-give-south -electoral-advantage/. Accessed September 21, 2019.

28. Direct Popular Election of the President and Vice President of the United States, Senate Judiciary Committee Report, May 1, 1979, pp. 28–29.

29. Emanuel Celler, House of Representatives, 70th Congress, 1st Session (May 17, 1928), p. 69: 9087.

5 One Person, One Vote

1. Editorial, "Last Call for Electoral Reform," *New York Times*, September 29, 1970, p. 42.

2. Interview with author, January 10, 2019.

3. "Remarks from Senator Birch Bayh," *Fordham Law Review*, Vol. 79, No. 3 (2011), p. 1091. https://ir.lawnet.fordham.edu/flr/vol79/iss3/12.

4. Stephen Ansolabehere and James M. Snyder Jr., *The End of Inequality: One Person, One Vote and the Transformation of American Politics* (New York: W. W. Norton, 2008), p. 241.

5. J. Douglas Smith, *On Democracy's Doorstep: The Inside Story of How the Supreme Court Brought "One Person, One Vote" to the United States* (New York: Hill and Wang, 2014), pp. 16–17.

6. Smith, *On Democracy's Doorstep*, pp. 19, 43.

7. *Colegrove v. Green*, 328 U.S. 549, 556 (1946).

8. *Baker v. Carr*, 369 U.S. 186 (1962).

9. Smith, *On Democracy's Doorstep*, p. 54.

10. Smith, *On Democracy's Doorstep*, p. 17.

11. *Gray v. Sanders*, 372 U.S. 368, 381 (1963).

12. *Wesberry v. Sanders*, 376 U.S. 1, 8 (1964).

13. *Reynolds v. Sims*, 377 U.S. 533, 562 (1964).
14. James Wilson, *Collected Works of James Wilson*, ed. Kermit L. Hall and Mark David Hall, with an Introduction by Kermit L. Hall, and a Bibliographical Essay by Mark David Hall, collected by Maynard Garrison (Indianapolis: Liberty Fund, 2007). https://oll.libertyfund.org/titles /2074#Wilson_4141_357. Accessed September 21, 2019.
15. Smith, *On Democracy's Doorstep*, p. 7
16. Michelle Goldberg, "Leave Drag Queen Story Hour Alone!" *New York Times*, June 7, 2019. https://www.nytimes.com/2019/06/07/opinion /conservatives-culture-trump.html. Accessed September 21, 2019.
17. Smith, *On Democracy's Doorstep*, p. 49.
18. Smith, *On Democracy's Doorstep*, p. 49.
19. Irving Kristol and Paul Weaver, "A Bad Idea Whose Time Has Come," *New York Times*, November 23, 1969. https://timesmachine.nytimes .com/timesmachine/1969/11/23/89147799.pdf. Accessed September 21, 2019.
20. In G. Edward White, *Earl Warren: A Public Life* (New York: Oxford University Press, 1987), p. 337.
21. *Gray v. Sanders*, 372 U.S. 368, 378 (1963). For a slightly less deferential perspective, consider the words of Robert H. Jackson, one of the great justices of the twentieth century. Before joining the Court he served as the U.S. Attorney General, in which capacity he gave a speech to the 1941 class of electors. Jackson told them, "Presidential electors belong to a land of constitutional make-believe, rather than to the world of practical politics." https://www.roberthjackson.org/speech-and-writing/a-progressive -democracy/. Accessed on September 21, 2019.
22. "Statement by Senator Birch Bayh," Election of the President, *Hearings Before the Subcommittee on Constitutional Amendments*, 89th Congress, 2d Session & 90th Congress, 1st Session (February 28, 1966), p. 22.
23. "Statement by Senator Birch Bayh," pp. 22–23.
24. Interview with author, June 28, 2018.
25. Birch Bayh, "Direct Popular Election of the President," *Congressional Record—Senate*, May 19, 1966, pp. 10998–11000. https://www.govinfo .gov/content/pkg/GPO-CRECB-1966-pt9/pdf/GPO-CRECB-1966 -pt9-1-1.pdf. Accessed September 21, 2019.
26. Statement of Senator Birch Bayh, *Congressional Record—Senate*, Vol. 112, Part 9, pp. 10998–11000, May 19, 1966, pp. 10479–81. http://fedora .dlib.indiana.edu/fedora/get/iudl:2384100/OVERVIEW. Accessed on September 23, 2019.
27. John F. Banzhaf III, "One Man, 3.312 Votes: A Mathematical Analysis of the Electoral College," *Villanova Law Review*, Vol. 13, No. 2 (1968), p. 304 FN3. https://digitalcommons.law.villanova.edu/cgi/viewcontent .cgi?article=1780&context=vlr.
28. "Electing the President," *American Bar Association Journal*, Vol. 53, No. 3 (1967), pp. 219–24. http://www.jstor.org/stable/25723942.

29. Neal Peirce and Lawrence D. Longley, *The People's President: The Electoral College in American History and the Direct Vote Alternative* (New Haven: Yale University Press, 1981), p. 182.
30. Russell Baker, *Our Next President: The Incredible Story of What Happened in the 1968 Elections* (New York: Atheneum, 1968), p. 101.
31. James A. Michener, *The Presidential Lottery* (New York: Dial, 1969), pp. 3, 15, 36.
32. Congressional Record, September 18, 1969, pp. 25990–91. https://www.govinfo.gov/content/pkg/GPO-CRECB-1969-pt19/pdf/GPO-CRECB-1969-pt19-6-1.pdf. Accessed November 2, 2019.
33. Warren Weaver Jr., "House Opens Debate on a Move to Wipe Out Electoral College," *New York Times*, September 11, 1969, p. 29.
34. Peirce and Longley, *The People's President*, p. 187.
35. Kristol and Weaver, "A Bad Idea Whose Time Has Come." Kristol and Weaver made no mention of the role of slavery in the College's origins, although they referred to the College as a "peculiar institution," a common nineteenth-century euphemism for slavery, as they surely must have known.
36. Warren Weaver Jr., "A Survey Finds 30 Legislatures Favor Direct Vote for President," *New York Times*, October 8, 1969, p. 1. https://www.nytimes.com/1969/10/08/archives/a-survey-finds-30-legislatures-favor-direct-vote-for-president.html.
37. *Fordham Law Review*, Vol. 79 (2010), p. 787.
38. Weaver Jr., "A Survey Finds 30 Legislatures Favor Direct Vote for President."
39. "Amend the Constitution to Abolish the Electoral College System," *Hearings Before the Subcomm. No. 1 of the House Comm. on the Judiciary*, 82d Cong., 1st Sess. (April 20, 1951), pp. 264–65.
40. "A Modern Father of Our Constitution: An Interview with Former Senator Birch Bayh," *Fordham Law Review*, Vol. 79, No. 3 (2010), p. 815. https://ir.lawnet.fordham.edu/flr/vol79/iss3/2.
41. Interview with author, June 28, 2018.
42. "A Modern Father of Our Constitution: An Interview with Former Senator Birch Bayh."
43. Interview with author, June 28, 2018.

6 Setting the Record Straight, Part One

1. Jamelle Bouie, "Getting Rid of the Electoral College Isn't Just About Trump," *New York Times*, March 21, 2019. https://www.nytimes.com/2019/03/21/opinion/electoral-college-warren-trump.html. Accessed September 21, 2019.
2. Nik DeCosta-Klipa, "Paul LePage Says Proposal to Sideline Electoral College Would Silence 'White People,'" *Boston Globe*, February 28, 2019. https://www.boston.com/news/politics/2019/02/28/paul-lepage-electoral-college-white-people. Accessed September 21, 2019.
3. Andrea Levien, "Following the Money: Campaign Donations and

Spending in the 2012 Presidential Race," FairVote, February 13, 2013. http://archive3.fairvote.org/research-and-analysis/presidential-elections /2012chart. Accessed September 23, 2019; "Two-Thirds of Presidential Campaign Is in Just 6 States," National Popular Vote, undated. https:// www.nationalpopularvote.com/campaign-events-2016. Accessed September 23, 2019.

4. Tom LoBianco, "Scott Walker: 12 States Will Elect Next President," CNN.com, September 1, 2015. https://www.cnn.com/2015/09/01 /politics/scott-walker-12-states-to-win/index.html. Accessed September 21, 2019.

5. Interview with author, May 23, 2019.

6. John Hudak, *Presidential Pork: White House Influence over the Distribution of Federal Grants* (Washington, D.C.: Brookings Institution Press, 2014).

7. From James Madison to George Hay, August 23, 1823. https://founders .archives.gov/documents/Madison/04-03-02-0109. Accessed September 21, 2019.

8. Interview with author, March 9, 2019.

9. John R. Koza, Barry Fadem, and Mark Grueskin, *Every Vote Equal: A State-Based Plan for Electing the President by National Popular Vote* (Los Altos, Calif.: National Popular Vote Press, 2013), pp. 457–67.

10. *Delaware v. New York*, 385 U.S. 964 (1966).

11. Todd Estes, "The Connecticut Effect: The Great Compromise of 1787 and the History of Small State Impact on Electoral College Outcomes," *The Historian*, Vol. 73, No. 2 (Summer 2011), pp. 255–83. http://www.jstor .org/stable/24455090.

12. Michael G. Neubauer and Joel Zeitlin, "Outcomes of Presidential Elections and the House Size," *Political Science and Politics*, October 2003, p. 721. https://doi.org/10.1017/S1049096503003019.

13. From James Madison to George Hay, August 23, 1823.

14. Richard Primus, "More on the Unprincipled Nature of the Senate: Further Conversation with Professor Dorf," Dorf on Law, November 28, 2018. http://www.dorfonlaw.org/2018/11/more-on-unprincipled-nature-of -senate.html. Accessed September 21, 2019.

15. Wendell Cox, "America's Most Urban States," *New Geography*, March 8, 2016. https://www.newgeography.com/content/005187-america-s-most -urban-states. Accessed September 21, 2019.

16. Timothy Williams, "With Most States Under One Party's Control, America Grows More Divided," *New York Times*, June 11, 2019. https://www .nytimes.com/2019/06/11/us/state-legislatures-partisan-polarized.html. Accessed September 21, 2019.

17. See, e.g., Charles Stewart III and Barry R. Weingast, "Stacking the Senate, Changing the Nation: Republican Rotten Boroughs, Statehood Politics, and American Political Development," *Studies in American Political Development*, Vol. 6, No. 2 (1992), pp. 223–71; Ian Millhiser, "The For-

gotten History of How Abraham Lincoln Helped Rig the Senate for Republicans," *ThinkProgress*, May 5, 2019. https://thinkprogress.org /how-abraham-lincoln-rigged-the-senate-for-republicans/. Accessed September 21, 2019. ("The history of the American statehood process is the history of political factions selectively admitting new states in order to bolster their own fortunes and harm those of their opponents.")

18. From James Madison to George Hay, August 23, 1823.

19. Michael Wines, "State Court Bars Using North Carolina House Map in 2020 Elections," *New York Times*, October 28, 2019. https://www. nytimes.com/2019/10/28/us/north-carolina-gerrymander-maps.html. Accessed November 3, 2019.

20. Claire Daviss and Rob Richie, "Fuzzy Math: Wrong Way Reforms for Allocating Electoral Votes," FairVote, January 2015, p. 11. https://fairvote .app.box.com/v/fuzzy-math-wrong-way-reforms. Accessed September 21, 2019.

21. *The Constitution of the United States of America: Analysis and Interpretation, Centennial Edition, Interim Edition: Analysis of Cases Decided by the Supreme Court of the United States to June 26, 2013* (Washington, D.C.: U.S. Government Printing Office, 2013), p. 49. https://www.govinfo.gov /content/pkg/GPO-CONAN-2013/pdf/GPO-CONAN-2013.pdf. Accessed September 23, 2019.

22. Neubauer and Zeitlin, "Outcomes of Presidential Elections and the House Size"; see also Nicholas R. Miller, "The House Size Effect and the Referendum Paradox in U.S. Elections," *Electoral Studies*, Vol. 35 (September 2014), pp. 265–71. https://doi.org/10.1016/j.electstud.2014.01.009. Accessed September 21, 2019.

7 The National Popular Vote Interstate Compact

1. "Asm Ray Haynes on National Popular Vote," YouTube, uploaded July 1, 2011. https://www.youtube.com/watch?v=PNDB9hMp-IY. Accessed September 21, 2019.

2. Interview with author, April 12, 2019.

3. John R. Koza, Barry Fadem, and Mark Grueskin, *Every Vote Equal: A State-Based Plan for Electing the President by National Popular Vote*, 4th ed. (Los Altos, Calif.: National Popular Vote Press, 2013).

4. Interview with author, April 12, 2019.

5. Kirk Johnson, "Coloradans to Consider Splitting Electoral College Votes," *New York Times*, September 19, 2004. https://www.nytimes .com/2004/09/19/politics/campaign/coloradans-to-consider-splitting -electoral-college-votes.html. Accessed September 21, 2019.

6. Dale Read Jr., "Direct Election of the President Without a Constitutional Amendment: A Call for State Action," *Washington Law Review*, Vol. 51 (1976), pp. 321–49. https://digitalcommons.law.uw.edu/cgi/viewcontent .cgi?article=2109&context=wlr. Accessed September 21, 2019.

7. Robert W. Bennett, "Popular Election of the President Without a

Constitutional Amendment," *Green Bag* (Spring 2001). http://www
.greenbag.org/v4n3/v4n3_articles_bennett.pdf. Accessed September 21,
2019.

8. Akhil Reed Amar and Vikram David Amar, "How to Achieve Direct National Election of the President Without Amending the Constitution:
Part Three of a Three-Part Series on the 2000 Election and the Electoral
College," FindLaw, December 28, 2001. https://supreme.findlaw.com
/legal-commentary/how-to-achieve-direct-national-election-of-the
-president-without-amending-the-constitution.html. Accessed September 21, 2019.

9. Koza et al., *Every Vote Equal*, pp. 206–8.

10. Hendrik Hertzberg, "Count 'Em," *The New Yorker*, February 26, 2006.
https://www.newyorker.com/magazine/2006/03/06/count-em-2. Accessed September 21, 2019.

11. Interview with author, March 9, 2019.

12. Interview with author, March 9, 2019.

13. "John Koza on the National Popular Vote," C-SPAN, March 9, 2019.
https://www.c-span.org/video/?c4787568/john-koza-national-popular
-vote. Accessed September 21, 2019.

14. Interview with author, March 10, 2019.

15. Author transcription of live feed of Colorado Senate debate on National
Popular Vote bill, January 28, 2019.

16. Author transcription of live feed of Colorado Senate debate on National
Popular Vote bill.

17. Interview with author, March 9, 2019.

18. Interview with author, March 9, 2019.

19. Interview with author, April 8, 2019.

20. Interview with author, April 8, 2019.

21. Interview with author, April 8, 2019.

22. Interview with author, April 12, 2019.

23. Interview with author, May 23, 2019.

24. Interview with author, May 23, 2019.

25. Interview with author, April 10, 2019.

26. Interview with author, March 9, 2019.

27. Interview with author, August 12, 2019.

28. Interview with author, May 23, 2019.

29. Interview with author, March 9, 2019.

30. Anna Staver, "Campaign to Overturn Colorado's National Popular Vote
Law Submits Record Number of Signatures," *Denver Post*, August 1, 2019.
https://www.denverpost.com/2019/08/01/colorado-national-popular
-vote-law-repeal/. Accessed September 21, 2019.

31. Anna Staver, "Challenge of National Popular Vote Compact Makes
Colorado's 2020 Ballot," *Denver Post*, August 29, 2019. https://www
.denverpost.com/2019/08/29/national-popular-vote-referendum-2020
-colorado/. Accessed September 21, 2019.

8 Setting the Record Straight, Part Two

1. Senator Charles Grassley, press release, "Grassley on Democrat Calls to Abolish the Electoral College," April 2, 2019. https://www.grassley .senate.gov/news/news-releases/grassley-democrat-calls-abolish-electoral -college. Accessed September 21, 2019.

2. Estes Kefauver, "The Electoral College: Old Reforms Take On a New Look," *Law and Contemporary Problems*, Vol. 27, No. 2 (Spring 1962), p. 196. https://scholarship.law.duke.edu/lcp/vol27/iss2/4.

3. United States Census Bureau, "QuickFacts: California; Florida; New York; Texas." https://www.census.gov/quickfacts/fact/table/CA,FL,NY,TX/ PST045218. Accessed September 23, 2019.

4. Interview with author, March 9, 2019.

5. Nate Cohn, "Why Trump Had an Edge in the Electoral College," *New York Times*, December 19, 2016. https://www.nytimes.com/2016/12/19 /upshot/why-trump-had-an-edge-in-the-electoral-college.html. Accessed September 21, 2019.

6. Nate Berg, "U.S. Urban Population Is Up . . . But What Does 'Urban' Really Mean?" *CityLab*, March 26, 2012. https://www.citylab.com/equity /2012/03/us-urban-population-what-does-urban-really-mean/1589/. Accessed September 21, 2019.

7. Nik DeCosta-Klipa, "Paul LePage Says Proposal to Sideline Electoral College Would Silence 'White People,'" *Boston Globe*, February 28, 2019. https://www.boston.com/news/politics/2019/02/28/paul-lepage-electoral -college-white-people. Accessed September 21, 2019.

8. J. Douglas Smith, *On Democracy's Doorstep: The Inside Story of How the Supreme Court Brought "One Person, One Vote" to the United States* (New York: Hill and Wang, 2014), p. 7 (quoting *Birmingham Post-Herald*, June 18, 1964).

9. John R. Koza, Barry Fadem, and Mark Grueskin, *Every Vote Equal: A State-Based Plan for Electing the President by National Popular Vote* (Los Altos, Calif.: National Popular Vote Press, 2013), pp. 491–95.

10. Koza et al., *Every Vote Equal*, pp. 491–95.

11. Koza et al., *Every Vote Equal*, p. 490.

12. Vikram David Amar, "Assessing the Challenge to Maine's Ranked-Choice Voting System for Congressional Elections," *Verdict*, November 30, 2018. https://verdict.justia.com/2018/11/30/assessing-the-challenge-to -maines-ranked-choice-voting-system-for-congressional-elections. Accessed September 21, 2019.

13. Maggie Astor, "Maine Voters Will Rank Their Top Presidential Candidates in 2020," *New York Times*, September 6, 2019. https://www.nytimes .com/2019/09/06/us/politics/maine-elections.html. Accessed September 22, 2019.

14. Damon Linker, "What If America Had 6 Political Parties?" *The Week*, May 28, 2019. https://theweek.com/articles/843773/what-america-6 -political-parties. Accessed September 21, 2019.

15. Pippa Norris, "Do Public Perceptions of Electoral Malpractice Undermine Democratic Satisfaction? The U.S. In Comparative Perspective," July 30, 2018. Paper for the Panel on Election Dynamics in the Developing World at the American Political Science Association Annual Convention, Boston. HKS Working Paper no. RWP18-022. https://papers.ssrn.com/sol3/papers.cfm?abstract_id=3222940. Accessed September 21, 2019.
16. Michael Kramer, "Bush Set to Fight an Electoral College Loss," New York Daily News, November 1, 2000. https://www.nydailynews.com/archives/news/bush-set-fight-electoral-college-loss-article-1.881690. Accessed September 21, 2019.
17. Jeff Greenfield, Oh, Waiter! One Order of Crow! (New York: Putnam, 2001), p. 14.
18. Interview with the author, October 31 and November 1, 2019.
19. Tomas McIntee, "The Electoral College Does Not Favor Republicans over Democrats," Medium/Politics, March 21, 2019. https://medium.com/@tomasmcintee/the-electoral-college-does-not-favor-republicans-over-democrats-a9ef3ff876e. Accessed September 21, 2019.
20. Michael Geruso, Dean Spears, and Ishaana Talesara, "Inversions in US Presidential Elections: 1836–2016," NBER Working Paper No. 26247, September 2019. https://www.nber.org/papers/w26247. Accessed September 25, 2019.
21. Nate Silver, "Will The Electoral College Doom the Democrats Again?" FiveThirtyEight, November 14, 2016. https://fivethirtyeight.com/features/will-the-electoral-college-doom-the-democrats-again/. Accessed September 21, 2019.
22. Koza et al., Every Vote Equal, pp. 703–4.
23. "Generations' Party Identification, Midterm Voting Preferences, Views of Trump," Pew Research Center, March 1, 2018. https://www.people-press.org/2018/03/01/1-generations-party-identification-midterm-voting-preferences-views-of-trump/. Accessed September 21, 2019; "Trends in Party Affiliation Among Demographic Groups," Pew Research Center, March 30, 2018. https://www.people-press.org/2018/03/20/1-trends-in-party-affiliation-among-demographic-groups/. Accessed September 21, 2019.
24. Lanae Erickson Hatalsky and Jim Kessler, "Why Demographics Weren't—and Won't Be—Destiny for Democrats," Washington Post, February 22, 2017. https://www.washingtonpost.com/opinions/why-demographics-werent--and-wont-be--destiny-for-democrats/2017/02/22/576a3a60-f91c-11e6-9845-576c69081518_story.html.
25. Emily Badger, "What If Everyone Voted?" New York Times, October 29, 2018. https://www.nytimes.com/2018/10/29/upshot/what-if-everyone-voted.html. Accessed September 21, 2019.
26. "Presidential Battleground States, 2016," Ballotpedia, undated. https://ballotpedia.org/Presidential_battleground_states,_2016. Accessed September 21, 2019.

27. United States Census Bureau, "Selected Characteristics of the Native and Foreign-Born Populations," 2015 American Community Survey 1-Year Estimates. https://factfinder.census.gov/faces/tableservices/jsf/pages /productview.xhtml?pid=ACS_15_1YR_S0501&prodType=table. Accessed September 21, 2019.

28. Leonard Steinhorn, "Without Voting, Noncitizens Could Swing the Election for Obama," *Washington Post*, October 5, 2012. https://www .washingtonpost.com/opinions/without-voting-noncitizens-could -swing-the-election-for-obama/2012/10/05/b9d99be8-0be9-11e2-bd1a -b868e65d57eb_story.html?utm_term=.ea6167fc2cce. Accessed September 21, 2019.

29. Allison Graves, "Fact-Check: Did 3 Million Undocumented Immigrants Vote in This Year's Election?" *Punditfact*, November 18, 2016. https:// www.politifact.com/punditfact/statements/2016/nov/18/blog-posting /no-3-million-undocumented-immigrants-did-not-vote-/. Accessed September 21, 2019.

30. Donald Trump, Twitter post, November 27, 2016. https://twitter.com /realDonaldTrump/status/802972944532209664. Accessed September 21, 2019.

31. Michael Wines, "All This Talk of Voter Fraud? Across U.S., Officials Found Next to None," *New York Times*, December 18, 2016. https:// www.nytimes.com/2016/12/18/us/voter-fraud.html?module=inline. Accessed September 21, 2019.

32. Art Swift, "Americans' Support for Electoral College Rises Sharply," *Gallup News*, December 2, 2016. https://news.gallup.com/poll/198917 /americans-support-electoral-college-rises-sharply.aspx. Accessed September 23, 2019.

33. Interview with author, April 8, 2019.

34. Interview with author, April 8, 2019.

9 Imagining a National Popular Vote

1. All of the quotes in this chapter are from interviews with the author, on the following dates: Chris Lehane, June 4, 2019; David Plouffe, April 25, 2019; Jennifer Palmieri, May 7, 2019; Jeremy Bird, April 25, 2019; Joel Benenson, May 20, 2019; Karl Rove, June 24, 2019; Matthew Dowd, May 6, 2019; Mitch Stewart, June 12, 2019; Stuart Stevens, April 24, 2019; Reed Hundt, March 6, June 16, July 21, December 4, 2018, and February 22 and April 29, 2019.

2. John Hudak, *Presidential Pork: White House Influence over the Distribution of Federal Grants* (Washington, D.C.: Brookings Institution Press, 2014).

3. John Hudak, "The Politics of Federal Grants: Presidential Influence over the Distribution of Federal Funds," Vanderbilt University Center for the Study of Democratic Institutions, Working Paper No. 01-2011, May 2010, p. 11.

4. Douglas Kriner and Andrew Reeves, "The Electoral College and Presidential Particularism," *Boston University Law Review*, Vol. 94 (2014), pp. 753–54.

5. Michael P. McDonald, "2016 November General Election Turnout Rates," United States Elections Project, last updated September 5, 2018. http://www.electproject.org/2016g. Accessed September 26, 2019.

6. "Voter Turnout," FairVote, undated. https://www.fairvote.org/voter _turnout#voter_turnout_101/. Accessed September 27, 2019.

7. Office of Communications, Federal Election Commission, "Official 2016 Presidential General Election Results" from state elections offices, January 30, 2017. https://transition.fec.gov/pubrec/fe2016/2016presgeresults .pdf.

INDEX